THE PENNSYLVANIA DUTCH
AND THEIR FURNITURE

THE PENNSYLVANIA DUTCH AND THEIR FURNITURE

John G. Shea

VNR VAN NOSTRAND REINHOLD COMPANY
New York   Cincinnati   Toronto   London   Melbourne

Other books by John G. Shea

Colonial Furniture Making for Everybody
(1964)
Woodworking for Everybody, Fourth Edition
(1970)
The American Shakers and Their Furniture
(1971)
Contemporary Furniture (1973)
Antique Country Furniture of North America
(1975)

Copyright © 1980 by Litton Educational Publishing, Inc.
Library of Congress Catalog Card Number 80–11149
ISBN 0–442–27546–3

Printed in the United States of America.

Published by Van Nostrand Reinhold Company
A division of Litton Educational Publishing, Inc.
135 West 50th Street, New York, NY 10020

Van Nostrand Reinhold Limited
1410 Birchmount Road
Scarborough, Ontario M1P 2E7, Canada

Van Nostrand Reinhold Australia Pty. Ltd.
17 Queen Street
Mitcham, Victoria 3132, Australia

Van Nostrand Reinhold Company Limited
Molly Millars Lane
Wokingham, Berkshire, England

16 15 14 13 12 11 10 9 8 7 6 5 4 3 2 1

Library of Congress Cataloging in Publication Data

Shea, John Gerald.
    The Pennsylvania Dutch and their furniture.

    Bibliography: p.
    Includes index.
    1. Furniture, Pennsylvania Dutch. 2. Pennsylvania
Dutch—Social life and customs. I. Title.
TT200.S4   749′.1′0287   80–11149
ISBN 0–442–27546–3

Acknowledgments

For their courteous cooperation in furnishing photographs and information, separately credited in this book, the author wishes to thank the following museums and historical sources:

American Museum in Britain, Bath, England; Mrs. Kay Bond, Curator.

Daniel Boone Homestead, Birdsboro, Pa. 19508; Dr. Lawrence Thurman, Curator.

Ephrata Cloister, Ephrata, Pa.; Mr. John L. Kraft, Curator.

Greenfield Village and Henry Ford Museum, Dearborn, Mich. 48121; Mrs. C. V. Hagler, Curator.

The Heritage Center of Lancaster County, Lancaster, Pa. 17604; Mr. Bruce G. Shoemaker, Administrator.

Hershey Museum of American Life, Hershey, Pa. 17033; Mrs. Eliza C. Harrison, Curator.

Historic Schaefferstown, Inc., Schaefferstown, Pa.; Mr. John D. Miller, Director.

Index of American Design, National Gallery of Art, Washington, D. C. 20565; Mrs. Lina Steele, Curator.

Annie S. Kemerer Museum, Bethlehem, Pa. 18918; Mrs. Byron G. Hayes, Director.

Lebanon County Historical Society, Lebanon, Pa. 17042; Mr. Ray S. Bowman, Director.

Mercer Museum, Doylestown, Pa.; Ms. Laurie J. Rufe, Curator.

The Metropolitan Museum of Art, New York, N.Y. 10028; Dora L. Pines, Librarian.

Moravian Museum of Bethlehem, Bethlehem, Pa. 18018; Mrs. C. A. Zug, Director.

Pennsylvania Farm Museum of Landis Valley, Lancaster, Pa. 17601; Carroll J. Hopf, Director.

Philadelphia Museum of Art, Philadelphia, Pa.; Mrs. Beatrice B. Garvan, Associate Curator.

William Penn Memorial Museum, Harrisburg, Pa. 17120; Ms. Cathryn J. McElroy, Curator of Decorative Arts.

Rock Ford Plantation, Lancaster, Pa. 17602; Henry J. Kauffman, Director.

Smithsonain Institution, Washington, D.C. 20560; Ms. Roberta A. Diemer (Photo Approval).

The Henry Francis du Pont Winterthur Museum, Winterthur, Del. 19735; Karol A. Schmeigel, Curator.

Most museums, listed above, were visited by the author, who is most grateful for the cordial welcomes extended by their curators. In most instances they were most generous of their time while they furnished detailed information on the historical background of their holdings. Some, in fact, extended their courtesy to take time to measure selected pieces of their furniture for inclusion in the measured drawings chapter of this book.

The following museums and historical places were listed for general reference and were contacted in correspondence.

American Canal Society, York, Pa. 17403; Mr. Thomas F. Hann, Secretary.

American Canal Society, York, Pa., 17403; Mr. Thomas F. Hann, Secretary.

The Historical Society of Berks County, Reading, Pa. 19601; Mrs. Harold Yoder, Curator.

The Historical Society of York County, York, Pa. 17403; Mrs. Richard C. Shultz, Director.

Lancaster Historical Society, Lancaster, Pa.; Mr. John Aunget, Archivist.

Lehigh County Historical Society, Allentown, Pa. 18104; Mrs. G. Spencer Allen, Librarian.

Newtown Historical Association, Inc., Newtown, Pa. 18940; Mrs. Robert S. Miller, President.

North Museum, Franklin and Marshall College, Lancaster, Pa., 17604; Mr. W. Fred Kinsey, Director.

Old Economy, Ambridge, Pa. 15003; Mr. Daniel Reibel, Director.

Pennsylvania Canal Society, Nazareth, Pa. 18064; C. P. Yoder, Curator.

Pennsylvania Dutch Folk Culture Society, Lenhartsville, Pa. 19534; Dr. Florence Baver, Director.

Railroad Museum of Pennsylvania, Strasburg, Pa. 17579.

Railroad and Trolley History, Columbia. Pa. 17512; Mr. John D. Denney, Historian.

The Reading Public Museum and Art Gallery, Reading Pa. 19602; Mr. Bruce L. Dietrich, Director.

The Valley Forge Historical Society, Valley Forge State Park, Valley Forge, Pa. 19481; Louise Kneass, Curator.

Of those who helped most directly in manuscript preparation, large portions of thanks and credit go to my bright and delightful daughters-in-law. First, there's Carol Wright Shea, the highly talented professional artist, who illustrated Chapters 4 and 5. Her outstanding talent seems to improve with each successive book of mine she illustrates—and is again expressed in this book; particularly in her precise interpretation of the *"hex signs"* in Chaper 5.

And, of course, Mary Anne Shea, wife of my younger son, who, at college, majored in history. Mary Anne did the research for Chapter 1 with such care and intensity that her detailed notes could easily be expanded to a full treatise on the subject, if book space allowed.

Then, my heartfelt thanks go to Mr. Joseph A. Romeo, the talented artist-draftsman who prepared precise pen and ink renderings of my measured drawings for the final chapter.

Thank you all!

Preface

Pennsylvania is located within 100 miles of my home, but up until the time that research of this book started, my wife and I had little reason to visit this state. Of course, many, many times we scooted back and forth across the Pennsylvania Turnpike enroute to the West. But we missed all the beautiful country lying north and south of Turnpike tracks.

In particular, we missed the Pennsylvania Dutch country located in the southern and eastern regions of the state. This is an area of rich farmlands and vast industrial projects that are owned and operated, mostly, by descendants of the original Pennsylvania Dutch settlers, who first came to this country during the latter years of the 18th century. Largely because of the rigid dictates of their religious faiths, they retained their original customs throughout the ensuing centuries—and even today, still observe the taboos and restrictions of their religions.

Today, this area is interlaced with ribbons of concrete—thruways, turnpikes and superhighways—speeding tourists to, through and away from the Pennsylvania Dutch country. Where once there were uninterrupted acres of farms and fertile pastures, now there are complexes of motels intermingled with gas stations, pizza huts and fast food franchises. Superficially, at least, it looks just like the rest of rural America!

But after you leave the concrete speedways and enter the sideroads and backroads, you can commence to observe the "Dutchness" of the countryside. You pass by acres of immaculately groomed farms—all with spacious barns usually decorated with quaint "hex" signs. Everything about these farms is impressive. If you get there in season, you will observe vast rows of crops, extending over the horizon in precise alignment. You will also see healthy livestock grazing in lush meadows and horses—yes, *"horses"*—in abundance. For the Pennsylvania Dutch farmers still depend on their horses to work their farms, just as they did centuries ago.

For an initial tour of the Pennsylvania Dutch country, it would be well to start in the northeast with the city of Bethlehem. You can then move west to the environs of Allentown. Following Route 78 you can drive toward the west until you arrive at Harrisburg. Along the way, you may wish to turn off the highway and travel short distances south to visit Lenhartsville, Lebanon and Hershey. Reversing your route, toward the East, you enter the heart of Pennsylvania Dutchland, visiting such places as Schaeffertown, Manheim, Lititz, Ephrata, Lancaster, Millersville, Reading, Intercourse, Birdsboro—and a scattering of innumerable other picturesque places in between.

If you have the good fortune to visit this country during the spring or fall seasons, you will marvel at the tidiness and good repair of everything you see. All the farm buildings and residences are freshly painted. Things do not lie about, willy-nilly, around the farmyards, but are placed or stacked in orderly fashion. The old addage, "a place for everything and everything in its place" is certainly put into practice, quite seriously, by the Pennsylvania Dutch farmers.

As you move along the backroads it behooves you to drive at careful pace. For along the way you will encounter many Amish horse n' buggies clip-clopping along the highways. Only recently were they required to put luminous reflectors on the backs of their buggies. Previously, numerous collisions were reported with oncoming, speeding automobiles.

My research trips into the Dutchland of Pennsylvania were spaced over two years. During this time, my wife and I made four separate visits, each of one week's duration, in the spring and fall of each year. Thus, while we spent one month visiting the rural museums and countryside of Pennsylvania, we were able to do so during the most favorable seasons of the year: in May when everything was bursting into bloom, and in October when the foliage was painted in vivid colors.

The first journey took us to the William Penn Memorial Museum, located in the capitol city of Harrisburg. Here, with the generous help of Curator McElroy, we had an opportunity to examine a spacious display of antique furniture, firearms, vehicles and folkcraft. We also became oriented to other displays, preserved by the Pennsylvania Historical Museum Commission and located in regional museums in other parts of Pennsylvania.

All in all, we ultimately visited more than 15 of these regional museums and gathered much important information and many useful photographs from them.

Traveling from museum to museum, one thing impressed us in particular: It was the abundance of Dower Chests displayed in each museum. On the average, each of these chests was approximately 200 years old, but they were maintained in perfect condition, their colorful decorations showing almost as brilliantly as the day they were first painted.

Equally impressive was the superb workmanship of the massive Pennsylvania *Kas*, of which there was at least one example displayed in every museum. Some of these ponderous cabinets must have required considerable time to construct. They are the best examples of the early Pennsylvania craftsman's superb skill at cabinetmaking.

Also, of special interest, were the abundant displays of firearms, including the famous ''Kentucky Rifles'' which were first made by the Pennsylvania Dutch, at Lancaster, centuries ago. These long-barreled, heavy rifles were considered to be much more accurate than any rifles made prior to their appearance.

It was also exciting to have an opportunity to look over so many of the flambuoyant old Canestoga Wagons, which are carefully restored and displayed in so many of the Pennsylvania museums. These, too, were an important invention and product of the Pennsylvania Dutch, and they were responsible for moving most of the commerce of Pennsylvania during the early days.

Now, a word about the content of this book: It seemed logical, at the start, to devote the first chapter to a comprehensive look at how Pennsylvania got to be settled with a description of the European colonists who emigrated to this state. Since religion played such an important part in their lives, it seemed appropriate to devote adequate space to descriptions of the many religions which governed their lives.

Then, Chapter 2 endeavors to explore the various occupations in which the Pennsylvania Dutch engaged. In the practice of many of their crafts and skills, their products were superior to those of the other colonies. And, particularly, in furniture making, their sophisticated skills, exemplified by the ornate furniture made in the urban centers of Philadelphia and elsewhere, set new standards of refinement for American craftmanship.

Chapter 3 explores the ramifications of designs of antique Pennsylvania country furniture. It is hoped that this chapter may catalog a comprehensive assortment of typical furniture made by the Pennsylvania Dutch.

Construction and old building techniques are discussed and illustrated in Chapter 4. This gets into old woodworking tools and devices used centuries ago to make furniture. At the same time, methods of joinery and common construction procedures are described and illustrated. Finally, a Dower Chest was especially built to illustrate, step-by-step, its constructional requirements.

Chapter 5 is devoted to important aspects of painting and decorating Pennsylvania Dutch furniture. The proper techniques of applying painted decorations are described and illustrated in step-by-step instructive sequences. It is hoped that this will help those who wish to try their hand at duplicating these decorations.

Also in Chapter 5, an assortment of hex sign designs are shown and instructions are given on their layout to help those who may desire to copy them.

Finally, Chapter 6 is devoted to presentation of over 50 actual Pennsylvania Dutch antique furniture designs with measured drawings to guide their reproduction. While many of these designs would require the skill of advanced craftsmen to assure satisfaction in their reproduction, there may be many skilled craftsmen among the readers of this book, and with drawings and dimensions given, they may proceed to make some of these handsome antiques. Others, less skilled, may try their hands at making the simpler pieces.

All in all, it is hoped that this may prove to be a *useful* book, and that all those who use it may find something interesting and helpful in its contents.

Contents

CHAPTER 1   COLONIZATION,
CUSTOMS & CREEDS   1
   Colonization, Customs & Creeds   3
   Causes of European Exodus   3
   Impact of the Reformation   3
   Direct Causes of Immigration to
      America   4
   William Penn's "Holy
      Experiment"   4
   The Voyage to America   5
   Perils of Passage   5
   The First Settlers   7
   The Second Wave of Settlers   8
   First Homes in America   8
   Life of the Early Colonists   9
   Variety of Religions   11
   The Plain People   11
   The Mennonites   12
   The Amish   13
   The Dunkards (or
      Baptist-Brethren)   15
   The Schwenkfelders   15
   River Brethren (or "Brethren in
      Christ")   17
   The Church People   17
   Lutherans   17
   Reformed Church   18
   The Moravians   18
   Ephrata Society (Seventh Day
      Baptist)   19
   Anabaptists   19
   Other Religious Sects   20

CHAPTER 2   OCCUPATIONS:
ARTS, CRAFTS & INDUSTRIES   21
   Occupations: Arts, Crafts &
      Industries   23
   Felling the Forest   23
   Agriculture   23
   Early Farmhouses   25
   Metalwork   26
   Textiles   32
   Fractur   34
   Ceramics   36
   Glass   37
   Woodenware & Carving   38
   Cooperage   39
   Transportation:
      Conestoga Wagons, Canal Boats &
      Trains   40

CHAPTER 3   FURNITURE
DESIGN   43
   Furniture Design   45
   Chairs   46
   Rockers   50
   Benches, Settees, Stools & Seats   52
   Tables   55
   Desks   61
   Dough Tables & Bins   63
   Stands & Stools   64
   Dower Chests   65
   Small Boxes & Chests   69
   Chests of Drawers   71
   Wall Cupboards & Hanging
      Shelves   72

Corner Cupboards   75
Utility Dressers   76
Cupboards   78
Schranks   80
Cradles   82
Beds   85
Boxes, Racks, Mirror & Stools   86
Kitchen Utility Furniture   88
Spinning Wheels, Looms & Reels   91
Pianos & Musical Instruments   93
Clocks   94
The Apostolic Clock   96

CHAPTER 4   FURNITURE
CONSTRUCTION   97
Old Construction   98
Felling & Hewing   99
Old Woodworking Tools   100
Early Hand Tools   100
Old Woodworking Devices   102
Old Hardware   104
Applied Moldings   106
Dado Joints   108
Edge Shapes   108
End Cleats   110
Edge Joints   110
Simple Carving   110
Lapped Joints   112
Pegleg Construction   112
Dovetail Joints   114
Dovetailed Construction   116
Hinged Joints   116
Mortise & Tenon Joints   118
How to Reproduce A Pennsylvania
    Dutch Dower Chest   120

CHAPTER 5   FURNITURE
PAINTING & DECORATING   127
Furniture Painting & Decorating   128
Decorative Painting   129
How to Apply Painted Decorations   130
How to Transfer Decorative
    Designs   131
Tools & Materials   132

Painting Procedures   132
Stencils   144
Hex Signs   148
Variations of Hex Designs   149
How to Lay Out Hex Designs   150
Variations of Hex Designs   152

CHAPTER 6   FURNITURE
MEASUREMENTS   155
Painted Kitchen Chair   156
"Judge's Chair"   157
"Moravian" Chair   158
Kitchen Stool   159
Pine Side Bench   160
Cricket-on-the-Hearth   161
Joint Table of Yellow Pine   162
Scrolled-Apron Bedside Table   164
Pennsylvania Desk-Table   165
Oval-Top Sawbuck Table   166
Occasional Table   167
Dower Chest   168
Dower Chest With Drawers   170
Kitchen Storage Cabinet   172
Hutch Table   173
Bench Table With Hutch   174
Chair Table With Hutch   175
Carpenter's Tool Box   176
Dough Bin   177
Dough Trough Table   178
Dough Trough Table (Design
    Variation)   179
Plate Rack   180
"Marbleized" Shelf   181
Adjustable Candle Stand   182
Betty Lamps With Threaded
    Standard   183
Turned Candle Stand   184
Miniature Chest of Drawers   185
Candle Box   186
Salt Box   187
Wall Boxes & Spoon Rack   188
Kitchen Utility Shelves   190
Pie Safe With Pierced Tin Panels   191
Pine Key Cupboard   192

Staghorn-Hinged Hanging
    Cupboard   193
Scrolled Wall Cupboard   194
Hanging Cupboard   195
Small Dovetailed Chest   196
Water Bench   197
Nazareth Hall School Desk   198
Schoolmaster's Desk   199
Drop-Lid Desk   200
Walnut Cradle   202
Hooded Cradle   203
''Cannonball'' Four-Poster Bed   204
Four-Poster Bed With Tester Top   206
Chest of Drawers   208
Chest of Drawers   210
Corner Cupboard   212
Open Cupboard   214
Pennsylvania Dutch Dresser   216

SELECTED BIBLIOGRAPHY   219
INDEX   223

Chapter 1

Colonization, Customs & Creeds

Ephrata Cloister. A preserved and restored group of medieval-style buildings erected in the 1730s by the pietistic Seventh Day Baptists. The large building is the *Saron*, or Sister's House. (*Photo by Karl G. Rath. Courtesy, Pennsylvania Historical and Museum Commission, Harrisburg, Pa.*)

COLONIZATION, CUSTOMS & CREEDS

They came from the Palatinate (in southern Germany) and other rich and fertile regions of the Rhine Valley: Wurtemberg, Baden and Alsace. They also emigrated from Switzerland, Sweden, Denmark, France, Silesia, Saxony and Moravia. And they settled in America in equally rich and fertile regions of southeastern Pennsylvania.

They came seeking religious freedom, economic betterment—or just adventure. Many endured incredible hardships both en route *to* and *in* their adopted land. But they arrived in such great numbers that Benjamin Franklin once worried aloud that Pennsylvania would soon become a German colony.

In America, the Pennsylvania Dutch lived apart from their Anglo neighbors—separated from them by language and customs. They were drawn to each other ethnically by their religions and ties of similar heritage. They were mainly agricultural people. But their abilities were mixed, and there were many skilled craftsmen and mechanics among them. Because of their diverse abilities, they were able to become a self-sufficient society. This tended to encourage their isolation and reinforce their ethnic independence from surrounding English-speaking settlements.

Originally, they were all called the "Deutsch" (or Germans) because among them the Germans were most numerous. But through the years, the pronunciation degenerated to "Dutch," and so the sobriquet "Pennsylvania Dutch" has endured.

CAUSES OF EUROPEAN EXODUS

The Germans and others who immigrated to America during the latter years of the 17th century were induced to make their moves because of intolerable conditions in their homelands. Seventeenth century Europe was suffering from the effects of polarizing and disastrous influences, causing wars and religious upheaval.

In the early 16th century, a Roman Catholic monk named Martin Luther, from Eisleben in the Harz Mountains, catalyzed a movement known as the Protestant Reformation. This started a chain of reactions throughout Europe which irrevocably altered the course of history.

In 1517, Luther published a list of 95 theses—a catalog of protest against alleged abuses and excesses within the Roman Catholic Church. Factions and splinter groups soon emerged in support or condemnation of the various aspects of the controversy. Eventually, religious and political considerations became confused and entangled.

Originally, there was no conscious decision to break away from the Roman Catholic Church. Those who agreed with Luther's dissatisfaction hoped that differences could be worked out within the Church. But as arguments became more heated and positions hardened, people were forced to choose sides. Eventually, those sides succumbed to wrath and endeavored to annihilate one another.

IMPACT OF THE REFORMATION

By the 17th century, the once powerful Holy Roman Empire had dissolved into little more than a loose federation of jealously independent German states. These numbered anywhere from 200 to 3,000—depending on whether one counted the scores of knights who lived on small estates and paid homage to no one but the Emperor. States' rights were vigorously enforced, with the ruler of each state determining the religion of his subjects.

This spelled disaster for German unity. For in the meantime, England, France, the Netherlands and Spain were centralizing and establishing their own national identities while the German states were regressing into a mosaic of feudalism.

By the early 17th century, various contending forces had emerged throughout Europe. These included Catholics vs. Protestants; States' Rights vs. Autocracy; France vs. the Hapsburgs; France vs. the Dutch. These controversies finally erupted into the Thirty Years' War (1618–1648). The Peace of Augsburg, which ended this war in 1648, put the finishing touches on the Holy Roman Empire, which then ceased to be an important force.

By the mid-17th century, western Europe was divided between Catholic and Protestant powers. Religious plurality had become recognized and accepted among the states, but not usually within them. Costly wars had been fought in the name of religion, but the political considerations were also substantial. The principle of States' Rights became firmly rooted in the Rhineland, as well as that of *cuius regio, cius religio* (whose the region, his the religion). The insecurity of the times was heightened by religious and political vacillation. Frequently, when a ruler changed, so did the religion. Those subjects who did not fall into line were either persecuted or killed.

In 1661, Louis XIV came to the throne of France. His ascension ushered in the Age of the Grand Monarch. Militarily he sought to expand his empire by attacking the Hapsburgs' holdings both in Spain and, to the east, along the Rhine. Domestically, he sought to enhance his personal comfort and image by sparing no expense in furnishing himself with extravagantly lavish surroundings. Many German states suffered grievously under the ravages of Louis' military campaigns. Homes were plundered and razed, and farmlands were burnt and destroyed. Two-thirds of the farm animals were killed or eaten by rampaging armies.

DIRECT CAUSES OF IMMIGRATION TO AMERICA

The Germans and others who immigrated to America during the latter years of the 17th century were induced to make their moves because of intolerable conditions in their homelands. As has already been noted, Germany was devastated by the Thirty Years' War. People were starving. There was constant conflict between religious factions: the followers of Luther, John Calvin and Ulrich Zwingli were antagonistic to the Catholics—and to each other—vying for control of the state church.

A multitude of obscure pietistic sects and esoteric cults swarmed in the urban and rural regions, and they persisted despite constant persecutions that were caused by the rapid change of rulers. Electors of the Palatinate changed religions 4 times in 4 successive reigns—and the people were expected to change religions in conformance with the current beliefs of their political leaders.

The burden of wars, misery and devastation visited on southern Germany and neighboring regions of the Rhine Valley looms large in the history of human misery. One authority says that between 1618 and 1700, the population of the Rhine Valley was reduced to one-tenth of its original size.

Religious toleration was then an unknown quantity in most of Europe, except for the Netherlands. When religious groups considered emigrating, their choices were few. They could go to the Netherlands and try to assimilate into the already established Dutch society, or they could take the greater risk of going to North America and establishing their own societies in the wilderness. Many of them chose the latter.

WILLIAM PENN'S "HOLY EXPERIMENT"

William Penn, an English Quaker, had been given a huge grant of land in North America by King Charles II. Here, he hoped to establish his "Holy Experiment"—a land where people of all beliefs would be welcome to live and practice their own religions in peace. Separation of church and state and religious liberty were regarded as highly radical concepts at that time. Nevertheless, Penn invited people of all beliefs, nationalities and opinions to join him in the development of his fertile colony.

Penn's Holy Experiment worked. Pennsylvania with its liberal philosophy of freedom, dedicated to the Quaker principles of pacifism and of opportunity for the oppressed, grew faster than any other colony in the 18th century.

William Penn invited a group of German Mennonites, whose beliefs were similar to the Quakers, to come to Pennsylvania. In 1683, Francis Daniel Pastorius, a German scholar, lawyer and leader, brought the first group of emigrés to Pennsylvania. Here they settled on acres of land purchased from the Penn family, in the vicinity of Philadelphia.

The strenuous journey across the Atlantic and the hardships encountered in hacking homesteads from the virgin forests were formidable. But living conditions for the first emigrés had been so intolerable in their homelands that they considered the risks encountered in the New World to be worth taking.

THE VOYAGE TO AMERICA

In his own personal account, called *Opportunities and Ways of Emigrating to this Country* (America), Pastorius described the ordeal as follows:

The German Society commissioned myself, Francis Daniel Pastorius, as their legal agent, to go to Pennsylvania and to superintend the purchase and survey of their lands.

From the month of April until the fall of every year there are vessels sailing to Pennsylvania, at frequent times, from England, principally from the port of Deal, although there is no fixed time or day for sailing, and persons are therefore compelled to watch their opportunity. Whenever there is a company of thirty-five or forty passengers together, exclusive of the ship's crew, a vessel is despatched. Every grown-up man pays for his passage the sum of 6 pounds sterling, or 36 rix dollars. For a female or servant, 22 rix dollars . . . .

After I had left London, where I had made my arrangements with Penn's agent, and arrived at Deal, I hired four male and two female servants, and on the 7th day of June

1683, set sail on the "Concord" with a company of eighty passengers. Our ship drew thirteen feet of water. Our fare on board was poor enough. The allowance of provision for ten persons per week was as follows: three pounds of butter; daily four cans of beer and one can of water, every noon; two dishes of peas; four times per week salt meat, and three times salt fish, which we were obliged to cook, each man for himself, and had daily to save enough from dinner to serve for our suppers also. And as these provisions were usually very poor, and the fish sometimes tainted, we were all compelled to make liberal use of liquors and other refreshments of a similar nature to preserve the health amid such hard fare. Moreover, it is the practice of the masters of these vessels to impose upon their passengers in a shameful manner by giving them very short allowances. It is therefore advisable not to pay the passage in full in England, but to withhold a part until the arriving in America, so that they are obliged to fulfill their part of the contract. Furthermore, it is advisable to endeavor to obtain passage in vessels bound to Philadelphia direct, inasmuch as those who come in such, landing at Upland, are subjected to many and grievous molestations.

PERILS OF PASSAGE

Of course, Pastorius did not dwell on the many additional hardships passengers had to endure en route to America. On one ship 100 to 150 passengers died of hunger. Ship fever was commonplace and came to be called "Palatine Fever." The journey to Philadelphia required 3 to 6 months at sea.

The sea voyage was made miserable because of the avaricious sea captains who only sought profit from their voyage at the expense and discomfort of their passengers. Ships were overcrowded and filthy. The food was scarce and was usually contaminated.

The journey of the emigrants did not begin with the sea voyage, but in their homelands in mid-Europe—many miles from England. Emigrants started out thinking they had enough

Open Fireplace of Saal Kitchen at Ephrata Cloister. The arduous monastic life endured by the pietistic Seventh Day Baptists of Ephrata allowed little physical comfort for the worshipers. (*Photo courtesy, Pennsylvania Historical and Museum Commission, Harrisburg, Pa.*)

money to pay for their voyage. But they were repeatedly cheated by unscrupulous operators. Their journey down the Rhine took perhaps 6 weeks during which they passed through 36 toll gates and customs houses. Every boat was subject to search at the whim of the customs officials, and spurious taxes and gratuities were extracted from the passengers.

Conditions on the emigrant ships, usually owned by English, Dutch or American operators, closely resembled those on African slave ships. The captains often starved and abused the passengers as badly as they did the slaves.

But to get back to Francis Daniel Pastorius. After their arduous sea voyage, he and his company journeyed on foot to the site of the land they had purchased from William Penn. Here they set to work laying the foundation for one of the most successful agricultural communities in the history of North America.

In his own personal account, Pastorius describes the development of Germantown as follows:

As relating to our newly laid-out town, Germanopolis, or Germantown, it is situated on deep and very fertile soil, and is blessed with an abundance of fine springs and fountains of fresh water. The main street is sixty and the cross street forty feet in width. Every family has a plot of ground for yard and garden three acres in size.

Thus prospered Pastorius and the group of Germans who joined him in colonizing the environs of Philadelphia. Thousands more soon followed. Ultimately, his tract of land between the Schuylkill and Delaware rivers was divided into four hamlets which no longer exist: Germantown, Krisheim, Krefeld and Sommerhausen.

THE FIRST SETTLERS

During the first wave of German immigration to Pennsylvania (1683–1727), people left their homelands because they were politically oppressed, economically impoverished, militarily devastated and religiously persecuted.

Central Hall and Prayer Room at Saal. The Seventh Day Baptist pietistic sect at Ephrata, Pa. was offered only bare comfort during endless sermons attended as part of their worship. (*Photo courtesy, Pennsylvania Historical and Museum Commission, Harrisburg, Pa.*)

They were honest, industrious people—agriculturally progressive, efficient and advanced. Many of them were educated. They paid their own passage over and bought their own land when they arrived in America.

As has already been noted, the first immigrants to arrive here with Pastorius settled in Germantown (which is now part of Philadelphia). These were largely Mennonites. Because of the similarities between Mennonites and Quakers, many of them converted to Quakerism.

In addition to Mennonites, the early religious sects included Pietists, Baptist Brethren, Lutherans, Amish, Schwenkfelders, Moravians and others. The Mennonites settled in Lancaster County; the Moravians in Bethlehem, Nazareth and Letitz; the Amish (a branch of the Mennonites) settled in Berks and Lancaster Counties; and the Lutherans received 22,377 acres at Manatawny—called The New German Tract, or "Falckner's Swamp." Members of the Reformed Church bought land from Penn's grantees near Neshaminy.

Soon the many Pennsylvania Dutch sects occupied lands in Dauphin, Northampton, York, Lebanon, Lancaster, Lehigh and Berks Counties. By 1730, they had made the land 100 miles east of the Susquehanna their domain.

Most of the early German immigrants were commoners, but a few aristocrats were mixed among them. They were primarily farmers, although artisans, craftsmen, teachers, doctors, preachers and other professions were represented. There were no court cavaliers or military men. These were the same Germans who had borne the burden of so many unhappy years in their homelands and who now dreamed of building an entirely new life in Pennsylvania.

THE SECOND WAVE OF SETTLERS

After 1727 most Germans arrived here in extreme poverty as indentured servants. For the most part, they lacked the education and cultural backgrounds of their predecessors. They were called Redemptioners and were recruited by ship owners and land agents who went through the Rhineland persuading the peasantry—often by misrepresentation and with false promises—to embark for Pennsylvania.

Usually the Redemptioners had to pledge from 2 to 7 years of their lives to serve out their indentures. Thus, they virtually became slaves to the ship owners and agents who provided their passage and, as such, they were sold to the highest bidders.

Fortunately, after the Redemptioners had served out their indentures in America, they were given a small plot of land and tools to work it, and thus became free citizens.

During the heaviest period of immigration (between 1749 and 1754), about 5,000 people per year immigrated to Pennsylvania. As has been pointed out, most of these were farmers, although many were experts in the mechanical arts. These skilled workers assisted substantially in the development of colonial manufacturing industries. The first census in 1790 revealed that 120,000 people—or one-third of the population of Pennsylvania—was of Germanic origin.

FIRST HOMES IN AMERICA

The first Germans arriving in Pennsylvania found a land very similar in terrain and climate—and in its potential for agricultural development—to their native Rhineland. The entire country was filled with dense forests sprinkled by fresh water streams and areas of rich mineral deposits. Woods and streams were alive with game and fish. Of course, much preliminary work was required to clear the land for farming.

Nothing was more important to the newly arrived immigrants than the character of the soil. They had learned that the richest soil lay beneath the densest forests. And the limestone valleys of eastern Pennsylvania were fabulously fertile.

So they toiled from dawn to dusk to clear

the woodlands. By wielding their saws and axes to bring down the trees, the pioneers also provided logs for their primitive cabins, fuel for heat and clearance of the land on which to sow their crops.

The immigrant's first home in America was apt to be a cave dug in the side of a hill, whose front opening was protected by overhanging branches. Or, a pit was dug by the river bank, deep enough for a man to lie down and tall enough for him to stand erect.

Soon, however, the dwellings in Pennsylvania imitated the half-timbered houses of northern Europe. Log cabins and "block houses" were built with whole trees squared into timber from rough logs and then laid in the form of a rectangle, one upon the other. The squared timbers were stacked high enough to provide head room. Tips of the timbers were notched into each other about one foot from the ends. Usually a peaked roof was raftered to receive a covering of split logs called *shooks*. All chinks and openings were stuffed with mud, clay and moss. Thus, a tight and warm little house was constructed and was heated by a great, open fireplace.

But dear to the hearts of all Pennsylvania Dutch farmers were their barns, and the erection of proper barns took first priority in their building programs.

At first, like their houses, they built their barns as large log cabins. But later they erected great barns, scientifically laid out and planned to serve the needs of livestock and storage. These barns were built better than their homes. Indeed, these people willingly sacrificed personal comfort for the sake of improving their barns and service buildings. The barn was always built first.

The Pennsylvania Dutch were partial to the building of *bank barns*, which were built against the side of a hill. In this way, horses pulling wagonloads of hay had easy access by ramp to the second floor. As a rule, animals were housed on the first floor, and grain and hay were stored above.

Usually, the barns were decorated with *hex signs*. These colorful devices are often regarded as superstitious symbols intended to ward off witches and other evil spirits which might otherwise bring harm to the occupants of the barn. However, although in Europe hex decorations did have religious connotations, in this country they are simply regarded as colorful decorations intended only to relieve the monotony of unadorned barns.

Incidentally, a number of typical hex designs are shown on pages 150–151—with instructions on how to reproduce them.

LIFE OF THE EARLY COLONISTS

Beginning with their arrival on the *Concord* in 1683, the German immigrants continued to come to Pennsylvania in significant numbers for nearly a century. The first wave of settlers, who arrived between 1683 and the 1720s, were the Sectarians—or Plain People—fleeing persecution for their religious beliefs and practices.

The second wave, which began in the 1720s and continued through the American Revolution, consisted more of members of the established churches—Lutheran and Reformed—and included Rhinelanders, Palatinates, Swiss, Swedes, Netherlanders, Danes and Huguenots. These people were fleeing the physical devastation of their homelands caused by international controversies that were often precipitated by religious interests and by aggressive France, which was flexing its muscles and seeking to expand its borders. Many of these refugees were Redemptioners.

The majority of these immigrants arrived in Pennsylvania with only the barest of necessities. Their material possessions were few. But their determination to establish a new life in this new land was magnificent, and their trust in God was complete. Many had been successful farmers and skilled craftsmen in their homelands, and their abilities were to serve them well in Pennsylvania.

Farmers were practical, efficient and wise in the ways of ecology. The land was their treasury and they treated it with supreme care.

Mennonite Barn Raising, in Lancaster County, Pa. Not only did the Pennsylvania Dutch farmers revere their barns; the entire religious community pitched in to help in the erection of new barns. *Barn raisings* are still regarded as recreational events by the religious communities. (*Photo by Mel Horst, Witmer, Pa., Copyright © 1970*)

Any waste or abuse of the land they considered wantonly sinful. They used natural fertilizers and developed systems of crop rotation, including the technique of periodically letting each field remain fallow to restore itself.

Pennsylvania had the highest concentration of craftsmen in colonial America, and a significant proportion of them was "Dutch." They made their own tools and built their own mills and forges.

In 1690, the first paper mill in America was built by Willem Ruettynhuysen on a branch of the Wissahickon River. The settlers in the area excelled in printing and began publishing German-language newspapers and a German-language Bible that appeared even before an English-language version. The settlers engaged in various forms of milling and manufacturing. They were tanners, wheelwrights, gunsmiths, coopers, weavers and carpenters. They manufactured iron, glass, pottery, textiles and numerous other commodities.

In summary, the Pennsylvania Dutch raised abundant and superior crops and tended to their own trades. They worshiped in their own churches and they supplied their own clergymen. They socialized and married within their own society and they spoke their own language. Thus, these Germanic inhabitants of southeastern Pennsylvania became comfortably isolated from the surrounding English-speaking colonists. They became a self-sufficient island of transplanted culture, absorbing from their new environment only the ways and mores that their pragmatic natures saw as useful and good.

Most immigrant groups retain their Old World ways for two or three generations before assimilating into their adopted culture. But not the Pennsylvania Dutch! Nearly three centuries have elapsed since the Concord first arrived in Philadelphia. But today, there are still groups of Pennsylvania Dutch who have retained a remarkable degree of ethnic integrity.

VARIETY OF RELIGIONS

A wide variety of Protestant religions were represented among the Pennsylvania Dutch. Among them were the Mennonites, Amish, Dunkards, Ephrata Pietists, Lutherans, Reformed, Moravians and a number of small eccentric cults—some quite fanatical in their expressions of religious zeal.

The religions, and hence the life styles, of the Pennsylvania Dutch fall into three main groups: the Plain People; the Church People; and the Moravians. Each of these groups has its own cultural pattern and each differs from the others.

The Plain People, or sectarians, are the most readily recognizable of the Pennsylvania Dutch. Their anachronistic dress and simple life style have set them apart and fostered the misconception that all Pennsylvania Dutch are Plain People. This is not true at all, for the Plain People make up only a very small percentage of the entire Pennsylvania Dutch community. The main groups among the Plain People are the Mennonites, the Amish, the Dunkards and the Schwenkfelders.

About 90 percent of the Pennsylvania Dutch are Church People. They belong to those churches which were officially recognized and tolerated in their homelands.

The Moravians came from contemporary Czechoslovakia. Of all the emigrés, they had the most refined culture. Whereas agriculture and crafts were the main contributions of the Plain People and Church People, the Moravians made their mark in the areas of music and education. They came to America as settlers and as missionaries to the Indians. Many Moravians were from the upper class; none came as Redemptioners.

THE PLAIN PEOPLE

The Sectarians had endured a surfeit of intolerance, wars and haughty aristocrats in Europe. That is why they fled to Pennsylvania to participate in William Penn's Holy Experiment. There they were free to embrace the beliefs they cherished and to repudiate those they found offensive. The Plain People were extreme pacifists, refusing to become involved in wars or disputes of any kind.

However, although they refused to fight, they were patriotic to the American cause. During the Revolution, they supplied food for the Continental Army and cared for the war casualties. The relief of human misery and misfortune has always been a high priority of the Plain People.

The earliest German settlers who came to this country were deeply concerned with the dignity of every person and with the individual's right to freedom. They believed in full respect for the human person as the supreme being of God's earthly creation.

In 1688, they were among the first people in North America to draw up a formal written protest against slavery. And in the decades before the Civil War, many Pennsylvania Dutchmen, along with their Quaker neighbors, became involved in the anti-slavery movement and in giving refuge and assistance to runaway slaves.

The unadorned dress and simple life style of the Plain People symbolize their rejection of the excesses and decadence of court life and high society in Europe. Their life style *is* their religion, and the family is central to everything they believe in. Thus they avoid the luxuries of modern technology, because they fear that too much material comfort will break down the family structure and destroy the wholesome closeness which they have so successfully preserved. Christ lived simply, and so do they.

Several generations of a family often live together on the same farm. Rooms or apartments are added to the house to accommodate the growing numbers. The father is the head of the family. He educates the boys in the family business, be it agriculture or trade, while the mother teaches the girls about the domestic side of life. There is no women's liberation movement among the Plain People! The man is unquestionably the dominant figure.

Weddings, funerals and barn raisings are social events that bring many of them together. Any social gathering is always attended by a sumptuous spread of food. The men take great pride in the bountiful products from their farms, and the women take perhaps even greater pride in their careful preparation. Pies, sausages, roasts, jams, jellies, fresh fruits and vegetables—huge quantities of wholesome and hearty food are always present at social gatherings.

The Plain People do not have a developed theology as the Church People do. Rather, theirs is a life style grounded in Christianity and tempered by the philosophy of the dignity of each individual and by the values of hard work, honesty, efficiency and simplicity. Theirs is a fundamentalist religion emphasizing a decent, moral life style and Bible reading. They are an agrarian society living in peace with each other and in harmony with nature.

THE MENNONITES

Members of the Mennonite Church came to Pennsylvania on the *Concord* in 1683 with Francis Daniel Pastorius. The church is one of the oldest Protestant denominations, having been founded in 1536 by Menno Simons, a priest from Switzerland who broke away from the Roman Catholic Church.

The Mennonites follow a fundamentalist approach to Christianity, adhering to the sacraments but emphasizing adult rather than infant baptism. The early Mennonites fled from persecution in Switzerland, moving first to southern Germany and from there to Pennsylvania.

Mennonite clergymen are untrained. They are chosen from the community *by lot* and serve for a lifetime. The lot system, leaving the ultimate choice to God, is a reflection of their complete trust in God's will. The lot has also been used to arrange marriages.

Although they are extreme pacifists, the Mennonites have always been loyal to American causes. Ever since colonial times, they have provided relief for war victims. The alleviation of human suffering has always been a matter of high priority for them.

After World War II, the American Mennonites, who constituted only one-tenth of 1 percent of the U.S. population, provided 40 percent of all non-government assistance! They provided food, clothing, medical supplies and personal and professional help both at home and in foreign countries. The Mennonite Disaster Service works along with the Salvation Army and the Red Cross as one of only three private agencies recognized by the U.S. government to provide aid in times of disaster. In the wake of floods, hurricanes, or tornadoes, the Mennonites mobilize volunteers and material to help the victims. It is their way of putting Christianity to work.

The Mennonites' lives and dress are simple. Women wear long, dark dresses, aprons, bonnets and shawls. Their hair is pulled back and braided. They use no makeup. The men wear broad-brimmed black hats and high-collared black coats. They shun worldly pleasures and keep only religious or technical books in their homes. They neither smoke nor drink and they avoid places of public entertainment. They allow no influences into their lives which would distract them from their ultimate goal: the worship of God through efficient, honest work.

The Mennonites are farmers par excellence: they stay on their farms for life. They use scientific and modern methods of agriculture —but not modern machinery. Even today, the horse is the mainstay of their farms for energy and transportation.

Because in Europe the politician was the tool of the state, who punished all dissenters, the Mennonites did not forget the punishment they had suffered, so they shunned and abhorred both politics and politicians. They also took a dim view of labor unions, motion pictures, horse races, fairs and picnics and similar social affairs.

Mennonites take no oaths—nor do the Brethren and Quakers—although they do practice the right to affirm. They may extend charity among their own people but will not tolerate acceptance of community or state welfare. They do not approve of life insurance. They shun worldly pleasures and worldly sins, believing that Christ's life was simple—and so must be theirs.

They believe that each person is blessed with an Inner Light which guides him in interpreting the Bible for himself. Their lack of a unifying theology, and the ultraconservative nature of the traditional Mennonite ways, has led to the development of many factions. Each faction expresses a varying degree of strictness in its adherence to original Mennonite doctrine. Among these factions are the Funkites, Pikers, Herrites, Weavers, Evangelicals, Brennemans, Wislerites, Martinites, Wengerites, Thirty-Fivers and Amish. There are varying degrees of strictness in adherence to original Mennonite doctrine in the disciplines of these many sects. For instance, the Black Bumper Mennonites permit the use of automobiles as long as their bumpers are painted black!

THE AMISH

The Amish are a group which separated from the Mennonites in the late 17th century. They were founded by Jacob Amman of Amenthal, Switzerland. Amman disagreed with the Mennonites over the treatment of unfaithful members. He advocated *meidung,* or total ostracism of the unfaithful. The Mennonites considered this too severe.

Amish are more conservative than their Mennonite brothers, whom they consider to be too worldly. The Bible is the handbook which guides their daily lives, which are strictly regulated. The rules are so rigid that many groups have splintered over disagreements about minor matters. Thus the Amish have within them some 30 groups, some separated from one another over such seemingly trivial matters as the proper pitch of a barn roof!

The Old Order Amish still hold to the 17th century teachings of Jacob Amman. He allowed no churches, no trained clergy and no

"The Country Fair," a painting made in 1824, pictures the rural scene, suggesting conditions existing on early Pennsylvania farms. Healthy livestock and well-kept farm buildings reflect characteristic care of Pennsylvania Dutch farmers. (*Photo courtesy, Smithsonian Institution, Washington, D.C.*)

occupation except farming. He also delineated strict regulations concerning dress and behavior.

Amish of the Old Order believe in well-disciplined communities, pacifism, adult baptism and a simple life, guarded by separation from the outside world. Forbidden items include central heating in their homes, bathrooms—even running water. They do not allow curtains on their windows or decorations on their walls. Everything about them must be useful, and that which is only decorative or pleasurable is ruled out.

These Plain People fall into two major groups: the House Amish and the Church Amish. The House Amish have no churches. They hold their Sunday services in the homes of the members. The men and women sit separately on backless wooden benches. Their services are conducted in German, and last from two to three hours. The Church Amish worship in churches and hold their services in English.

During services, singing is permitted, but instrumental music is forbidden. The Amish have the oldest Protestant hymnal still in use today. But it contains only words—no musical notes. The tunes have been passed down orally through the generations.

Amish attire has remained much the same over the centuries. Married men may grow beards, but no mustaches! (The mustache is regarded as a sign of pride and historically the mark of a military man.) They use no buttons on their clothing. The ostentatious use of buttons on military uniforms in the 17th and 18th centuries became symbolic of wars and military oppression. Neckties are also considered too worldly; they prefer instead to wear brightly colored shirts under their black coats. Men's hair is usually worn short, is parted in the middle and is topped off by a black hat.

The women wear brightly colored dresses, aprons, black hats and shawls. A colored kerchief indicates a woman is married, whereas a white one means that she is single. Even babies wear the traditional garb.

Like so many others, the Amish came to America to escape religious persecution. By the middle of the 18th century, nearly all the Amish had left Europe. Today they are spread in communities throughout the United States, Canada and Paraguay.

Those who stayed in Pennsylvania are now concentrated in Lancaster County, which has become the most fertile and bountiful farmland in the United States: its farms lead the nation in production per acre.

Amish farmers practice crop rotation, diversified planting and natural fertilization. Few of them smoke cigarettes, but they do grow tobacco as a lucrative money crop. They stay on their farms until they die, at which time the land is passed on to the youngest son.

Today's Amish are the direct descendants of the 18th century immigrants. They seek no new members or converts. There are approximately 15,000 of them living in Pennsylvania. Intramarriage has been so commonly practiced that only about 30 different surnames remain.

Over the years the Amish have managed to escape poverty and unemployment. They look after their own, will not accept community or state welfare assistance and refuse all forms of government aid—including Social Security. They do not buy insurance, because they believe that this would show lack of faith in Divine Providence. Because of the restrictions of their faith, the government has ruled them exempt from the requirement to make Social Security payments.

During recent years, the positions taken by the Amish in regard to education have been highly controversial. The Amish are the only established religious group specifically opposed to secondary education on religious grounds. But they provide for *alternative* education in line with their beliefs and priorities.

Notwithstanding their many religious restrictions, the Amish are not an entirely somber people. Although they frown on dancing and the use of musical instruments, they do allow singing and get much enjoyment from attending barn raisings, quilting bees, songfests, auctions and similar social activities.

THE DUNKARDS (or BAPTIST-BRETHREN)

The Dunkards first came to Pennsylvania in 1719. Their name derives from their unique baptism ceremony which requires complete immersion—or dunking—three times, face forward, in a stream. Many Dunkard brethren were originally members of the Reformed Church. After their separation, the parent church became bitter and resorted to persecution to stamp out this rebellious new sect.

To escape persecution, the Dunkards first fled to Krefeld on the Rhine. Then, learning that William Penn was offering land and freedom of religious choice in America, they started to emigrate to this country. In 1719, 120 Dunkards arrived in Philadelphia and settled in Germantown. Within the next decade, practically all the Dunkards of Europe had migrated to America.

Like the Quakers and Mennonites, the Dunkards were non-belligerents, and their early dress was anachronistic.

THE SCHWENKFELDERS

The first Schwenkfelders arrived in Pennsylvania on September 24, 1734. They were followers of an Anabaptist mystic named Kasper Schwenkfeld von Ossig. He disagreed

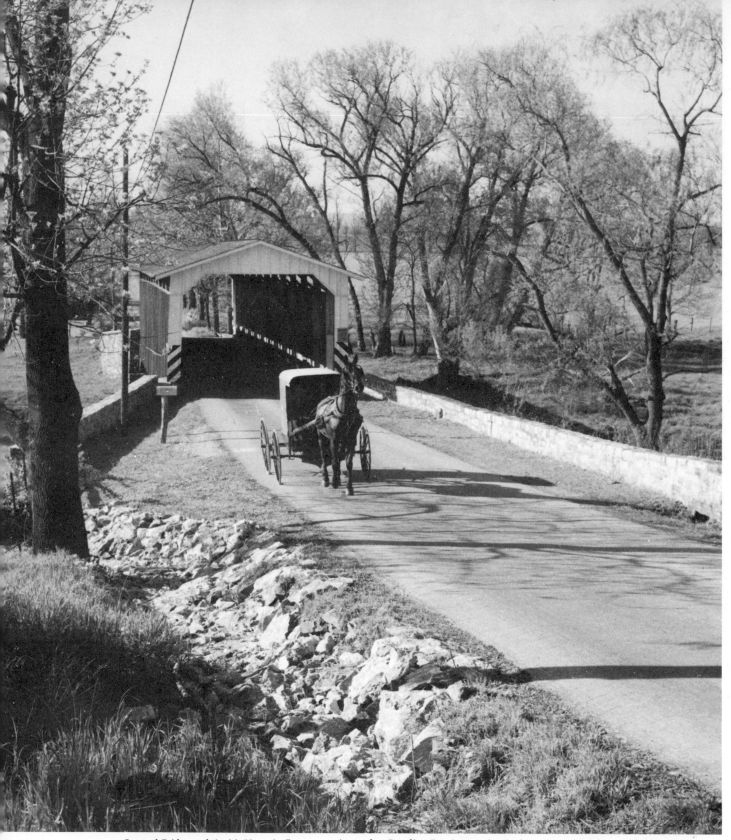

Covered Bridge and Amish Horse 'n Buggy, on the road to Paradise, Pa. Among the Amish, who eschew the use of automobiles, these covered buggies are still commonly used. (*Photo by Mel Horst, Witmer, Pa., Copyright © 1970.*)

with Martin Luther, believing that the spirit of Christ exists in man and is revealed by an Inner Light. Schwenkfeld did not allow baptism or communion rites. He contended that these were superficialities and that Christ was central to, and above, all other beliefs. In Europe, Schwenkfeld and his followers were persecuted for their beliefs, so they all emigrated to America to secure their religious freedom. None remained in Europe.

At first, the Schwenkfelders were regarded as "Plain People." They wore the same attire and followed the quiet customs of the Mennonites and Amish. However, with the passage of time, they started to dress in contemporary fashions and become more worldly in their attitude toward modern inventions and institutions.

RIVER BRETHREN (or "BRETHREN IN CHRIST")

The River Brethren practiced the virtues of simplicity, naturalness, modesty and integrity. They separated from the Mennonites because of their belief in baptism by immersion. (The prefix "River" was attached to their name because they settled near the Susquehanna River.) Like the House Amish, they had no churches; instead, they rotated their religious services in the homes of their members.

Characterized as a quiet people, with a strong strain of mysticism in their makeup, the River Brethren preferred to withdraw from the social and political activities of the world. Ardent pacifists, generous to their own and charitable to the world at large, the River Brethren live their Christianity. Incidentally, President Dwight D. Eisenhower's mother was a member of the River Brethren sect.

THE CHURCH PEOPLE

The Church People are those who belong to the Protestant churches which grew out of the Reformation and were officially recognized in Europe. The majority of the Pennsylvania Dutch fall into this category, approximately 90 percent of them belonging to the Lutheran and Reformed Churches. Frequently this vast majority of the Pennsylvania Dutch community is forgotten because its members have assimilated into the population so naturally. The religious restrictions and taboos of the Plain People do not affect the Church People: their clergymen are formally educated, and they live in a modern world and enjoy its comforts and conveniences.

There are, however, some common ties which link all Pennsylvania Dutch, regardless of their religion. First unlike the Puritans of New England, who wrote down and recorded all their deeds voluminously, the early Pennsylvania Dutch were not a literary society— theirs was a spoken language rather than a written one. Hence, much of their history has been orally recorded and passed along from generation to generation by word of mouth only. Also, regardless of religious denomination, they all believed in man's right to complete religious freedom and in the equality of all men before God.

LUTHERANS

Over 60 percent of Pennsylvania Dutch immigrants in the 18th century were Lutherans. They were the largest religious group among the German colonists in Pennsylvania.

The Lutherans were founded by Martin Luther, who taught that man's relationship with God did not require the mediation of a priest or a church. Luther believed that grace and faith alone would accomplish the salvation of man.

Lutheran and Reformed Churches and all other Protestant churches of the Pennsylvania Dutch were greatly influenced by the pietist movement of the 17th and 18th centuries. Pietism stressed Christianity as a way of life rather than as a creed.

The biggest difference between Lutheran and Reformed Churches is over their concepts of communion. In their church services, the Lutherans accept bread and wine as the *true* body and blood of Christ; members of the

Reformed Church regard bread and wine as being only *symbolic.*

Most Lutherans came to Pennsylvania to better themselves economically. Among them were many members of the nobility, including German princes.

Relations between the Lutherans and the Reformed Church in this country were generally amiable, although the Lutheran Church is more ritualistic and conservative than the Reformed. Both Lutheran and Reformed Church members enjoyed educational and cultural traditions. They encouraged art and music. Together, they founded Franklin College in 1787.

Today, the Lutheran Church is the main Protestant church in Germany, and it is also the state church of Norway, Sweden and Denmark.

REFORMED CHURCH

The Reformed Church was started in Switzerland by Ulrich Zwingli. It interprets the philosophy of the Reformation *liberally* rather than *literally.* The system of church government which it follows allows the layman to share authority with the clergy. This system has also been adopted by many other Protestant religions.

After the Peace of Augsburg in 1555, the principle was established that in religious worship a man must follow his ruler. Since some Germanic princes were Lutherans, members of the Reformed Church who lived under their rule were persecuted and banished.

As a result, more members of the Reformed Church than of the Lutheran Church emigrated to America during the early 18th century. In 1730, more than half the Pennsylvania Germans were Reformed, but by the late 18th century the Lutherans outnumbered them.

THE MORAVIANS

The Moravian Church—the oldest Protestant church still in existence—traces its origin back to the preaching of *John of Husinec,* more commonly known as *John Hus,* who was burned at the stake for his beliefs on July 6, 1415. The Moravian Church, which he started, emphasized the suffering of Christ.

After suffering persecution and banishment in Europe, the Moravians started emigrating to America early in the 18th century. They were led by Bishop Spangenberg and first settled in the state of Georgia. In 1740, some of them went north to Pennsylvania with a Methodist minister named Whitefield. William Penn's promises of freedom of religion and his philosophy of pacifism attracted them to establish permanent colonies in Pennsylvania.

When they arrived there, the Moravians first settled on the "Barony of Nazareth," a 5,000 acre tract granted by the Penn family for the payment of "one red rose on the 24th day of June yearly, if the same shall be demanded, in full (payment) of all services, customs and rents." The Moravians also bought 500 acres of land at the present site of Bethlehem, and they acquired additional land at Nazareth and Lititz.

Moravian settlers were generally better educated and more sophisticated than their Pennsylvania Dutch neighbors. Several members of the European nobility came over with them—including one of their leaders, Count Zinzendorf. They were people of gentle manners with exceptional sensitivity to the higher arts, especially music. They encouraged higher education and cultural development. During the early years of their settlement, they started the Moravian College at Bethlehem and the Moravian Academy, which is one of the oldest schools in America.

Bethlehem became the musical center of colonial America. The Moravians excelled in both vocal and instrumental music, and from their earliest days in Pennsylvania they encouraged enjoyment of this art. As early as 1744, they established the *Collegium Musicum,* a symphony of sorts with 14 musicians. In 1754, the Moravian Trombone Choir was organized. It is still functioning today, and has had the longest continuous existence of any musical group in the United States. Even today the Bach Festival is held annually at Bethlehem. Nazareth and Lititz also enjoy rich musical heritages.

The Moravian community was divided into two groups: the "Pilgergemeine" (or missionaries), whose work concentrated on the conversion of both whites and Indians to the Moravian faith; and the "Hausgemeine," whose job it was to build, farm and establish the settlements.

The Moravian missionaries traveled to places no other Christian missionaries had ever been. They penetrated into isolated parts of Maryland, Virginia, the Carolinas and Georgia, as well as New York and New England. They quickly made friends with the Indians and converted them to their faith—they even intermarried with them. Unlike the other settlers, the Moravians always paid the Indians for the land they took.

In time, Bethlehem became one of the most progressive towns of the American colonies. In 1754 the Moravians of Bethlehem built the first waterworks in America. By 1762 they imported America's first fire engine. The first apothecary shop in America was opened in Bethlehem by Dr. Frederick Otto in 1743.

There were many other "firsts" and an abundance of other progressive projects undertaken by the Moravians of Bethlehem, Nazareth and Lititz. By 1783, nearly all the congregation in Bethlehem was bilingual and the town was well known for its many schools and musical programs.

EPHRATA SOCIETY
(SEVENTH DAY BAPTISTS)

Perhaps the most curious of the early Pennsylvania Dutch religions was the Ephrata Society, which was founded early in the 18th century by Johann Conrad Beissel at Ephrata, Pennsylvania. Beissel had been banished from the Palatinate because of his religious beliefs.

Ephrata was a communistic society, not unlike the early Moravian church. The members eschewed physical pleasure of any sort and, attired in monks' robes, led a monastic life.

Beissel believed in the Seventh-Day Sabbath and preached the advantages of celibacy. He was against the use of meat and dairy products and advocated a strict vegetarian diet. He was anti-war and even anti-*iron*, insisting that wooden pegs be used instead of iron nails and that, wherever possible, wood be substituted for metal in the making of hinges, hasps and hardware.

The brothers and sisters of Ephrata lived under extremely harsh, ascetic conditions: they slept on planks with wooden blocks for pillows, and they suffered through cold winter nights in unheated 5'-by-10' cells. In lieu of horses, they let themselves be harnessed to plows for tilling the land. Their life style was so punitively extreme that fanaticism inevitably developed among them.

Conrad Beissel wanted to build a new age and a new way of life. One of his main accomplishments was to start singing schools, in order to bring harmony to a new country recently inhabited by savages. In May 1793, the Ephrata Singing School opened under the direction of Margretha Thomme. She assisted Conrad Beissel in conducting this school and also prepared—and illuminated—its great choral books. It was Margretha Thomme who illuminated, in *fractur,* the three great manuscripts of Ephrata, two of which were dedicated to Beissel. To this day, Ephrata is noted for its excellent examples of *fractur* and handsome calligraphy.

Ephrata had *three* orders: unmarried brothers, unmarried sisters and married householders. The householders farmed their own land, but were joined to the congregation both religiously and economically. The unmarried orders, living in cloisters, performed the crafts.

During its later years, Ephrata became more productive in poetry, art, music and other creative pursuits.

ANABAPTISTS

Throughout their early history, the Anabaptists were cruelly punished. Among their other unorthodox beliefs, the Anabaptists opposed infant baptism and required all adults to be rebaptized. Their unique contentions offended the Lutherans and Calvinists as well as the Roman and Greek theologians. As a result, there has hardly been a region of Christendom, excepting Pennsylvania and Rhode Island, where such contradictions of general ecclesiastical law could escape punishment. Consequently, prior to their arrival in Pennsylvania, where they became free to practice their religion as they pleased, the Anabaptists were persecuted wherever they went.

In 1520, during the Diet of Spires, for example, it was decreed that all Anabaptists were to be executed without a trial. They were regarded as being disloyal, heretical, rebellious and untrustworthy. Thereafter they fled to Munster, where the Bishop of Munster sent troops to slaughter them.

OTHER RELIGIOUS SECTS

Among the other religions practiced by the Pennsylvania Dutch are many splinter factions of main groups, some small factions that eventually joined main groups and many odd sects that flirted with strange or even fanatical ideas.

Of the latter, mention should be made of the "Society of Women in the Wilderness,"

which arrived in Philadelphia from Europe on June 23, 1694. Their leader was Johannes Kelpius, a mystic of Altdore. They lived in a celibate, monastic settlement where they prayed and watched for the Second Coming of Christ. After Kelpius's death, in 1708, the sect gradually fell apart.

Then, there was the "New-Geboren" sect in which the members regarded themselves as sinless. Like Adam before the fall, they believed themselves not only to be sinless but also to be incapable of sin.

Another sect, the "New Mooners," believed that for prayers to be effective, they had to be offered only during the rise of the new moon. Still another faction, the "Inspirationalists," thought they possessed true gifts of prophecy. The "Millerites" believed that the year 1843 would bring the Millenium, the Second Coming of Christ. Needless to say, the year passed normally and the Millerites were disappointed.

As well as these esoteric sects, there were many others with less radical views. The "United Brethren," originally known as the "Church of the United Brethren in Christ," merged in 1947 with the Evangelical Association to form the "Evangelical United Brethren." Both churches are products of the Pennsylvania Dutch Methodist Revival.

Chapter 2

Occupations: Arts, Crafts & Industries

Typical virgin forest. This is how the early Pennsylvania Dutch settlers found the land when they first arrived. Soon, however, they felled the forest with saws and axes, and planted their crops in the lime-rich soil. (*Courtesy, Weyerhaeuser Co.*)

22

OCCUPATIONS: ARTS, CRAFTS & INDUSTRIES

FELLING THE FOREST

First came the forest. For although the state of Pennsylvania was rich in natural resources (including heavy deposits of iron, coal and other minerals), the soil first had to be uncovered in order to get at these treasures. Thus, when the first European settlers arrived, they found the soil shrouded under heavy growths of forest. They also observed that these forests contained enormous amounts of valuable lumber that was ideally suited for building their dwellings and farm structures.

Such woods as ash, cedar, walnut, fir, butternut, maple, hickory, birch, pine, cherry, chestnut, oak and poplar—as well as numerous other species—grew in abundance. Beneath these trees, the virgin soil lay rich and fertile with limestone deposits that had accumulated since the earliest days of the planet. All the settlers had to do was to fell the forest in order to expose this planters' paradise.

So the first settlers devoted their labor to the task of clearing the land. With axes and handsaws they laboriously cut down the forest, thus releasing acres of farmland for planting. As a by-product of their labor, they also harvested huge stocks of timber suitable for building their barns, homes and furniture —and for supplying fuel to keep them warm.

During an era when wood was used for making tools and utility items—as well as buildings and furniture—the colonial craftsman had his choice of the most adaptable woods for making different things. For instance, he fashioned working parts (like wagon axles and the bent backs of chairs) from tough and bendable hickory. Cedar, which resisted moisture, was used for making pails, tubs, barrels and other liquid containers. Walnut and butternut—as well as oak, pine and maple—were ideal for building furniture. So the settlers simply browsed through their forests until they found particular trees that were best suited for the objects they wished to make.

Another means of facilitating the colonists' early lumbering operations was provided by the unusual number of rivers and streams which crisscrossed the Pennsylvania woodlands. These waterways served ideally for transporting logs to sawmills, or to the places where they were used. In many instances, swift-running streams powered the water-wheels of sawmills used for sawing the logs.

AGRICULTURE

As the land was cleared, the settlers proceeded to plow and cultivate the rich soil. Soon they had small plots under cultivation, but in time their acreage increased.

Pennsylvania Dutch farmers were truly remarkable in their agricultural accomplishments. By practicing crop rotation and proper fertilization and by following the most advanced scientific methods, they kept their farms in superb shape to produce maximum yields of crops.

Every early farmer was of necessity a jack-of-all-trades, and so was his wife. Cloth was spun from the flax and hemp grown on their farms. They produced woolen fabrics from their sheep. They made shoes from their own leather. They dried and preserved their fruits, vegetables and meats, and produced their own honey and maple syrup.

Although the Pennsylvania Dutch farmer and his family had to perform assorted tasks, he was assisted in the performance of special chores by traveling groups of artisans. Blacksmiths, wagonmakers, weavers, shoemakers, tinkers, millers, tanners, tinsmiths, gunsmiths, foundrymen, potters and other itinerant craftsmen traveled to the farms to perform their chores. Regional mills also produced many of the goods that farmers required.

Wheat was their principal crop, but their farms were also stocked with prize breeds of livestock grazing in lush pastures. Vegetable gardens (frequently tended by the women), fruit orchards and acreage planted with grain, corn and oats kept their granaries, barns and

As well as planting his acres with numerous crops, the Pennsylvania Dutch farmer also raised prize breeds of livestock. In this serene summer scene, contented cows rest in the tidy pasture of a well-stocked Pennsylvania farm. (*Photo courtesy, Mel Horst.*)

cellars abundantly filled. From the adjoining forests came building materials, as well as wild berries, herbs, honey and maple syrup.

Writing to the Bishop of Exeter in 1747, George Thomas, then colonial governor of Pennsylvania, lauded the Germans in his colony: "The State of Pennsylvania is so much indebted for her prosperity and reputation to the German part of her citizens."

EARLY FARMHOUSES

The first farmhouses in Pennsylvania imitated the half-timbered construction of northern Europe. Block houses or log cabins were built with the whole trees squared from the rough logs and then stacked to form a rectangle, one upon the other, as high as headroom required. The ends of the timbers were notched into each other about one foot from each end. Usually a peaked roof was raftered to receive a covering of split logs, or *shooks*. All chinks and openings were stuffed with mud, clay and moss. Thus, a tight and warm little house was built, heated by a great open fireplace.

Log farmhouse built in the Oley Valley of Pennsylvania by Peter Herbein in 1747. Squared logs were notched together to form the walls. Note adjoining bake oven at right. (*Photo by author. Courtesy, Daniel Boone Homestead, Birdsboro, Pa.*)

Cast-iron side of 6-plate stove, made by Heinrich Wilhelm Stiegel at his Elizabeth Furnace, Manheim, Lancaster County, Pa. in 1769. (*Courtesy, National Gallery of Art, Index of American Design, Washington, D.C.*)

Cast-iron stove plate, made in 1763 by George Stevenson. Note careful detailing of decorative motifs. These designs first had to be carved on a wooden pattern to provide a mold for the iron casting. (*Courtesy National Gallery of Art, Index of American Design, Washington, D.C.*)

METALWORK
Iron

With widespread deposits of iron ore and limestone and an abundance of wood for making charcoal, Pennsylvania soon became a leader in the production of iron and steel. As early as 1742, Colebrookdale was erected as the first iron-melting furnace in Pennsylvania. A number of other furnaces soon followed, and additional furnaces were later opened in western Pennsylvania.

Much of the production of the early furnaces consisted of crude pig iron, which was later worked into products either in Pennsylvania or abroad. But there was also some manufacturing of stove parts, Franklin fireplaces, cannon, grave markers, chain, pipe, fences, holloware and parts of machinery. However, it was not until the iron foundry first appeared around 1787 that production branched out into the making of many different products.

Cast-iron objects were made from wooden patterns which duplicated the shape of the casting. The making of patterns required skilled patternmakers who were familiar with the casting process and who also had a craftsman's knowledge of wood joinery. They also had to be clever carvers in order to make patterns of the intricate decorative details which usually appeared on ornamental ironwork.

Other important processes of ironwork were performed by blacksmiths. Of all the metalworkers in Pennsylvania during the 18th century, blacksmiths were the most numerous. In addition to shoeing horses, the blacksmith—with his hearth, sledge and anvil—was ready to produce the innumerable iron utility items so urgently needed in homes and farms.

Thus, the blacksmith hammered out the hardware, ornaments, pots, andirons, scissors, tools, weather vanes, grills, trivets, candlestands, door pulls, latches, spoons, scoops, scales and other iron items that the colonists required. Obviously, the blacksmith's services were in constant demand.

Many Pennsylvania blacksmiths maintained their own shops. Others, who were itinerant craftsmen, visited farms in their regions to perform their work at regular intervals. Their visits signaled a time of rejoicing for the farmer and his wife. For during the blacksmith's visit, the worn-out pots and household utensils were repaired—or were replaced with new items—and the farmer's iron tools and equipment were restored to good working order.

Perhaps the most attractive work of the skilled ironworker was evident in his fashioning of highly embellished and ornate cast-iron fences and decorative gates. In many instances, these were artistic masterpieces: they consisted of scrolled, turned, curved and spiraled parts brought together to produce a highly attractive overall effect.

Among the most noted Pennsylvania ironmasters was William Perkins of Philadelphia, who produced some of the most noteworthy fences and gates in that city. Another was Mr. S. Wheeler, who during the 18th century made the superb iron gate at Trinity Church and the corner posts of a balcony on Congress Hall.

It is interesting to note that before he attained success at making fine glass, "Baron" Wilhelm Stiegel started his American career by operating an iron-casting furnace. His "Elizabeth" furnace (named after his wife) manufactured stoves and cast-iron parts. Like his glass, his ironwork was of superb quality. His business prospered and soon expanded to include several other furnaces. "Baron" Stiegel's furnaces remained in operation until he became fascinated by glassmaking. Then he suddenly abandoned his role as an outstanding ironmaster and devoted the ensuing years to the manufacture of fine glass.

This ironbound sea chest was probably made in Europe and used to carry the possessions of an early German immigrant to America. The wrought-iron decorations, however, are typical of work performed in Pennsylvania. (*Photo by author, Courtesy, the Moravian Museum of Bethlehem, Bethlehem, Pa.*)

Wrought-iron hardware, produced by metalworkers of Pennsylvania, includes many artistic designs. Metalcraftsmen competed to create the most ornate designs. Note the intricate scrolls and shapes which distinguish these hinges, door pulls, and key plates. (*Photo by author. Courtesy, The Heritage Center of Lancaster County, Lancaster, Pa.*)

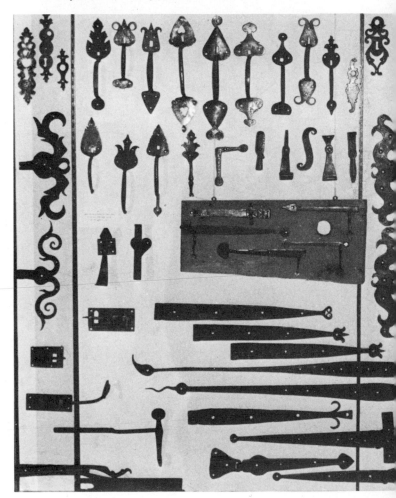

Toleware coffee pot made of tinned sheet iron with painted foliage decorations. Toleware was often given as birthday or wedding presents—*and was never used.* Hence, its fine present state of preservation. (*Courtesy, National Gallery of Art, Index of American Design, Washington, D.C.*)

Toleware & Punched Tin

For the farmwife, who was accustomed to handling pots, pans and cooking utensils of heavy ironware or massive earthenware, the introduction of light *tinware* came as a welcome relief. The manufacture of tinware entailed the coating with tin plate of thin sheets of iron.

Of itself, tin is a soft white metal with a low melting point. However, when plated on thin sheets of iron, it provides protection against rust and also gives a more pleasing and "finished" appearance to the sheet iron.

Tin was used to make all kinds of utensils, containers, appliances and general equipment for homes and farms. An 18th century tinsmith's advertisement lists 54 different items he made of tinplate.

Although most articles of tinware were undecorated, some were brightly painted with Pennsylvania Dutch motifs, including hearts, flowers, fruits, birds and foliage. This decoration, which usually appeared on tea and coffee pots, serving trays and tin boxes, identified these objects as *toleware*. Many handsome pieces of Pennsylvania toleware survived over the centuries and are now displayed in museums.

Another form of decoration was made by punching design outlines around the sides of coffee pots. This was done with a blunt punch to avoid piercing the tin. However, in making the tin panels of pie safes, where ventilation was required—and in making tin lanterns where candlelight shone through the indentations—the decorative designs were made to pierce the tin, by punching openings *through* the metal.

Toward the end of the 18th century, tinsmiths prospered throughout the Pennsylvania Dutch country. Many of them operated their own factories and sold their wares to stores in Pennsylvania and elsewhere.

Punched tin coffee pot was made in Pennsylvania around 1830. Punched designs of floral and geometric forms, outlined with extruded dots. (*Courtesy, National Gallery of Art, Index of American Design, Washington, D.C.*)

Copper & Pewter

Many different metals were worked by Pennsylvania craftsmen. Silversmiths plied their trade in Philadelphia and other urban centers. But in the provinces of the Pennsylvania Dutch country, copper and pewter were apt to take the place of silver for making teapots, candlestands, spoons, cups and bowls.

The homes of the more affluent farmers were often adorned with rows of shining copper saucepans of graduated sizes, hanging above the hearth. These were augmented by copper ladles, pots and molds, which were often tinned on the inside. Of special appeal were the copper kettles with large bail handles and gracefully shaped spouts and lids.

Pewter (an alloy of tin, lead, brass or copper) is malleable and easy to work. In sheet form, it could be beaten or molded into all kinds of shapes, or it could be melted and poured into molds of various designs. In addition to fulfilling many household needs, it was also used for making sacramental vessels.

Many of the early Pennsylvania pewter pieces are as beautifully shaped and designed as their silver counterparts that were made by sophisticated silversmiths of the urban centers. Although only craftsmen of exceptionally good taste could produce these exquisite pewter pieces, their quality may also be attributed to the exceptionally workable nature of the alloy itself. It could be bent to produce the most delicate curves, or it could be cast in complex shapes that were readily smoothed down and polished.

It is interesting to note that early pewter did double duty by first being used to make household utensils and then being melted down to make bullets for the Continental army to shoot at the British. (Some years earlier, to circumvent the British tax on American-made pewter, many craftsmen disguised the metal by stamping it "London," and thus deceived the British colonial authorities!)

Copper kettles, displayed at the Heritage Center of Lancaster County, were made by five different coppersmiths. These fine designs express the artistic acumen of the craftsmen. (*Photo by author. Courtesy, The Heritage Center of Lancaster County, Lancaster, Pa.*)

This display of ecclesiastical pewter designs originated at Lancaster, Pa. between 1715 and 1781. Most of these articles were made by the master metalsmith, Johann Christoph Heyne. (*Photo by author. Courtesy, The Heritage Center of Lancaster County, Lancaster, Pa.*)

Elaborate display of Kentucky rifles at Hershey Museum includes different models made by many individual gunsmiths. (*Photo courtesy, Hershey Museum of American Life, Hershey, Pa.*)

Detailed view of superbly shaped stock of Kentucky rifle, showing delicate craftsmanship of inlaid metal parts. Note hinged brass patchbox. (*Courtesy, Hershey Museum of American Life, Hershey, Pa.*)

Firearms

Of all types of metalworkers, those regarded as the elite were the gunsmiths. These highly dexterous craftsmen combined the separate skills of blacksmith, brass founder, woodworker, engraver and locksmith. Frequently, the guns of Pennsylvania were made by a number of craftsmen, each contributing his specialized skill. However, just as often, the complete gun was made entirely by one man.

The most famous gun designed and produced by Pennsylvania Dutch gunsmiths was the so-called *Kentucky rifle.* This rifle was dubbed "Kentucky" because it was used extensively by pioneering scouts, soldiers and settlers venturing into Kentucky and the Western Territories. Daniel Boone used this rifle during his exploratory visits into Kentucky.

The Kentucky rifle—which was longer, lighter and far more accurate than either the British smoothbore musket or the German snubnosed gun which preceded it—was masterfully made with a handsome carved walnut stock. It was embellished with decorative brass

inlays, butt plates and trigger guards. The brass patchbox embedded in the stock was invented in Lancaster and was first used around 1725. The long barrel of this rifle was accurately bored to shoot with utmost precision.

Although the innovative Pennsylvania rifle contributed significantly to winning the Revolutionary War (it was far more accurate, more easily loaded and more generally adaptable than the smoothbore muskets borne by the British), it was not as a weapon of war that this rifle gained its greatest renown. The man of the frontier regarded his rifle as an indispensable tool for coping with primitive conditions. It was used to shoot wild game, so necessary for survival; for defense against hostile Indians; and, not least, as an implement of sports competition at turkey shoots and target-shooting contests.

The pistols made in Pennsylvania (also often called Kentucky pistols) were masterpieces of fine craftsmanship. The wooden parts were usually made of burled or figured walnut, while inlaid ornamentation of brass (or sometimes silver) was elaborately engraved.

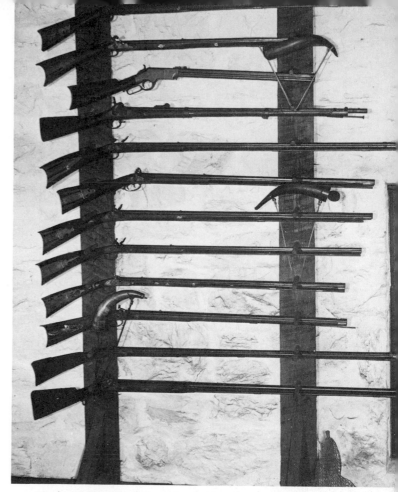

Museum display of early Pennsylvania rifles and powder horns includes rifles of different types and makes. Note Winchester repeating rifle (third from top), which was invented many decades after the other models shown. (*Photo courtesy, Pennsylvania Historical and Museum Commission, Harrisburg, Pa.*)

Flintlock pistol, made by J. P. Beck for Col. Robert Coleman between 1775 and 1780. Beck was an armorer in Coleman's command during the Revolutionary War. Note curly maple wooden parts and engraved silver inlays. (*Photo by author. Courtesy, The Heritage Center of Lancaster County, Lancaster, Pa.*)

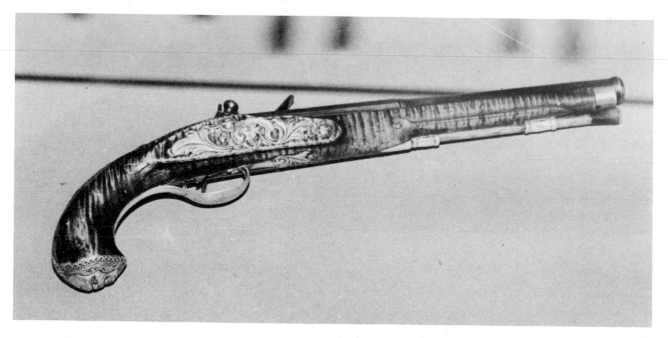

31

Assorted spinning devices on display at Lebanon County Historical Society include *wool wheel*, at extreme left, and *reel*, second from right. Yarn for Jacquard coverlets, hanging on wall, was produced with such wheels. (*Photo by author. Courtesy, Lebanon County Historical Society.*)

TEXTILES

With the founding of Germantown, the textile industry in Pennsylvania was already flourishing. As the 18th century advanced, the home-based looms were augmented by textile factories operating at regional mills or by itinerant professional weavers.

As early as 1736, Pennsylvania Dutch farmers engaged in sheep raising, but the early settlers were quite conservative in their use of wool. Thus, when weaving their textiles, they mixed wool with flax to produce the celebrated colonial fabric called "linsey-woolsey."

This homemade cloth was tough and durable, but it was also stiff and uncomfortable to wear. Ultimately, it was replaced by softer and more pliable fabrics.

Cloth, woven wholly of wool, was used for the best Sunday-meeting garments. Woolen material for men's clothes was woven only of the finest yarn. It was then taken, by the farmer, to the *fulling mill* where—after being washed, dyed and finished—it emerged as *fulled cloth* ready to be made into garments.

Linen, of course, was woven of flax to produce men's and women's garments as well as bed sheets, pillowcases, tablecloths, towels and numerous other household necessities. Frequently, towels, tablecloths and other fine linen pieces were decorated with cross-stitch and drawn decorations.

Colorful coverlets were also woven by the Pennsylvania Dutch. Many of these are masterpieces of inventive design. Nowhere else in America were coverlets produced of such creative designs and vivid colors as those made by the Pennsylvania Dutch.

The invention of the four-harness Jacquard loom early in the 18th century made possible the weaving of contrasting materials (like bleached and unbleached linen or linen and wool) into large, one-piece sections. This loom also increased the output of professional weavers, who had emigrated in great numbers with the early settlers. Itinerant weavers acquired these looms and used them to advantage in response to the housewives' demand for professionally made textiles.

Coverlet, woven on Jacquard loom at Bucks County, Pa., in 1859, shows refinement of design development. This may have been used as a weaver's sampler. (*Courtesy, National Gallery of Art, Index of American Design, Washington, D.C.*)

Working with an old loom. Considering the many complicated procedures involved in weaving, it is remarkable that such beautiful designs were produced. (*Photo courtesy, Pennsylvania Historical and Museum Commission, Harrisburg, Pa.*)

Letter from the Ephrata alphabet book shows perfection of manuscript lettering performed during the 18th century at Ephrata Cloister, (*Courtesy, Pennsylvania Historical and Museum Commission, Harrisburg, Pa.*)

infrequently, a large heart occupied the center of the composition.

Also among the fractur renderings were handlettered and decorated sheets of psalms, proverbs, and hymn books illuminated with ornate compositions of birds, flowers and foliage, interworked with lettering of divine injunctions, decorated rosters of children's birth dates and other ornamental wall displays.

Often a fractur copybook, called a *vorsschrift,* was used by schoolchildren to guide their efforts at fractur writing and drawing. The vorschrift was usually produced by the schoolmaster and was sometimes given as a present to a favored pupil.

Birth and baptismal certificates were called *taufscheine.* Usually they were produced by the schoolmaster. Aside from drawing and lettering taufscheine, the fractur artist was in constant demand for illuminating family records, making book plates and *haus-segen*— the German name for wall placards imploring the blessings of God on family and dwelling.

FRACTUR

The most interesting artwork performed by the Pennsylvania Dutch was the highly embellished and illuminated writing-drawing they called *fractur.* This art form, which was rendered as colored pen-paintings, seems to have been retained in Pennsylvania as a continuation of the medieval Germanic art of manuscript illumination. In its Pennsylvania expression, it ranged from the crude work of untutored individuals to the masterful manuscripts produced at Ephrata Cloister. Indeed, the work performed during the early 18th century at Ephrata contains some nearly perfect examples of fractur lettering and decoration.

Fractur drawings were used to illuminate legal papers, decorative displays and documents. Often this highly ornate penwork appeared on birth and baptismal certificates. On these documents, all significant data was handlettered in precise German script. Not

Hymn book *fractur* decoration was crudely ornamented and lettered, indicating it was probably made by a student or amateur. (*Courtesy, National Gallery of Art, Index of American Design, Washington, D.C.*)

34

Birth and baptismal certificate of Levi Bingeman was rendered in ornate fractur in 1828. This was typical of the *taufscheine* drawn and lettered by artists of varying degrees of skill throughout the Pennsylvania Dutch country. (*Courtesy, Philadelphia Museum of Art, Philadelphia, Pa.*)

Sgraffito plate, made in 1793, has peacock and foliage decorations. This is typical of the red earthenware pottery produced during the 18th century in eastern Pennsylvania. (*Courtesy, National Gallery of Art, Index of American Design, Washington, D.C.*)

CERAMICS

As well as providing rich deposits of iron ore, and other minerals, the soil of Pennsylvania also contained an ample supply of *potters' clay.* From this, the early potters produced pots, pans, plates, platters, jugs and utensils, as well as roofing tiles for their homes.

Pottery produced during the 17th and early 18th centuries was *unglazed* and made for strictly utilitarian purposes. However, during the second phase of pottery making, which began about 1760, the pottery was glazed and decorated.

Decoration was done in one of two ways:
1. By tracing a design in *slip.* (Slip is potters' clay in liquid form, used for decoration.)
2. By scraping a design through the glaze, to reveal the red clay beneath.

The first method, known as *slip decoration,* was ornamented with birds, flowers, foliage or lettering. Pottery made by the second method, called *sgraffito,* was usually decorated with lettered mottos or proverbs. Fish, birds, mounted soldiers, flowers and foliage usually appeared inside the lettered borders.

Among the finer varieties of imported crockery was *spatterware,* which was so highly prized by Pennsylvania Dutch housewives and which appeared between 1800 and 1850. Spatterware is a Staffordshire product which seems to have been made and distributed solely for the Pennsylvania Dutch trade. It was decorated in vivid colors, always with an Adams concept of a *peafowl* as the focal motif.

Another type of imported crockery was called *Gaudy Dutch.* This also came from Staffordshire, England, between the years 1785 and 1815. Gaudy Dutch was freehand decorated on a white background. It was truly "gaudy" in design and color.

Included among the native accomplishments of the Pennsylvania Dutch was the early manufacture of *chalkware.* This called for the molding of animals, birds, dishes and miniature human figures in a plaster of paris composition, called *chalk.* Frequently the pieces remained pure white, although they were also painted in vivid colors.

Covered jar, which originated in Pennsylvania in 1830, has lead glaze on common clay. Sgraffito tulip and leaf designs are bordered by yellow, red and green glaze. (*Courtesy, National Gallery of Art, Index of American Design, Washington, D.C.*)

Right. Chalkware displayed in Pennsylvania Dutch dresser includes animals, birds, vases, ornamental foliage and caricatured human figures. Dresser was built between 1760 and 1780. (*Courtesy, American Museum in Britain, Bath, England.*)

Below right. Glass flask is decorated with blue, green, yellow and white enamel in the Stiegel manner. It is likely that these two renderings were made of authentic Stiegel originals. (*Courtesy, National Gallery of Art, Index of American Design, Washington, D.C.*)

Below left. Stiegel-type glass vase, below left, was faithfully made and decorated in the Stiegel manner. (*Courtesy, National Gallery of Art, Index of American Design, Washington, D.C.*)

GLASS

Glass was produced in Pennsylvania as early as 1693, when a glassmaker by the name of Joshua Tatery first operated a glassmaking factory for the Quakers of Philadelphia. However, it was not until "Baron" Wilhelm Stiegel started his Elizabeth glass factory in the Lancaster Valley that the making of glass in America attained any real growth or distinction.

Stiegel brought traditional glassmaking techniques (and artisans) over from his native city of Cologne. (His importation of the noble title "Baron," however, was spurious and was motivated purely by vanity.) So successful was *Stiegel Glass* that soon it was sold in other American colonies and exported abroad. Genuine "Stiegel" had so many imitators that nowadays it is practically impossible for collectors to identify authentic pieces. Hence, today all alleged "Stiegel Glass" must be referred to as "Stiegel-type" glass.

Butter mold, carved to produce tulip imprint, is lathe-turned with nondetachable handle. (*Courtesy, National Gallery of Art, Index of American Design, Washington, D.C.*)

Carved cutlery board shows simple flower and geometric designs which distinguish it as a practical wall decoration. (*Courtesy, The Metropolitan Museum of Art, New York, N.Y.*)

Door panel of 18th century Pennsylvania Dutch wall cupboard is crudely carved with distelfink and geometric designs. (*Courtesy, National Gallery of Art, Index of American Design, Washington, D.C.*)

WOODENWARE & CARVING

With enormous tracts of woodland flourishing all around him, it was natural for the Pennsylvania settler to construct his buildings, tools, implements and furnishings of wood. Many things which today would be made of metal or plastic were originally made of wood because of the abundance of this material. These included such items as rolling pins, scoops, spoons, butter molds and paddles, dough boards, flour bins, salt boxes, trays, chests, hat boxes and turned woodenware. But aside from these items and numerous others, the farmer used wood to make most of his farm tools, vehicles and working implements.

Many items made of wood were decoratively carved. In fact, carving was a popular pastime of the early era. It was practiced by young and old, and it produced many interesting objects including toys, decorative birds and animals, as well as incised designs carved into butter and cookie molds. There were also carved spoon racks, small boxes and chests. All of these objects were hand-whittled in various attractive designs. The carving was usually done with a sharp penknife.

Many amateur whittlers carved crude birds, animals and human figures, apparently to enjoy the relaxation which carving affords. Aside from their use as *for-fancy* parlor decorations, these crudely carved objects had little practical value (although, when vividly painted, they made colorful objets d'art).

With the disappearance of skilled wood carvers, which took place in the middle of the 19th century, the hand carving of wooden objects became a lost art. Some craftsmen persisted, however, and took to the roads as itinerant artisans. They left behind them carved roosters, eagles, peafowl and other ornaments at the farmhouses and taverns they visited along the way. There were also many dedicated woodcarvers (most notably Noah Weis, who lived from 1842 to 1907) who continued to whittle exquisite wood carvings throughout their lives. These individuals remained so involved in their craft that they produced a wealth of impressive carvings which now fortunately are displayed in state and national museums.

COOPERAGE

Ever since the Middle Ages, the cooper has been regarded as a highly specialized craftsman. For the cooper engaged in the intricate craft of fitting together barrels, pails, casks, buckets, firkins, churns and other round containers made of meticulous, edge-fitted wooden staves.

Because of the different types of containers they made, there were two different kinds of coopers. One kind, known as *wet* or *tight* coopers, made waterproof containers for whiskey, molasses, cider, vinegar and other liquids. The other kind, known as *white* or *dry* coopers, constructed containers for flour, sugar, meal and other nonliquid substances. Obviously, the more highly skilled were the wet coopers, who had to bevel the edges of their staves so accurately that no liquid could escape. The wet coopers used white oak for their staves to assure precise craftsmanship.

Usually, the cooper cut down white oak trees from his own forest. Ash, chestnut and hickory were also commonly used for dry cooperage. After a period of seasoning, the cooper shaped his staves and beveled the edges to form barrels or other round containers. Hickory was used to make the hoops which whipped the staves together for final assembly.

Some Pennsylvania Dutch farmers made their own barrels, although they usually made the dry type to hold grain rather than liquids. Thus, the joints did not have to be made precisely watertight.

(One interesting sidelight: during the early 19th century, professional coopers sold 100-pound butter tubs for 15¢, while large sap buckets went for 6¢ apiece. It should also be noted that the first American cooper was John Alden, of *Priscilla* fame. Alden had served as a cooper on the Mayflower and continued to ply his trade in the Plymouth colony.)

Laundry tub—made in Bucks County, Pa., early in the 19th century—was originally equipped with a wooden pestle for agitating and pounding clothes in process of laundering. (*Photo by author.*)

Cooperage shop showing barrels made by early craftsmen. Typical cooperage tools are shown in background. (*Photo by author.*)

Conestoga Wagons provided the principal means of transportation for people and produce during early settlement days. Drawn by 6 to 8 heavy draft horses, these bold vehicles traveled in trains of up to 100 wagons on the Reading and Lancaster roads. They were painted light blue with wheels and running gear of vermillion. Ironwork was painted black, and the top was made of white, homespun canvas. (*Photo courtesy, Pennsylvania Historical and Museum Commission, Harrisburg, Pa.*)

TRANSPORTATION: CONESTOGA WAGONS, CANAL BOATS & TRAINS

Rolling along the early turnpikes of Pennsylvania—sometimes in trains extending to 100 or more vehicles—the Dutch-built *Conestoga Wagons* moved people and produce during the early settlement period. Practically every day of the year, 50 to 100 wagons, moving at the rate of 12 to 15 miles per day, passed along the Lancaster and Reading roads.

This great vehicle was boat-shaped with slanted ends and a sag in the center of the wagon bed, both crosswise and lengthwise, to make sure the load would settle in the middle. Heavy back wheels were approximately 6 feet in diameter. Hickory bows supported the homespun canvas top, which was overhung at both front and rear for protection against rain or snow.

Conestoga Wagons were drawn by as many as 8 large horses; the usual number, however, was 6. Since each loaded wagon carried about

8 tons, special breeds of powerful horses were required to pull them. The horses, bred in the Conestoga Valley, were enormous draft animals, standing from 16 to 17½ hands high and weighing around 1,600 pounds.

These huge Conestoga Wagons hauled glass, pottery, linen, sugar, salt, tobacco, grain, flour, flaxseed, whiskey, cider, fruit, coal, charcoal, iron ore and pig iron, among other cargos. George Washington was supplied by these wagons at Valley Forge. Year by year, the number of Conestoga Wagons increased until by 1830, there were over 3,000 of them traveling each day on the road from Philadelphia to Pittsburgh and moving beyond to carry people and freight westward. (It should also be noted that the Conestoga Wagon, which always moved along the right side of the road, is credited with starting the American practice of driving on the right side of the road.)

As it traveled along the early Pennsylvania turnpikes, the Conestoga Wagon was a bold sight to behold. The body of the wagon was

painted light blue; the great wheels and running gear were vermillion; the ironwork was black and the homespun canvas top was white. The tool box, attached to the left side of the wagon, was beautifully detailed with wrought-iron decorations. To add a musical note, a row of bells was attached to the harness over one or more of the horses. These rang in harmony to announce the approach of a Conestoga train.

After 1830, the rapid excavation and widespread utilization of canals for transporting people and goods heralded the demise of the Conestoga Wagon as the principal means of transportation. Soon there were numerous canals in southeastern Pennsylvania, canals that lined the banks of the Delaware to Easton —and then on to Lehigh. The Schuylkill river had a canal opening to Pottsville.

Along the Susquehanna River, there was a canal connecting Bellefonte with the West Bend and another linking Pittstown on the North Branch with Sunbury. Another canal was dug along the Juniata to Hollidaysburg

Early Pennsylvania canal boat, drawn by a mule, enters a toll station. By 1840, there were 954 miles of canals in operation in Pennsylvania—more than in any other state. (*Photo courtesy, Pennsylvania Historical and Museum Commission, Harrisburg, Pa.*)

Cumberland Valley Railroad operated between Chambersburg and the Susquehanna, a distance of 49 miles. Later its route was extended by a bridge built across the Susquehanna for direct access to Harrisburg. Train above was used around 1850. (*Photo courtesy, Pennsylvania Historical and Museum Commission, Harrisburg, Pa.*)

and another from Cordorus to York. Conestoga and Lancaster were soon joined by a canal, and the Union Canal joined the Susquehanna at Middletown with the Schuylkill at Reading. This canal passed under a tunnel that was built in 1823 near Lebanon.

After 1835, there were 601 miles of canals in the state of Pennsylvania. By 1840, there were 954 miles of canals in operation, more than in any other state.

The coming of the railroads spelled the doom of the canals. As early as 1839, the Reading Railroad completed the laying of tracks between Reading and Philadelphia. Later, in 1855, the Lehigh Valley Railroad connected Allentown, Bethlehem and Easton with New Jersey and New York.

Among the railroads most commonly used by the Pennsylvania Dutch were the Reading and Lehigh Valley Railroad and the Pennsylvania Railroad. But they were also served by less ambitious railroads—including the Cumberland Valley Railroad, which ran from Chambersburg to the Susquehanna for a distance of 49 miles. Later, this railroad was extended by a bridge built across the Susquehanna for direct access to Harrisburg. The Portsmouth, Mount Joy & Lancaster Railroad was opened for its full 36-mile length in 1838.

Some of the regional railroads operated on extremely short routes. For instance, the Strasburg Railroad was only 4½ miles long; while the Catasauqua & Fogelsville, Cornwall & Lebanon, Middletown & Hummelstown, Bellefonte Central and the Quakertown & Eastern were each less than 30 miles long.

The Philadelphia & Reading Railroad soon became one of the leading carriers of Pennsylvania. As early as 1842, its tracks extended to Pottsville and Mount Carmel. Thus, it connected the coal mines with Philadelphia and also transported crops from the rich agricultural regions around Reading. By 1847, the Reading Railroad was one of the greatest freight-carrying roads in the United States. During that year it carried more freight than the Erie Canal and at much lower cost. For example, prior to the construction of the railroad, anthracite coal sold for $14 per ton. A few years later, when coal was carried by railroad, the price was reduced to $5.50–$6.00 per ton.

By 1846, the Reading Railroad was carrying over 88,000 passengers each year. Its crack train, *The Queen of the Valley,* was hailed by generations of Pennsylvania Dutchmen as a thing of great beauty and tremendous purpose.

But, like the Conestoga Wagon and the canal boats which preceded them, the railroads, too, had to abandon many of their routes toward the end of the 20th century. Trains were replaced by trucks for transporting freight over the ever-expanding highways and turnpikes of Pennsylvania. Fleets of motorbuses carried people to even the most out-of-the-way places. And the burgeoning airlines furnished fast transportation for both people and cargo to and from many places throughout the state, and connected them directly with places all over the world.

Chapter 3

Furniture Design

Kirshner—Pennsylvania Dutch parlor of the 18th century—is reconstructed at Winterthur museum. Displayed here are architectural details and furniture of the German Renaissance period. Beside the walnut sawbuck table are Moravian Splay-legged plank chairs as well as wainscot armchairs of early origin. In the corner stands a massive German *schrank*, while a painted dower chest (dated 1774) stands between the windows. On top of this, a bible box holds a German bible printed in 1748. (*Courtesy, The Henry Francis du Pont Winterthur Museum, Winterthur, Del.*)

FURNITURE DESIGN

While most of the Germans who emigrated to Pennsylvania were farmers, there were also many skilled mechanics among them. These craftsmen created a distinctive Pennsylvania Dutch style of furniture, which was inspired largely by work they had previously performed in the old country.

Perhaps the most striking feature of Pennsylvania Dutch furniture is its flamboyant display of painted decorations. This is particularly true of the dower chests shown in this chapter. Frequently these were painted a soft blue, brown or red color. Over this were painted various decorative motifs, including flowers, fruits, birds, angels, unicorns, soldiers, stars and other devices. Many dower chests are inscribed with the name of the owner and the date it was made.

Impressive among the many Pennsylvania Dutch furniture designs is the outsized cupboard, or *schrank,* which occupied much floor space in most homes. The *schrank,* which was built along Gargantuan lines, could be either painted or finished in natural tones of walnut or cherry wood. Usually the painted versions were decorated with fruit or floral motifs, while those finished of natural wood were elaborately inlaid.

Top. Construction of this simple chair has biblical implications. It was used as a "treatment chair" by a "powwow doctor" in the Manheim area of Pennsylvania, over 100 years ago. (*Photo by author. Courtesy, Historic Schaefferstown, Schaefferstown, Pa.*)

Above. Plain, kitchen-utility chair was made by local Pennsylvania Dutch craftsmen during early 19th century. (*Photo courtesy, Hershey Museum of American Life, Hershey, Pa.*)

Left. One of a set of four chairs made in Pennsylvania around 1810. Note free-hand painted decorations. (*Courtesy, The Henry Ford Museum, Dearborn, Mich.*)

45

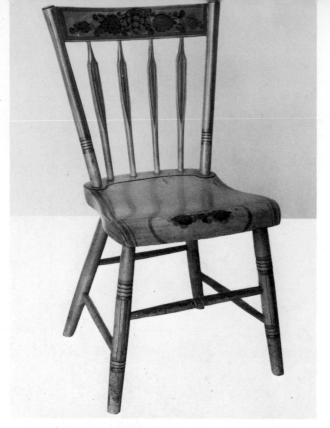

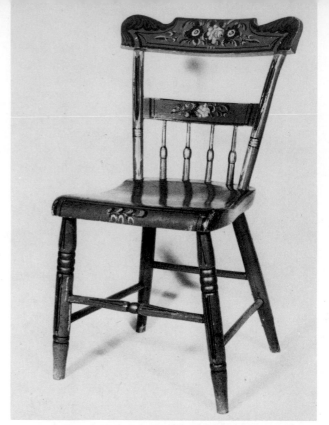

Arrowback utility chair of pleasing proportions is lightly decorated in the Pennsylvania Dutch manner. (*Courtesy, Philadelphia Museum of Art, Philadelphia, Pa.*)

Elaborately painted decorations and unusual structure of back spindles and rails, distinguish this 19th century kitchen chair. (*Courtesy, William Penn Memorial Museum, Harrisburg, Pa.*)

CHAIRS

Although all chairs on this page are basically of the same design, contrasts appear in the design of details. Note the broad shield back of this example. (*Courtesy, The Henry Ford Museum, Dearborn, Mich.*)

Again, by combining good design with attention to distinctive detailing of shapes and painted motifs, this early 19th century chair acquires its attractive appearance. (*Courtesy, The Henry Ford Museum, Dearborn, Mich.*)

This massive wainscot armchair—made in Chester County, Pa., early in the 18th century— was reserved for the exclusive use of the master of the house. (*Photo courtesy, The Metropolitan Museum of Art, New York, N.Y., Anonymous Gift, 1948.*)

Wainscot, slatback armchair, built in Pennsylvania around 1750, is made somewhat lighter than most early wainscots. Parts are shaved down to finer proportions and, unlike other examples, it has a woven splint seat. (*Courtesy, The Henry Francis du Pont Winterthur Museum, Winterthur, Del.*)

Heavy, walnut wainscot armchair of unusually sturdy construction and large size, originated in Pennsylvania late in the 17th century. (*Courtesy, Philadelphia Museum of Art, Philadelphia, Pa., The Titus C. Geesey Collection.*)

Tastefully turned details and large size distinguish this wainscot armchair, which was made in Chester County, Pa., around 1725. (*Courtesy, The Henry Francis du Pont Winterthur Museum, Winterthur, Del.*)

"Moravian" chair, made in Pennsylvania during the 17th and 18th centuries, followed the same designs as earlier examples made in Germany. (*Courtesy, The Henry Francis du Pont Winterthur Museum, Winterthur, Del.*)

Plank chair, from Ephrata Cloister, was probably made by the Moravians during the 18th century. This is constructed with back tenons penetrating through the seat and secured with keys underneath. See measured drawing, page 158. (*Photo by author. Courtesy, Ephrata Cloister, Ephrata, Pa.*)

Known as the "judge's chair," this unusual armchair of tiger maple originated in Pennsylvania around 1835. See measured drawing, page 157. (*Courtesy, Hershey Museum of American Life, Hershey, Pa.*)

Windsor armchair, made of hickory and maple, originated in Pennsylvania (probably Philadelphia) between 1765 and 1800. (*Courtesy, The Henry Francis du Pont Winterthur Museum, Winterthur, Del.*)

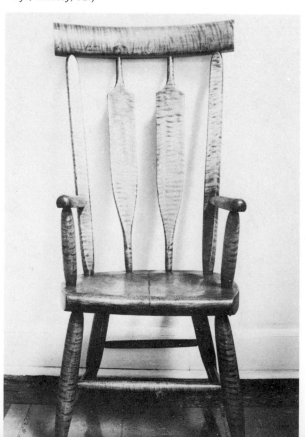

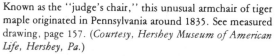

Typical Pennsylvania Dutch armchair of the 18th century. This ladderback chair with splint-woven seat was originally painted mottled red. (*Courtesy, The Metropolitan Museum of Art, New York, N.Y. Gift of Mrs. Robert W. de Forest, 1933.*)

Commonly made and used throughout New England during the 18th century, this writing-arm windsor chair may have come to Pennsylvania via another colony. However, abbreviated comb back differs from New England counterparts. (*Photo by author, courtesy, Rock Ford Plantation, Lancaster, Pa.*)

Maple side chair originated in Pennsylvania early in the 18th century. Note unusually fine turning. (*Courtesy, William Penn Memorial Museum, Harrisburg, Pa.*)

Windsor high chair of exceptionally fine design originated in Pennsylvania during the early 1800s. (*Courtesy, William Penn Memorial Museum, Harrisburg, Pa.*)

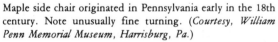

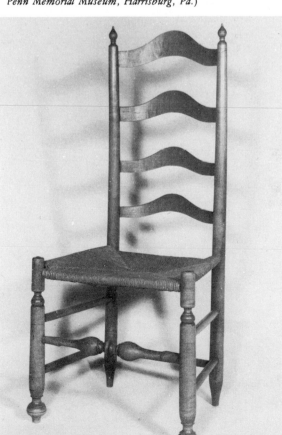

ROCKERS

Pennsylvania Dutch rockers were made of many different designs. They ranged from massive, copiously carved and painted designs to the less ponderous slatback types. Some were simply shaped of solid planks, while others were constructed with arrowback slats and gracefully shaped arms which added a note of refinement to their appearance. Another unique type had rockers attached parallel to the front legs and the back legs. Hence, its rocking motion was *sidewise*!

Most Pennsylvania rockers were built during the 19th century. Some are marvels of curved and bent-wood construction. The slab seats are fully contoured and matched to the angle of the back for maximum comfort. Rockers of this type, illustrated here and on the next page, are of opulent proportions and size.

Child's commode rocker of walnut is gracefully shaped and decorated with a heart-shaped cut-out in the back. This little rocker was made in Pennsylvania early in the 19th century. (*Courtesy, Philadelphia Museum of Art, The Titus C. Geesey Collection, Philadelphia, Pa.*)

Tall, severe, rush-seated rocker has unusually high back constructed with six slats. (*Photo by author. Courtesy, Daniel Boone Homestead, Birdsboro, Pa.*)

Side rocker, believed to have been made in Pennsylvania around 1820, offers a new sidewise twist to rocking motion. (*Courtesy, National Gallery of Art, Index of American Design, Washington, D.C.*)

Spacious and comfortable old rocker, made in Pennsylvania during the 19th century, is attractively painted with striping borders as well as fruit and floral designs. (*Photo by author. Courtesy, Pennsylvania Farm Museum of Landis Valley, Lancaster, Pa.*)

Another example of wood sculpturing produced a rocker with huge arched back and all related parts contoured for comfort. (*Photo by author. Courtesy, Pennsylvania Farm Museum of Landis Valley, Lancaster, Pa.*)

Arrowback walnut rocker was built by Reuben Luckenbach of Bethlehem, Pa., in 1850. It offers maximum comfort with contoured seat and carefully curved back and arm rests. (*Photo by author. Courtesy, Moravian Museum of Bethlehem, Bethlehem, Pa.*)

This novel rocker, made with one-piece sides and slat back, was built near Bethlehem, Pa., during the 19th century. (*Photo by author. Courtesy, Moravian Museum of Bethlehem, Bethlehem, Pa.*)

BENCHES, SETTEES, STOOLS & SEATS

An abundance of elongated benches were built throughout the Pennsylvania Dutch regions during the 18th and 19th centuries. Most often used as seats in churches and meeting houses, these benches and settees also found their way into the parlors and kitchens of most early homes. For in addition to being decoratively turned, they were usually well designed and attractively painted to grace the domestic scene.

Among these designs were the formal wainscot settees, which were produced during the

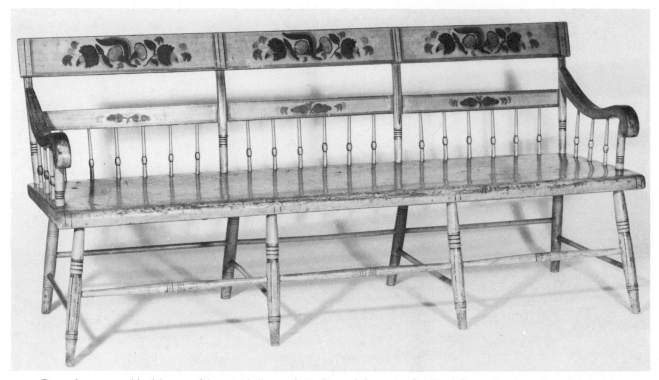

Decorative settee, with eight turned legs, 24 ball-turned spindles and decorative floral and fruit painted stencils, originated in Pennsylvania early in the 19th century. (*Courtesy, Mercer Museum, Doylestown, Pa.*)

Wainscot settee originated in Pennsylvania around 1730. This formal piece was probably designed for use in a church or meeting house. (*Courtesy, The Henry Francis du Pont Winterthur Museum, Winterthur, Del.*)

18th century, mostly for use in churches. Other benches, seats and stools were designed strictly for utility purposes: some were made with hinged, lidded seats for storage; others were made for dual use, both in the home and as wagon seats. The tall, narrow enclosed *throne,* shown at the bottom of the facing page, was probably designed to eliminate cold drafts when someone was sitting on it by the open fire.

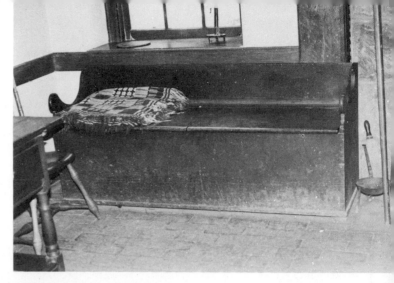

Pennsylvania wagon bench was built around 1780. It was designed for alternate service between wagon and home. (*Courtesy, National Gallery of Art, Index of American Design, Washington, D.C.*)

Nestled beside the fireplace, this bench provides both seating and storage (beneath the seat) for firewood. It was built near Lancaster, Pa., around 1820. (*Photo by author. Courtesy, Pennsylvania Farm Museum of Landis Valley, Lancaster, Pa.*)

Cherry bench was built in Pennsylvania around 1750. Design is painted with floral decorations. (*Courtesy, The Metropolitan Museum of Art, New York, N.Y., Gift of Mrs. Robert W. de Forest, 1933.*)

This massive enclosed seat was probably designed to protect the users from the cold drafts so prevalent in early homes. (*Courtesy, National Gallery of Art, Index of American Design, Washington, D.C.*)

On the walls of the Fractur Room, reconstructed at Winterthur Museum, are examples of *fractur*, the medieval art of illuminated writing used by the Pennsylvania Dutch to embellish important documents. The room paneling was taken from a stone farmhouse built in 1783 by David Hotenstein, near Kutztown in Berks County. Around the sawbuck table are walnut wainscot chairs made in Chester County. In the far corner, a red and blue painted desk shows an interesting combination of the classical Philadelphia Chippendale style yielding to provincial folk art painted decorations. To the left of the desk is a painted dower chest from Berks County. It is decorated with unicorns and mounted horsemen. (*Courtesy, The Henry Francis du Pont Winterthur Museum, Winterthur, Del.*)

TABLES

As illustrated on these pages, Pennsylvania Dutch tables were made in a wide variety of designs: some were elaborately turned and embellished with scrollwork, while others were perfectly plain.

Perhaps the most common and typically Pennsylvania Dutch were the sawbuck tables, shown here and on the facing page. These were often constructed of walnut. The sawbuck ends were sometimes gracefully carved, and were curved to modify their sturdy structure. Pierced by keys, end tenons of the center rail, these tables were so structurally strong that original models of them, now well over 200 years old, are still in usable condition.

The scope of Pennsylvania Dutch tables otherwise included tastefully turned designs with scalloped aprons. Square "turned" tables were made early in the 18th century, apparently when turned effects were desired but when turning lathes were not yet available. Artisans also produced a vast assortment of elongated tavern tables, small stands and sturdy gateleg tables.

Sawbuck table made of oak and walnut, originated in Pennsylvania early in the 18th century. Sturdy, scrolled sawbuck ends, large-key-tenoned center rail and spacious drawer all contributed to convenience and strength of this Table. (*Courtesy, The Metropolitan Museum of Art, New York, N.Y., Gift of Mrs. Robert W. de Forest, 1933*)

Small walnut sawbuck table was made at Ephrata Cloister early in the 18th century. (*Photo by author. Courtesy, Ephrata Cloister, Ephrata, Pa.*)

Large walnut sawbuck table is beautifully proportioned and designed to modify its massive size. The sturdy rails and key-tenoned construction endowed these tables with enduring strength. (*Courtesy, The Henry Francis du Pont Winterthur Museum, Winterthur, Del.*)

This graceful little three-legged table has exceptionally beautiful vase and ball turning. It originated in Pennsylvania between the years 1700 and 1750. (*Photo courtesy, The Henry Francis du Pont Winterthur Museum, Winterthur, Del.*)

Tall three-legged pine table was probably originally used as a candlestand. This one was made in Pennsylvania between 1725 and 1775. (*Courtesy, The Henry Francis du Pont Winterthur Museum, Winterthur, Del.*)

This attractive scrolled-apron table was made in Pennsylvania around the middle of the 18th century. Note unusually wide slant of legs—characteristic of early Pennsylvania Dutch design. (*Courtesy, Philadelphia Museum of Art, Philadelphia, Pa., Gift of J. Stogdell Stokes.*)

Large refectory table of oak was made in Pennsylvania around 1700. Enlarged vase turning of legs, and protruding structure of bottom rails, are reminiscent of earlier gothic tables. Side *forms* (or elongated stools) are made of pearwood. (*Courtesy, Philadelphia Museum of Art, Philadelphia, Pa., Gift of J. Stogdell Stokes.*)

Above left. Stretcher table of maple and pine was built in Pennsylvania around 1725–1750. (*Courtesy, The Henry Ford Museum, Dearborn, Mich.*)

Above right. Unusual turning and scrollwork of this 18th century Pennsylvania Dutch table contribute to its interesting design. (*Courtesy, National Gallery of Art, Index of American Design, Washington, D.C.*)

Left. Walnut stretcher table, with two-drawer and fluted apron, originated in Pennsylvania during the 18th century. (*Courtesy, William Penn Memorial Museum, Harrisburg, Pa.*)

Below left. Pennsylvania walnut desk-table, circa 1730–1750, was designed with wide and narrow drawers and elaborately scrolled front apron. Top swings up on peg-pivoted cleats, allowing access to "hidden" compartments. See measured drawing, page 165. (*Courtesy, Philadelphia Museum of Art, Philadelphia, Pa.*)

Below right. Sophisticated stretcher table of early 18th century origin has ornate brass hardware. (*Courtesy, The Henry Francis du Pont Winterthur Museum, Winterthur, Del.*)

Above left. Walnut table of early 18th century origin; has square "turning," extruded bottom rail and elaborately scrolled aprons. (*Courtesy, Philadelphia Museum of Art, Philadelphia, Pa.*)

Above right. Square "turned" tables such as this one originated during 18th century in rural Pennsylvania Dutch communities. Obviously, they lacked turning lathes and substituted square shapes for round turning. (*Courtesy, The Henry Francis du Pont Winterthur Museum, Winterthur, Del.*)

Right. Oval-top, stretcher-base table was used during the 18th century in Postlewaits Tavern on the Conestoga Turnpike. (*Photo by author. Courtesy, the Heritage Center of Lancaster County, Lancaster, Pa.*)

Below left. Unusual small walnut trestle table was made in Pennsylvania early in the 18th century. (*Courtesy, The Metropolitan Museum of Art, New York, N.Y., Gift of Mrs. Robert W. de Forrest, 1933.*)

Below right. Joint table of yellow pine was made in Pennsylvania around 1750. See measured drawing page 162. (*Courtesy, The Metropolitan Museum of Art, New York, N.Y., gift of Mrs. Robert W. de Forrest, 1933.*)

Walnut gateleg table is made somewhat heavier than New England counterparts, and displays turned shapes made only by Pennsylvania Dutch craftsmen of the 18th century. (*Photo by author. Courtesy, Daniel Boone Homestead, Birdsboro, Pa.*)

Massive, X-trestle table (sawbuck table) with oak understructure and pine top was used in the kitchen of the Daniel Boone Homestead during the 18th century (*Photo by author. Courtesy, Daniel Boone Homestead, Birdsboro, Pa.*)

Sawbuck table originated around 1800 in southeastern Pennsylvania. Note graceful tapering of "X" members. (*Photo by author. Courtesy, Farm Museum of Landis Valley, Lancaster, Pa.*)

60

Built around 1800, at Linglestown, Pa., this poplar school-master's desk was severely designed to stand up to the stern requirements of the schoolmaster. (*Courtesy, Hershey Museum of American Life, Hershey, Pa.*)

This cherry schoolmaster's desk was used in 1819 by John F. Frueauff, who was then principal of the Bethlehem Female Seminary, a Moravian school for girls. (*Photo by author. Courtesy, Moravian Museum of Bethlehem, Bethlehem, Pa.*)

DESKS

Pennsylvania Dutch desks vary in design from the most primitive to the most sophisticated. Many of the schoolmaster's desks (as pictured above) were totally undecorated and consisted merely of a box at the top with a hinged lid. Usually, there were also a couple of drawers to hold writing accessories and incidentals.

Others, like the Moravian schoolmaster's desk, shown above at right, were of more elaborate design. This desk is made with a delicate spindled gallery at the top, and gracefully turned legs. Apparently, early schoolmasters taught in a standing position.

Another type of desk, shown at right, could double as a washstand. The top could accommodate a washbowl with room for the pitcher on the shelf below.

The elaborately inlaid walnut drop-leaf desk, shown at bottom right, originated in Chester County, Pennsylvania, between 1720 and 1750. This represents the ultimate in elegant design. For its fine proportions and superb inlaid craftsmanship, it even exceeds work performed at the time by the cabinet-makers of the urban colonial centers.

Right. This handsome inlaid walnut desk—built in Chester County, Pa. between 1720 and 1750—exemplifies the great skill of some Pennsylvania Dutch craftsmen. (*Courtesy, The Henry Francis du Pont Winterthur Museum, Winterthur, Del.*)

Cherry desk, built by John Christ of Nazareth, Pa., during early 19th century. This desk could double as a washstand. (*Photo by author. Courtesy, Annie S. Kemerer Museum, Bethlehem, Pa.*)

This sturdy kneading trough (dough table) made of unstained white pine was built in Pennsylvania around the middle of the 18th century. (*Courtesy, Philadelphia Museum of Art, Philadelphia, Pa., Gift of J. Stogdell Stokes.*)

Dough table of poplar, painted white, is believed to have been built in Pennsylvania around 1840. See measured drawing, page 179. (*Courtesy, Hershey Museum of American Life, Hershey, Pa.*)

Dough trough table with removable top; doubles as a spacious eating table and as a bin for kneading dough. It was made during the early years of the 19th century in southeastern Pennsylvania. See measured drawing, page 178. (*Courtesy, Mercer Museum, Doylestown, Pa.*)

DOUGH TABLES & BINS

In practically all the colonies, dough tables and bins were essential items of kitchen equipment. Without them, how could the colonists' "daily bread" have been produced? Usually, these items were made of pine, poplar or similar softwoods. Some of the most handsome models were made of walnut.

One interesting point about the design and construction of Pennsylvania dough tables and bins is that you rarely see two of them that were designed exactly the same. Although the top bins are all shaped with slanted sides and ends, the understructure is designed and turned differently in each instance.

Of the bins shown on this page, the most remarkable is the one at the bottom with the decorative painted designs. This was made of poplar in Dauphin County, Pennsylvania, between 1780 and 1800.

The design at the top (which was made at Lebanon, Pennsylvania, around the middle of the 19th century) is decorated with straight and wavy combed graining. The middle design is typical, with shaped, cleat handles spanning the lid.

Simulated graining, of straight and wavy lines, distinguishes the decoration of this dough bin, which was made in Pennsylvania in the mid-19th century. (*Courtesy, William Penn Memorial Museum, Harrisburg, Pa.*)

Dough bins were sometimes called "kneading trays." This typical design is believed to have originated near Steelton, Pa., around the middle of the 19th century. (*Courtesy, William Penn Memorial Museum, Harrisburg, Pa.*)

This excellent design of Pennsylvania dough bin is believed to have originated near the end of the 18th century in Dauphin County. Note the attractive painted decorations. (*Courtesy, The Metropolitan Museum of Art, New York, N.Y., Gift of Mrs. Robert W. de Forrest, 1932.*)

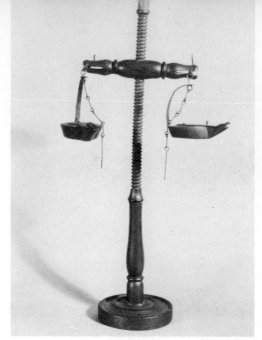

This 18th century Pennsylvania Dutch candlestand has a threaded stem for raising and lowering the candle bracket. Note the legs, broadly splayed, for added stability. (*Courtesy, The Metropolitan Museum of Art, New York, N.Y., Gift of Mrs. Russell Sage, 1909.*)

Betty lamps were used in Pennsylvania during the 18th century. Threaded stem facilitated raising and lowering the lamps. See measured drawing, page 183. (*Courtesy, Philadelphia Museum of Art, Philadelphia, Pa., Gift of J. Stogdell Stokes.*)

STANDS & STOOLS

Candlestands were commonly used for holding tallow candles in early Pennsylvania Dutch homes. Some of these were ingeniously made with threaded stems for elevating and lowering the candle bracket. Others (like the little turned stand below) were made with heavy bases to avoid tipping the candle.

In some early colonies where candles were not available, *Betty lamps* (like the one shown above, at right) provided the necessary illumination. Their small iron pots, suspended by metal links to the crossarm, were filled with oil into which a wick was inserted and lighted.

The handsome windsor turned stool shown below was made in Pennsylvania late in the 18th century.

Turned candlestand, of early 18th century Pennsylvania origin, is strongly built with through mortise and tenon joints connecting cross-lapped base and top cleats. See measured drawing, page 184. (*Courtesy, Philadelphia Museum of Art, Philadelphia, Pa.*)

Gracefully turned windsor stool was made in Pennsylvania between 1760 and 1800. Stool is made low enough (22 1/8″) for conventional seating. (*Courtesy, The Henry Francis du Pont Winterthur Museum, Winterthur, Del.*)

Highly decorative dower chest features a central panel painted with prancing unicorns. On right and left panels, crowned images of the king are painted in company with mounted horsemen. Chest is otherwise painted with stippled designs including swirls and intricate patterns. This dower chest was built in Berks County late in the 18th century. See measured drawing of similar design, page 170, and patterns for decorative panels, page 141. *(Courtesy, The Henry Francis du Pont Winterthur Museum, Winterthur, Del.)*

DOWER CHESTS

Referred to by the Pennsylvania Dutch as *Ausschteier Kischt,* the dower chest has come to be known and loved as the most representative article of Pennsylvania Dutch furniture. According to Germanic custom, it was built specifically for a girl and was given to her when she reached the age of eight or ten. Her name and usually the date of presentation was painted on the chest when the gift was made. Into the chest went all the things the girl made, was given, or purchased in anticipation of her marriage. On her wedding day, her fully packed dower chest was proudly carried to the "wedding wagon" and was driven to her new home.

Many dower chests have survived and their variety of designs, dimensions and construction (not to mention the wide diversification of their painted decorations) would indicate that no craftsman copied the designs of another. However, he may have made duplicate copies of his own work.

It is possible to recognize regional patterns in the design of chests and thus to categorize them as having been made, or painted, in certain regions of the state by recognized craftsmen. Thus, the work of Christian Selzer, which first appeared in Lebanon County around the middle of the 18th century, has been widely recognized, and several of his chests are displayed in museums of Pennsylvania.

A single physical characteristic is the basis for distinguishing the different designs of all dower chests: some are drawerless, whereas others are made with bottom drawers.

This dower chest was made at Lebanon County late in the 18th century. (*Courtesy, The Henry Ford Museum, Dearborn, Mich.*)

Scatter-painted dower chest with unusual block feet is self-dated, "1794." (*Photo by Derek Balmer. Courtesy, The American Museum in Britain, Bath, England.*)

Line-decorated chest, dated 1781, has hearts painted on corners. (*Courtesy, National Gallery of Art, Index of American Design, Washington, D.C.*)

Built in Pennsylvania in 1774, this dower chest is of unusually heavy construction. (*Courtesy, The Henry Francis du Pont Winterthur Museum, Winterthur, Del.*)

Dower chest from Bucks County, Pa., was made in 1784. (*Courtesy, National Gallery of Art, Index of American Design, Washington, D.C.*)

Decorated with simple, painted panels and a large valentine heart, this dower chest was built for Mary Shultz in 1818. (*Photos by author. Courtesy, The Heritage Center of Lancaster County, Lancaster, Pa.*)

A large heart-shaped cartouche frames the name "Maria Stoller" to identify this 1788 dower chest. (*Photo by author. Courtesy, the Heritage Center of Lancaster County, Lancaster, Pa.*)

Dower chest inscribed with name "Christina Ern-stin" was made in the Lehigh Valley, late in the 18th century. (*Courtesy, National Gallery of Art, Index of American Design, Washington, D.C.*)

Stencils may have been used to produce the symmetrical panel decorations of this dower chest, built in Berks County, Pa., in 1785. (*Courtesy, The American Museum in Britain, Bath, England.*)

Another dower chest built and painted by Christian Selzer (1789–1831). This one, built between 1771 and 1796, is primly painted with floral panels. (*Photo by author. Courtesy, Lebanon County Historical Society, Lebanon, Pa.*)

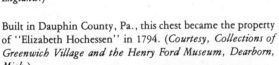

Built in Dauphin County, Pa., this chest became the property of "Elizabeth Hochessen" in 1794. (*Courtesy, Collections of Greenwich Village and the Henry Ford Museum, Dearborn, Mich.*)

Another unicorn chest of tulipwood and pine was built at Berks County, around 1780. (*Courtesy, the Metropolitan Museum of Art, New York, N.Y., Rogers Fund, 1923.*)

Two panels, each picturing a large-petaled blossom, frame the bold decoration of this dower chest. Corners of the chest are painted with hearts alternating with tulips. This chest was built in Lebanon County, Pa., in 1786. (*Courtesy, The Metropolitan Museum of Art, New York, N.Y., Rogers Fund, 1944.*)

Dower chest of more recent make (1850), at left, has free-hand decorations on front, with inscription of name: "M. Brenaman." Stenciled chest at right has initials "C Y" and date "1879" inscribed with faded decorations on front. (*Both chests, courtesy, the Henry Ford Museum, Dearborn, Mich.*)

SMALL BOXES & CHESTS

Pennsylvania Dutch craftsmen were famous for their production of a vast variety of little boxes and chests. These were used for the storage of valuables and precious papers, or as a repository for the family bible. Whatever their purpose, they were all handsomely designed and colorfully finished.

With their love of flamboyant painted decorations, it was inevitable that many of their small chests were vividly painted with bold floral, fruit and geometrical patterns. Others were made of walnut and delicately inlaid with white wood. Some of the inlaid designs are quite intricate, consisting of circles, elliptical swirls or sometimes the inlaid outlines of vines bearing fruit.

When feet were attached to these little chests, they were usually turned (of turnip shape). The best small chests seem to have originated during the final years of the 18th century.

Attractively painted box is 7 3/4" high, 17 3/4" long and 10 3/4" deep. It was built around 1775. (*Courtesy, The Henry Francis du Pont Winterthur Museum, Winterthur, Del.*)

Walnut spice box is 22" high, 17 ½" wide and 11" deep. It was made in Chester County, Pa., between 1700 and 1725. Delicate geometrical wax-inlaid design depicts 8-pointed star and vines bearing fruit. (*Courtesy, William Penn Memorial Museum, Harrisburg, Pa.*)

Inlaid, walnut chest is 17 1/2" high, 15 3/8" long and 8 1/2" deep. It was made in Chester County, Pa., some time between 1725 and 1775. (*Courtesy, The Henry Francis du Pont Winterthur Museum, Winterthur, Del.*)

Small, dovetailed chest was made in Pennsylvania in 1840. Ball or *turnip* feet were frequently used by Pennyslvania craftsmen. (*Courtesy, Hershey Museum of American Life, Hershey, Pa.*)

Tastefully decorated with floral and distelfink designs, this chest of drawers was made in Snyder County, Pa., around 1834. Note progressive size graduations of distelfink drawer paintings to correspond with increased widths of drawers. See graphed decorative designs, page 152, and measured drawing, page 208. *(Courtesy, Philadelphia Museum of Art, Philadelphia, Pa.)*

CHESTS OF DRAWERS

Pennsylvania Dutch chests of drawers were made and decorated with painted designs in the usual peasant style. Chests shown here display typical bird and floral painted decorations. The design below also includes scrollwork along the top and base aprons.

In the 19th century, the transition from the inherited Germanic forms became noticeable. Painted decorations of the 19th century became somewhat more subdued, and there was a tendency to copy the designs of other American colonies.

The four chests of drawers shown on these pages are typical of early 19th century Pennsylvania Dutch production.

This chest of drawers—decorated with distelfinks, flowers and hex stars—was built in the Mahantongo Valley of Schuylkill County, Pa., in 1834. (*Courtesy, The Henry Francis du Pont Winterthur Museum, Winterthur, Del.*)

Made of pine and decoratively painted with stippled stars, augmented by rows of "A" marks, this chest of drawers—which originated in Pennsylvania around 1830—shows another method of painted ornamentation. (*Courtesy, The Henry Ford Museum, Dearborn, Mich.*)

Elaborate scrollwork, simulated wood graining and stenciled end panels distinguish this chest of drawers, which is otherwise identified with initials "R W" and date "1850." (*Courtesy, The Henry Ford Museum, Dearborn, Mich.*)

WALL CUPBOARDS & HANGING SHELVES

Above left. This little key cupboard was made around 1800. See graphed design, page 138, and measured drawing, page 192. *(Courtesy, The Metropolitan Museum of Art, New York, N.Y., Gift of Mrs. Robert W. de Forrest, 1933.)*

Above right. This unusually fine hanging corner cupboard was made in Pennsylvania around the middle of the 18th century. *(Courtesy, Philadelphia Museum of Art, Philadelphia, Pa., Gift of J. Stogell Stokes.)*

Left. Typical Pennsylvania Dutch corner cupboard is believed to have been built around 1750. *(Photo by author. Courtesy, Daniel Boone Homestead, Birdsboro, Pa.)*

Below left. Hanging cupboard, with ample drawers; measures 36 7/16" high, 38 5/8" wide and 18" deep. *(Courtesy, The Henry Francis du Pont Winterthur Museum, Winterthur, Del.)*

Below right. Inlaid hanging cupboard was built in Pennsylvania in 1772. *(Courtesy, Philadelphia Museum of Art, Philadelphia, Pa., The Titus C. Geesey Collection.)*

Above left. Pennsylvania Dutch hanging wall cupboard of the 18th century is nicely detailed with fully scrolled apron. See measured drawing, page 194. *(Photo by Ron Sprules. Courtesy, American Museum in Britain, Bath, England.)*

Above right. Plate rack of early 19th century origin shows typical Pennsylvania Dutch detailing of fretwork, carving and cutouts of heart-shaped apertures. See measured drawing, page 180. *(Photo by Ron Sprules. Courtesy, The American Museum in Britain, Bath, England.)*

Right. This heavy walnut cupboard with elaborately scrolled hinges originated in Pennsylvania around 1725. See measured drawing, page 193. *(Courtesy, The Metropolitan Museum of Art, New York, N.Y., Gift of Mrs. Robert W. de Forrest, 1933.)*

Below left. This handsome wall cupboard was built in central Pennsylvania around 1780. *(Photo by author. Courtesy, Pennsylvania Farm Museum of Landis Valley, Lancaster, Pa.)*

Below right. Unusual scrolled corner shelves were designed to hold crockery and cutlery. *(Courtesy, The Metropolitan Museum of Art, New York, N.Y., Gift of Mrs. Robert W. de Forrest, 1933.)*

Massive pine corner cupboard was built in the Delaware Valley of Pennsylvania between 1770 and 1785. This cupboard is 98 ½ " tall, which was the ceiling height of many early homes. Apparently it was originally painted, but was recently restored to natural wood (stain) finish, which exposes the beautiful wood graining. (*Courtesy, William Penn Memorial Museum, Harrisburg, Pa.*)

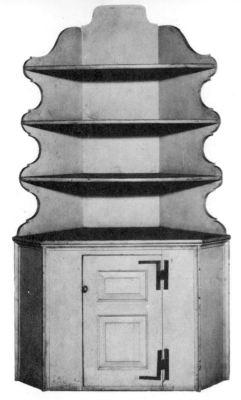

Open corner cupboard, made in Pennsylvania during the 18th century, has sides and shelves made of pine boards measuring a full inch thick. See measured drawing of adapted design, page 212. (*Courtesy, Philadelphia Museum of Art, Philadelphia, Pa.*)

Spacious corner cupboard with broad crown molding was built in Pennsylvania between 1760 and 1780. (*Courtesy, Hershey Museum of American Life, Hershey, Pa.*)

CORNER CUPBOARDS

Glass-front corner cupboard of early 19th century origin is decorated along the sides with split turnings. (*Photo by author. Courtesy, Hershey Museum of American Life, Hershey, Pa.*)

Spacious corner cupboard (c. 1800) with glazed doors has ample shelf space for display of prized glass and crockery. (*Photo by author. Courtesy, Hershey Museum of American Life, Hershey, Pa.*)

UTILITY DRESSERS

Of more elementary design than the glazed cupboards shown on the following pages, the Pennsylvania utility dressers (or *Welch* dressers, as they are sometimes called) are of simple, sturdy construction. They predate the glazed cupboards, having been built in this country since the early 17th century.

These dressers were usually relegated to the kitchen, where they were used to store and display household collections of crockery, glassware, tin and pewter. They were usually plainly made, sometimes with simple scrollwork along the top and sides to relieve their unadorned design. Most often they were painted in drab tones of red, blue or brown.

The Pennsylvania Dutch referred to the dresser as a "kiche shonk," which translates into English as "kitchen cupboard." Since many of them still remain in museums, they may be regarded as part of the rich heritage of Pennsylvania's past.

The Pennsylvania Folk Art Room at Winterthur Museum brings together furniture and decorative objects made in Pennsylvania during the 18th and 19th centuries. On the shelves of the old pine dressers are earthenware plates and jars with *slip* and *sgraffito* decoration. The table is an unusual example of late 17th century gate leg, made in Pennsylvania. Armchairs beside the table are of early wainscot type. In the corner, another early armchair, chest and wall cupboard complete the picture. (*Courtesy, The Henry Francis du Pont Winterthur Museum, Winterthur, Del.*)

Pine dresser, made in Pennsylvania in the middle of the 18th century, is plainly designed with scrolled sides, crown top and slab feet. (*Courtesy, Philadelphia Museum of Art, Philadelphia, Pa., Gift of J. Stogell Stokes.*)

This typical "Welch" dresser was built in Berks County, Pa., between 1750 and 1780. (*Photo by author. Courtesy, the Heritage Center of Lancaster County, Lancaster, Pa.*)

This perfectly plain, open cupboard was built in Pennyslvania around the turn of the 19th century. Here it displays an attractive collection of Pennsylvania Dutch painted tinware. See measured drawing, page 214. (*Courtesy, The American Museum in Britain, Bath, England.*)

"Kiche shonk" is the German name for this early utility dresser which was built in Pennsylvania some time between 1750 and 1800. (*Courtesy, The Henry Francis du Pont Winterthur Museum, Winterthur, Del.*)

CUPBOARDS

Above left. This rare cupboard, circa 1760, has graceful proportions which focus attention on its delicately carved scalloping. (*Courtesy, Philadelphia Museum of Art, Philadelphia, Pa., The Titus C. Geesey Collection.*)

Above right. Stenciled cupboard, made at Johnstown, Pa., has initials "O E" and date "1851" stenciled on drawer fronts. (*Courtesy, Collections of Greenfield Village and the Henry Ford Museum, Dearborn, Mich.*)

Left. Handsome walnut cupboard, with glazed top and graduated row of front drawers, was made in Pennsylvania around 1750. (*Courtesy, Philadelphia Museum of Art, Philadelphia, Pa., The Titus C. Geesey Collection.*)

Below left. Heavily decorated cupboard, displaying rural chalkware, was built in Pennsylvania between 1760 and 1780. (*Courtesy, The American Museum in Britain, Bath, England.*)

Below right. Unusual glazed cupboard is decorated with abundance of painted designs, including landscapes painted on the door panels. It was built between 1800 and 1830. (*Courtesy, The Henry Francis du Pont Winterthur Museum, Winterthur, Del.*)

Made entirely of walnut, this masterpiece of Pennsylvania Dutch craftsmanship originated in eastern Pennsylvania during the early years of the 18th century. This highly decorative cupboard is of somewhat complicated construction. Ornamental hardware, including bail handles, rattail hinges and unusual door hasps, all contribute to its interesting appearance. See measured drawing page 216. *(Courtesy, The Metropolitan Museum of Art, New York, N.Y., Rogers Fund, 1945.)*

George Huber's *schrank*—with name, date and decorations cleverly inlaid on doors and front—was built in Berks County in 1779. This is regarded by many as the finest piece of Pennsylvania Dutch furniture in existence. (*Courtesy, Philadelphia Museum of Art, Philadelphia, Pa., Purchased.*)

Martin Eisenhauer's schrank, dated 1794, is designed with symmetrically matched panels of varying sizes. On this design, intricate inlays replace the elaborate carving of earlier Germanic models. (*Courtesy, Philadelphia Museum of Art, Philadelphia, Pa., Purchased: Museum Annual Membership Fund.*)

Another walnut schrank, closely resembling the one above, at right, is dated 1768. It probably originated in Lancaster County. White sulfur inlays on door panels spell out indistinguishable names. (*Courtesy, The Henry Francis du Pont Winterthur Museum, Winterthur, Del.*)

This handsome, inlaid walnut schrank was built in Lancaster County, Pa. in 1766. Apparently it was made for, or built by, "I. H. Kauffman" and "A. N. Kauffman," whose names are inlaid on the upper door panels. Note carved lilies on corners of door panels. (*Courtesy, William Penn Memorial Museum, Harrisburg, Pa.*)

This elaborately painted pine schrank is believed to have originated in Berks County, Pa., in 1790. With its flamboyant brushwork on drawers and floral door panels, this is an unusually colorful piece. (*Courtesy, The Henry Ford Museum, Dearborn, Mich.*)

This hooded cradle of poplar was built near Ephrata, Pa., around 1800. See measured drawing, page 203. *(Photo by author. Courtesy, Ephrata Cloister, Ephrata, Pa.)*

Open cradle was built at Bethlehem, Pa., in 1780. Note intricate top cutting of ends and crude decorations. *(Photo by author. Courtesy, Moravian Museum of Bethlehem, Bethlehem, Pa.)*

CRADLES

Since the Middle Ages and right up to the 20th century, cradles have been regarded as an essential household item for the upbringing of infants. All over the world, they are made in a great variety of types and sizes.

As illustrated on these pages, the design of Pennsylvania cradles ranged from hooded types; to trestle, suspended models; to plain, open designs with delicate scrolled sides. As a token of affection, a loving heart was usually cut through the end panels.

This attractively scrolled open cradle was built near Hershey, Pa. late in the 18th century. *(Courtesy, Hershey Museum of American Life, Hershey, Pa.)*

Walnut trestle cradle was made at Bethlehem, Pa., late in the 19th century. Crib is suspended on trestles to be rocked from the top. Note flamboyant hand-woven fabric in background. (*Photo by author. Courtesy, Lebanon County Historical Society, Lebanon, Pa.*)

Open cradle, believed to have originated in Pennsylvania between 1800 and 1830. Note rope-fastening knobs used to secure infant. (*Courtesy, William Penn Memorial Museum, Harrisburg, Pa.*)

Heavily constructed open cradle made of tiger maple has unusual heart-shaped cutouts on ends. This cradle is believed to have been built around 1800. (*Courtesy, William Penn Memorial Museum, Harrisburg, Pa.*)

Cleverly designed little open cradle of walnut was built in Pennsylvania between 1750 and 1775. (*Courtesy, The Henry Francis du Pont Winterthur Museum, Winterthur, Del.*)

In this late 18th century Lebanon bedroom, the furniture combines early and late forms. The pencil-post bed stands in the center of the room to clear the sloping ceiling. A green painted armchair represents a form of Pennsylvania slatback design popular throughout the region. Next to the chair stands an 18th century candlestand. In the foreground at right is a walnut cradle, its scalloped end pierced with the popular heart motif. A large tin chandelier hangs above, the candlelight reflected by strips of mirrored glass. (*Courtesy, The Henry Francis du Pont Winterthur Museum, Winterthur, Del.*)

84

Four-poster bed with tester top was built in Pennsylvania around the turn of the 19th century. Note unusual stippled finish. See measured drawing, page 206. *(Courtesy, Philadelphia Museum of Art, Philadelphia, Pa.)*

Four-poster, canopy-top bed, made of maple, was built for the master bedroom of an 1815 Pennsylvania farmhouse. *(Courtesy, William Penn Memorial Museum, Harrisburg, Pa.)*

BEDS

Beds seem to have been more thoughtfully developed by Pennsylvania Dutch craftsmen than by the craftsmen of other colonies. Indeed, many of the early designs illustrated here would be most welcome in our modern homes.

Most early beds were made with rope platforms, which wound around wooden pegs inserted in the rails. Usually the ropes supported mattresses filled with feathers, straw or hay.

Children's beds were apt to be of simpler design, narrower and made with shallow headboards. Beds were frequently finished in natural wood tones or were painted and stippled for decorative effect.

Cannonball four-poster bed was built for the Miess family in 1840. Bed is massively constructed of poplar and white pine. See measured drawing, page 204. *(Courtesy, Hershey Museum of American Life, Hershey, Pa.)*

BOXES, RACKS, MIRROR & STOOLS

Above left. Bright, painted floral decorations of this slide-lid Pennsylvania candle box associate it with the best examples of early Germanic decorative art. It was made in 1783. See graphed patterns of decorations, page 139 and measured drawing, page 186. (*Courtesy, National Gallery of Art, Index of American Design, Washington, D. C.*)

Above right. Salt box, believed to have been built in Pennsylvania around 1840, is strongly constructed with dovetail joints. (*Courtesy, Pennsylvania Farm Museum of Landis Valley, Lancaster, Pa.*)

Left. Pine candle box, stencil-decorated, is believed to have originated around 1800. (*Courtesy, The Metropolitan Museum of Art, New York, N.Y.*)

Below left. Bride's box, highly decorated, with Revolutionary soldier painted on cover, was made in Pennsylvania during the 18th century. (*Courtesy, Mercer Museum, Doylestown, Pa.*)

Below right. Highly decorated salt box was made in 1797 as gift to "Anne Leterman." See measured drawing, page 187. (*Courtesy, National Gallery of Art, Index of American Design, Washington, D.C.*)

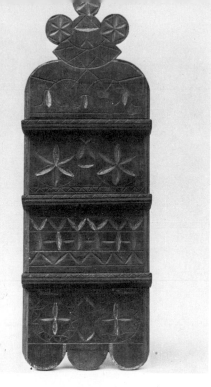

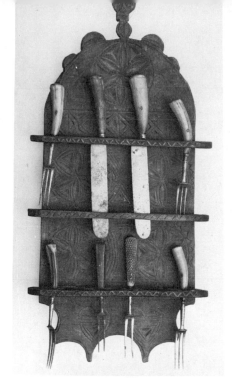

Above left. 18th century Pennsylvania Dutch spoon rack is pleasantly shaped and chip-carved in simple designs. (*Courtesy, The Metropolitan Museum of Art, New York, N.Y., Gift of Mrs. Robert W. de Forest, 1933.*)

Above right. Cutlery rack of 18th century Pennsylvania origin is distinctively shaped to hold assorted knives and forks. (*Courtesy, The Metropolitan Museum of Art, New York, N.Y., Gift of Mrs. Robert W. de Forest, 1933.*)

Right. Early 18th century mirror displays simple crested design commonly found throughout the colonies. (*Photo by author. Courtesy, Daniel Boone Homestead, Birdsboro, Pa.*)

Below left. Simple, scrolled foot stool is 6 15/16″ wide, 13 13/16″ long and 7 ½″ high. It is of 18th century Pennsylvania origin. (*Courtesy, The Henry Francis du Pont Winterthur Museum, Winterthur, Del.*)

Below right. This *cricket-on-the-hearth* is one of a variety of little foot stools made in Pennsylvania during the 18th and 19th centuries. See measured drawing, page 161. (*Photo by author. Courtesy, Rock Ford Plantation, Lancaster, Pa.*)

KITCHEN UTILITY FURNITURE

The kitchen of every farmhouse in the Pennsylvania Dutch regions needed a variety of utility furniture to perform the multitude of household chores. Although this furniture did not function as efficiently as our furniture and appliances of today, it nevertheless did relieve the good housewives of unnecessary work.

For instance, what could be handier for storing huge jars of preserves, pickles, cider, molasses and vinegar, than the sturdy shelves pictured at the left? And the dry sinks, water benches, storage chests, hutch tables and pie safes, all pictured on these pages, had their important uses.

All of these items were hand-made, of solid wood—usually pine. They continued to be built and used throughout these provinces until the advent of the 20th century.

Above left. Standing utility shelves are strongly built with shelves mortised and tenoned through the sides and top dovetailed. See measured drawing, page 190. *(Photo by author. Courtesy, Rock Ford Plantation, Lancaster, Pa.)*

Left. This Pennsylvania Dutch dry sink was made in Lancaster County between 1850 and 1870. It is built of pine, with original ochre grained finish. *(Photo by author. Courtesy, Pennsylvania Farm Museum of Landis Valley, Lancaster, Pa.)*

Below left. Water bench, built at Strausstown, Pa. between 1825 and 1850, was originally designed to hold buckets of water drawn from a nearby well. *(Photo by author. Courtesy, Annie S. Kemerer Museum, Bethlehem, Pa.)*

Below right. Called a *kitchen dresser for storage*, this utility chest was built at Ephrata Cloister during the early years of the 18th century. All hardware—hinges, hasps and catches—are made of hardwood. See measured drawing, page 172. *(Photo by author. Courtesy, Ephrata Cloister, Ephrata, Pa.)*

Sturdy hutch table serves dual purposes of table and bench. Lidded seat is hinged to provide ample storage space below. See measured drawing, page 173. *(Photo by author. Courtesy, Rock Ford Plantation, Lancaster, Pa.)*

Handsome pie safe has hundreds of holes, forming decorative designs on tin panels of doors and ends. See measured drawing, page 191. *(Photo by author. Courtesy, Rock Ford Plantation, Lancaster, Pa.)*

Cozy corner grouping at the Pennsylvania Farm Museum includes traditional sawbuck table, flanked by windsor chairs and plain slab chair. Heating stove at left is set in sandbox for safety. *(Photo by author. Courtesy, Pennsylvania Farm Museum of Landis Valley, Lancaster, Pa.)*

Massive, Germanic beam loom was built at Lancaster, Pa. around 1750. This is heavily constructed with keyed tenons protruding through mortises of upright members. Sample of fabric woven on this loom hangs on back wall. (*Photo by author. Courtesy, Pennsylvania Farm Museum of Landis Valley, Lancaster, Pa.*)

Wool wheel, spinning wheel and clock reel, all of 18th century origin, stand in front of patterned fabrics they helped produce. (*Photo by author. Courtesy, Lebanon County Historical Society, Lebanon, Pa.*)

Dated "1767," this sturdy spinning wheel with widely splayed legs probably originated somewhere around Lancaster, Pa. (*Photo by author. Courtesy, Pennsylvania Farm Museum of Landis Valley, Lancaster, Pa.*)

SPINNING WHEELS, LOOMS & REELS

The spinning wheel, with its related looms and reels, played an important part in the 18th century and early 19th century Pennsylvania Dutch household. Without these devices, it would have been impossible for the settlers to weave the cloth required for their clothing, as well as the bed covers, tablecloths, rugs and other fabrics required in their daily lives.

Large beam looms, like the one pictured on the facing page, could handle sizeable sections of material. Others, not so massively built, were used for producing finer fabrics.

There were two kinds of spinning wheels: one had a large wheel for spinning wool; the other had smaller wheels for spinning linen thread and cotton.

Clock reel, left, and spinning wheel, right, originated at (or near) the Ephrata Cloister early in the 19th century. Wheel was used mostly for spinning linen thread. (*Photo by author. Courtesy, Ephrata Cloister, Ephrata, Pa.*)

Spinning wheel for spinning linen thread was built by "P. Klauser" early in the 19th century. In some regions of Pennsylvania, spinning wheels continued to be used well into the 20th century. (*Photo by author. Courtesy, Ephrata Cloister, Ephrata, Pa.*)

Flax wheels, also known as *clock winders or weazels*, were used in southeastern Pennsylvania around 1750. These were strongly constructed of oak and pine. (*Photo by author. Courtesy, Daniel Boone Homestead, Birdsboro, Pa.*)

Display of assorted spinning devices includes spinning wheel of late 18th century origin, placed in front of a clock reel and various peg-legged stools used for weaving. (*Photo by author. Courtesy, Pennsylvania Farm Museum of Landis Valley, Lancaster, Pa.*)

This handsome piano was built by John C. Melthaner of Bethlehem, Pa. in 1850. Mr. Melthaner built pianos at Bethlehem between 1837 and 1873.

Clavier, below, was built by Jacob C. Till at Bethlehem in 1825. It was owned by J. Fred Wolle, founder and director of the Bethlehem Bach Choir. (*Both photos by author. Courtesy, Moravian Museum of Bethlehem, Bethlehem, Pa.*)

Piano, built in 1815 by Charles Pommer of Philadelphia, is handsomely made of mahogany with maple inlays. (*Photo by author. Courtesy, Pennsylvania Farm Museum of Landis Valley, Lancaster, Pa.*)

PIANOS & MUSICAL INSTRUMENTS

The music-loving Pennsylvania Dutch produced their own musical instruments long before Steinway became a household name. Indeed, many of their pianos, now in museums, are regarded as works of art—and at the time they were used, their pitch was undoubtedly perfect.

Pianos shown on these pages were played mostly by the Moravians. These ardent music lovers, led by Bishop Christian Gregor (known as the "Father of Moravian Hymnody"), wrote and arranged many of the hymns and chorale tunes still sung at Moravian religious services.

This lovely old harpsichord was owned by the Boughter family, prominent Lebanon County bankers. It is believed to have been built around 1790. (*Photo by author. Courtesy, Lebanon County Historical Society, Lebanon, Pa.*)

This *trombone chair* was built at Bethlehem in 1790. When used by trombonist in the orchestra, the chair was high enough to prevent extended trombone from hitting the floor. *Photo by author. Courtesy, Moravian Museum of Bethlehem, Bethlehem, Pa.*)

Assorted clocks at Hershey Museum include, from left to right (dots): • Clock by Christian Eby, 30-hour local dial, walnut case with inlaid corners, 1805, Manheim, Pennsylvania; • Jacob Eby's 8-day clock, with center sweep hand, moon phase, walnut case and American eagle inlay. Made in 1820 in Manheim, Pa. • John Heinselman's 8-day walnut case clock with spruce inlay shows moon phase. Made at Manheim, Pa., in 1805. • Heinselman's 30-hour clock with moon phase, American face, Chippendale cherry case with fluted quarter columns. Made in 1790 at Manheim, Pa. (*Courtesy, Hershey Museum of American Life, Hershey, Pa.*)

Grandfather's clock, *left,* built by Charles F. Beckel at Bethlehem, Pa. between 1826 and 1830. Charles F. Beckel served his clockmaking apprenticeship with Samuel Krause and Jedediah Weiss. He started his own business in 1826 with Henry D. Bishop as his apprentice. He gave up his clockmaking business in 1830 to build an iron foundry. (*Photo by author. Courtesy, Annie S. Kemerer Museum, Bethlehem, Pa.*)

Bracket clock, made in 1770 by George Hoff, Sr., of Lancaster, Pa., has a handsome walnut case and ornately embellished face. (*Photo by author. Courtesy, Heritage Center of Lancaster County, Lancaster, Pa.*)

CLOCKS

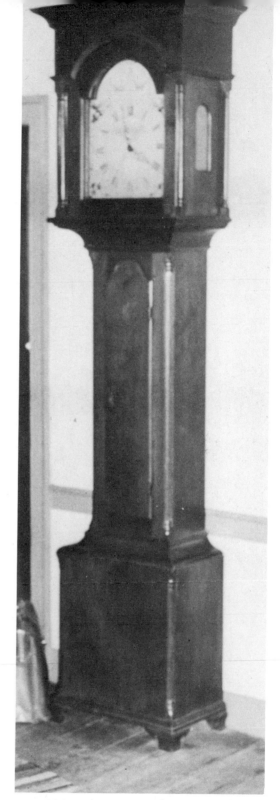

Elegant grandfather's clock with 30-hour brass works was built by Martin Shriner of Lancaster County in 1800. The case is made of select-grain walnut. (*Photo by author. Courtesy, Pennsylvania Farm Museum of Landis Valley, Lancaster, Pa.*)

Cherry case grandfather's clock has moon dial, inlaid Hepplewhite case and 8-day movement. It was built by Jacob Guthart of Lebanon, Pa., between 1800 and 1820. Pictures representing the four seasons are inscribed on corners of the face. A sailing ship and grist mill are pictured on the moon dial. (*Photo by author. Courtesy, Lebanon County Historical Society, Lebanon, Pa.*)

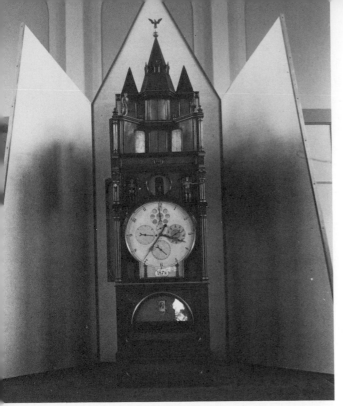

Dramatic setting of the apostolic clock shows its overall design. The patient craftsman who made this clock spent eleven years mastering its mechanical intricacies. Later, to compensate for a friend's kindness, he gave him the clock as a gift. (*Courtesy, Hershey Museum of American Life, Hershey, Pa.*)

Top of clock, showing entrance-ways of carved apostolic figures. Apostles move in procession in the upper sections. Figures of Christ, St. Peter, Judas and the three virgins (at top center), as well as the devil, move in and out during procession. (*Courtesy, Hershey Museum of American Life, Pa.*)

THE APOSTOLIC CLOCK

This remarkable clock was finished in 1878 by John Fiester, who was then 32 years old and a native of Lancaster County, Pennsylvania. Mr. Fiester had devoted 11 years of his life to producing this masterpiece.

The clock consists of three sections. The lower section houses a music box which plays upon the appearance of the trumpeters (carved figures) at the time the Apostles' procession starts in the upper section.

Centered above the face, a form representing *childhood* appears at the approach of the first quarter hour. Father Time then strikes "one" with his scythe. At the second quarter, *youth* appears and Father Time strikes "two." On the approach of the third quarter, *middle age* appears and Father Time strikes "three." At the fourth quarter, *old age* appears and Father Time strikes "four." Then the skeleton, representing death, also strikes the hour. Meanwhile, the procession of Apostles continues, enacting the betrayal of Christ.

Close-up of face shows the seconds, minutes and hours; the day of the week; the day of the month; the month itself; the signs of the Zodiac and the phases of the moon. Figures of Father Time and death (skeleton), at top, perform pantomime indicating inevitable passage of time and constant approach of death. (*Courtesy, Hershey Museum of American Life, Hershey, Pa.*)

Chapter 4

Furniture Construction

Cabinetmaker's workbench, circa 1870—1880. This oak bench was built by Charles V. Arnold of Lebanon, Pa., to pass his test from apprentice to cabinetmaker. Note sturdy, slanted leg with vise attached. This assures stability when work is being planed or sawed. (*Photo by author. Courtesy, Lebanon County Historical Society.*)

OLD CONSTRUCTION

Many of the old furniture-making skills practiced by Pennsylvania Dutch craftsmen stemmed from ancient origins. But they brought to America the native skills of their homelands in Europe, and their early furniture copied what they had previously made abroad.

In America, the craftsmen found an abundance of excellent construction materials, including immense forests flourishing with choice cabinet woods—oak, ash, pine, maple, birch, cherry, walnut, chestnut, elm, hickory and poplar, to mention only a few. Thus, while clearing acres of the forest for their farms, the early settlers reaped the enormous by-product of harvesting vast quantities of timber to construct their homes, barns and furniture, and to use as well to fuel the fires that kept them warm.

After a period of outdoor seasoning, local craftsmen sawed and smoothed their rough planks into furniture parts. Following traditional procedures learned in the old country,

they joined boards together with sturdy mortise and tenon joints, pegs, tongue and grooves, dados, cross-laps, dovetails and other joinery methods. (Much of their early work was performed before the discovery of glue.) Hence, the parts of their furniture and all other wood construction had to be pegged, keyed and wedged in such a way as to stay together virtually of its own substance.

As is noted on the following pages, many of the old tools and woodworking devices have disappeared from common use. Today, with instant electricity available to provide power for numerous tools, the old hand methods and tools are no longer required.

However, it is well to study old construction methods in order to appreciate the way in which early furniture was actually built. Indeed, many skilled hand craftsmen of our present era may for nostalgic reasons wish to try their hands with the tools and practices of more than 200 years ago—if they have the good fortune to find antique tools with which to do so!

FELLING & HEWING

Arriving in Pennsylvania, the colonists found plenty of native timber for building their homes, barns and furniture. But an enormous amount of labor was required to fell the trees and to render them into the shape of construction lumber. Although a few enterprising settlers did erect sawmills powered by wind or water, most lumber was cut by hand by the arduous *pitsawing* method.

As illustrated at right, the felled timber was first roughly squared with a broadax, then was dressed for smoother surfaces with an adze. Following this, it was placed on a platform above a shallow pit, where two men—one on the platform above and the other in the pit below—heaved at each end of a *long saw* until the plank was separated. (Sometimes a large *frame saw* was used instead of the long saw.)

After sawing off the planks in order to prevent warping and splitting, the men stacked the pieces outdoors for a period of seasoning. Then, if the lumber was needed for making furniture, it was stacked indoors until it was thoroughly dry. After this, the lumber was ready for fine sawing, planing and shaping into furniture parts.

Early Pennsylvania craftsmen were not too strict about their selection of a single species of wood to make an entire piece of furniture. Indeed, several kinds of wood were generally used, often for good reason. For instance, hickory was easily bent and therefore was well adapted for making bent parts. Pine, which grew in abundance—and usually to great girth—was ideal for making wide tabletops and other broad surface areas. Legs and rails of chairs and tables, which were subjected to abusive wear, were generally made of hardwoods such as maple or oak.

The following pages try to convey an understanding of the old ways of furniture making by picturing and describing the old tools, woodworking devices, materials, shapes, processes and joinery methods commonly employed. These construction features apply to all the early Pennsylvania Dutch furniture shown in this book.

Hewing and squaring with broadaxe

Dressing the rough beam with an adze

Pitsawing plank from squared beam

OLD WOODWORKING TOOLS

Many of the old woodworking tools shown on these pages have been discarded. Others have been so altered in design that their modern counterparts are barely recognizable. But in their own time, all of these tools played an important part in constructing the buildings and furniture of early America.

Some of these old hand items are now as obsolete as the archaic names they bear. Hardware dealers today would be puzzled if they were asked to fill orders for froes, holzaxts, beetles, crozes, wimbles, twibles, rivers and scorpers. But these were important hand woodworking tools used by the Pennsylvania Dutch, as well as by other early American craftsmen.

The *froe,* for example, was made with a heavy blade, sharpened along the lower edge, and secured (like an ax) to a short handle. The top edge was pounded with a mallet to split rough staves from log sections. The *twible* was shaped like a pickax, with a horizontal adze blade at one end and a narrow hatchet at the other. It was a general cutting tool used mostly for cutting rough mortises.

Early Pennsylvania saws, like those of other colonial craftsmen, came in various types and sizes. The earliest models of crosscut and rip saws were often made with metal handles and oddly shaped blades. Two-man *long saws,* with handles at each end, were used for cutting timber. *Frame saws,* their narrow blades held taut under the tension of a twisted leather thong, were used for straight cutting and for sawing curved shapes.

All Pennsylvania woodworking shops were equipped with an abundance of planes. They varied from the long wooden types to an infinite assortment of *molding planes* with cutters ground for rabbeting, grooving, routing, rounding and forming an infinite variety of molded edge shapes.

Early tools used by the Pennsylvania Dutch for boring holes were crude and primitive when compared to those we know today. Spiral auger bits, with T handles, were used for boring large holes. Braces, which seemed too narrow to provide proper leverage, were used to turn the smaller bits. Sharp-edged gouges were also used for cutting holes.

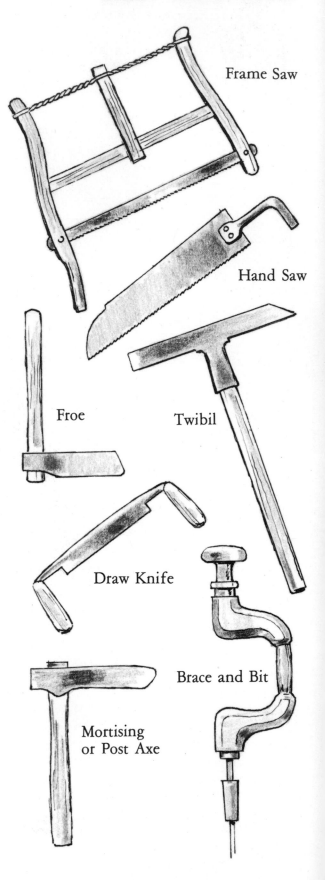

Frame Saw

Hand Saw

Froe

Twibil

Draw Knife

Brace and Bit

Mortising
or Post Axe

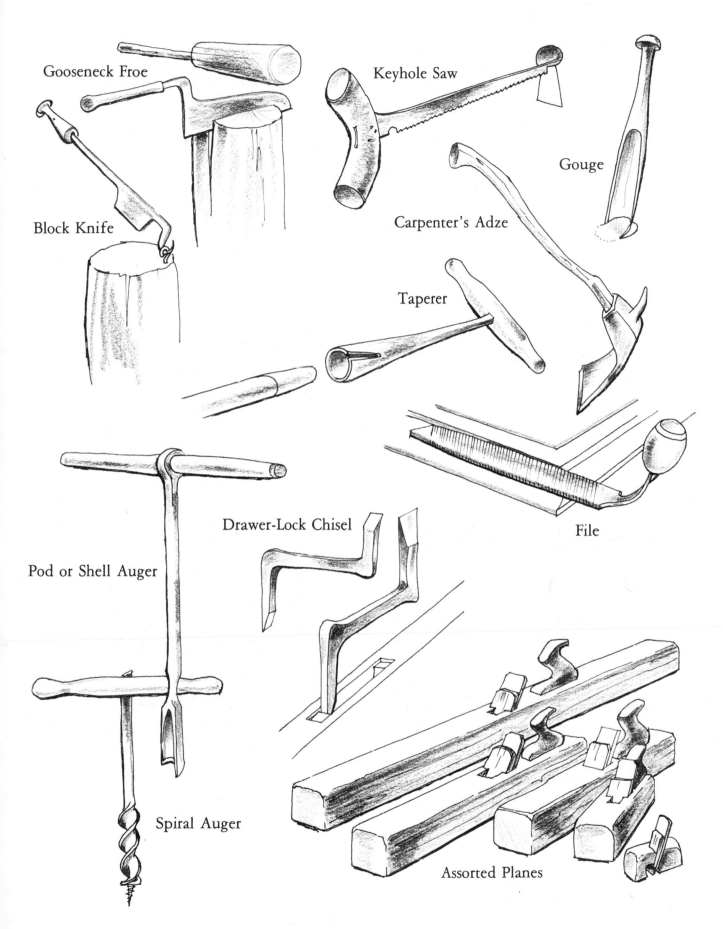

Gooseneck Froe

Keyhole Saw

Gouge

Block Knife

Carpenter's Adze

Taperer

File

Drawer-Lock Chisel

Pod or Shell Auger

Spiral Auger

Assorted Planes

101

OLD WOODWORKING DEVICES

Although they were too rudimentary to be called "machines," a variety of devices were made by early Pennsylvania craftsmen to help them in their work. As an example, for drilling small holes, the craftsmen utilized *bow drills* or *pump drills*. The bow utilized the thong of a bow (of bow and arrow type) looped around a drill spindle. As the bow was drawn back and forth, the drill spindle revolved.

The pump drill, illustrated at right, worked on the flywheel principle. It revolved as pressure was applied to a yoke attached to two leather thongs wound around the shaft.

Considering the exquisite wood turning displayed in the design of early Pennsylvania furniture, we can marvel at the patience and persistence of the pioneer craftsmen, especially because the lathes of that era left much to be desired.

The *spring-pole lathe*, illustrated at right, revolved the work in cutting direction only when the operator pressed down on the foot lever. As the craftsman released pressure on the spring pole, the work revolved in the reverse direction until the foot lever was up and ready for the next turning thrust.

An improvement over the spring-pole lathe was the *treadle lathe*, which operated in sewing machine fashion with a heavy flywheel turned by a foot treadle.

Before electrical power became available, the two-man *great wheel lathe*, shown at right, was undoubtedly the best producer of turned parts. At least this lathe left the operator free to attend to his work. For while the apprentice boy labored at cranking the big wheel, the master craftsman could concentrate on cutting the shapes of his turned designs.

Other devices, such as the *planing jack* shown at right, were designed to help in production of work. This device assisted in the planing of edges by adding gravity to reduce pushing effort.

A variety of true woodworking machines, including *pole-* and *treadle-action jigsaws, mortising jigs, tongue and groove cutters,* and many other labor-saving gadgets were introduced as the years progressed to increase the production of Pennsylvania craftsmen.

Pump Drill

Spring-Pole Lathe

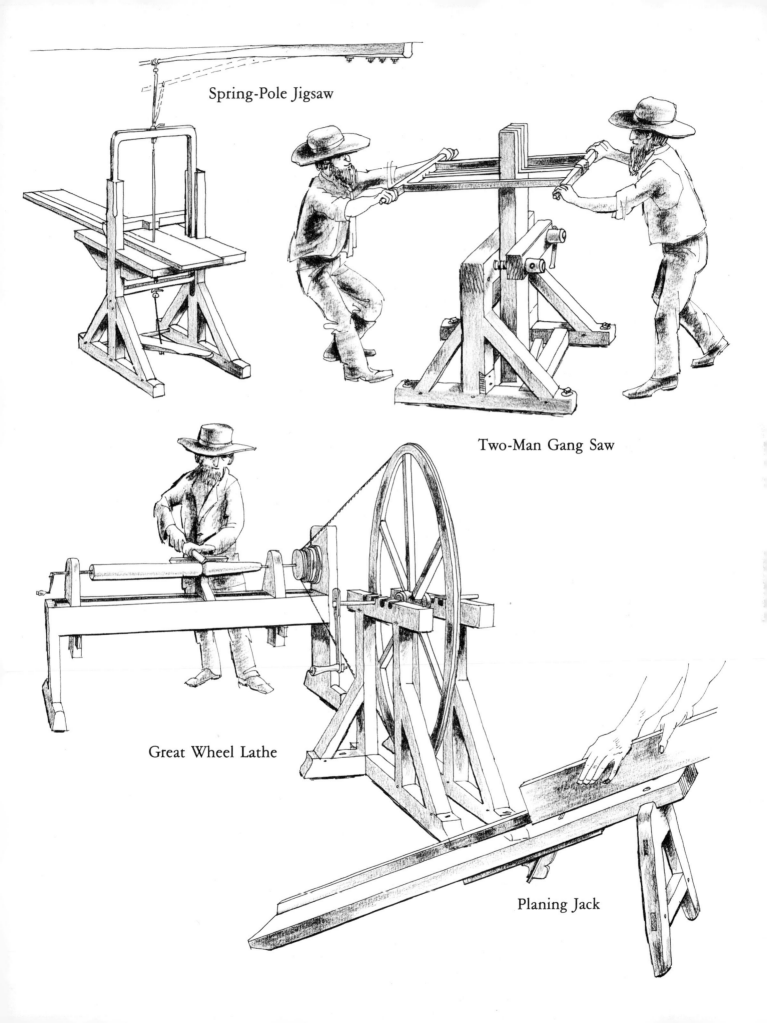

Spring-Pole Jigsaw

Two-Man Gang Saw

Great Wheel Lathe

Planing Jack

OLD HARDWARE

Combined with their excellence as woodworkers and furniture makers, the Pennsylvania Dutch were also superb metalsmiths. As early as the 17th century, iron foundries were established throughout the ore-rich hills and streams of Pennsylvania, and production of various metal objects became a major enterprise.

Most notable were the many different types of metal hasps, hinges, door latches, key plates and decorative ornaments which emerged from their forges. Many of the objects shown on these pages were designed for artistic effect—exquisitely scrolled shapes were intended to decorate the furniture on which they were used.

Different kinds of hinges were made, varying from the "H" and "HL" types to the more elaborately designed *strap hinges, rattail hinges* and highly decorative *staghorn hinges,* shown here.

The unusual collection of Pennsylvania Dutch hardware displayed at the Heritage Center of Lancaster County (photo, below) shows the geometrically shaped finials of their door latches, as well as the intricately shaped staghorn and strap hinges. All of these were hand-wrought of native iron.

Assorted Pennsylvania Dutch door latches, key plates and hinges. (*Photo by author. Courtesy, the Heritage Center of Lancaster County, Lancaster, Pa.*)

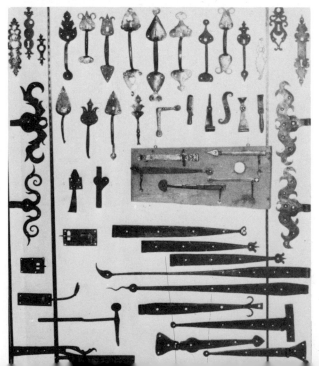

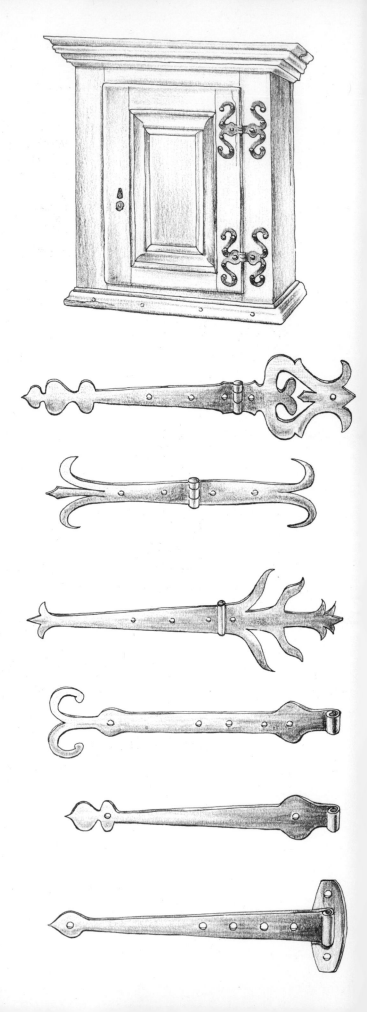

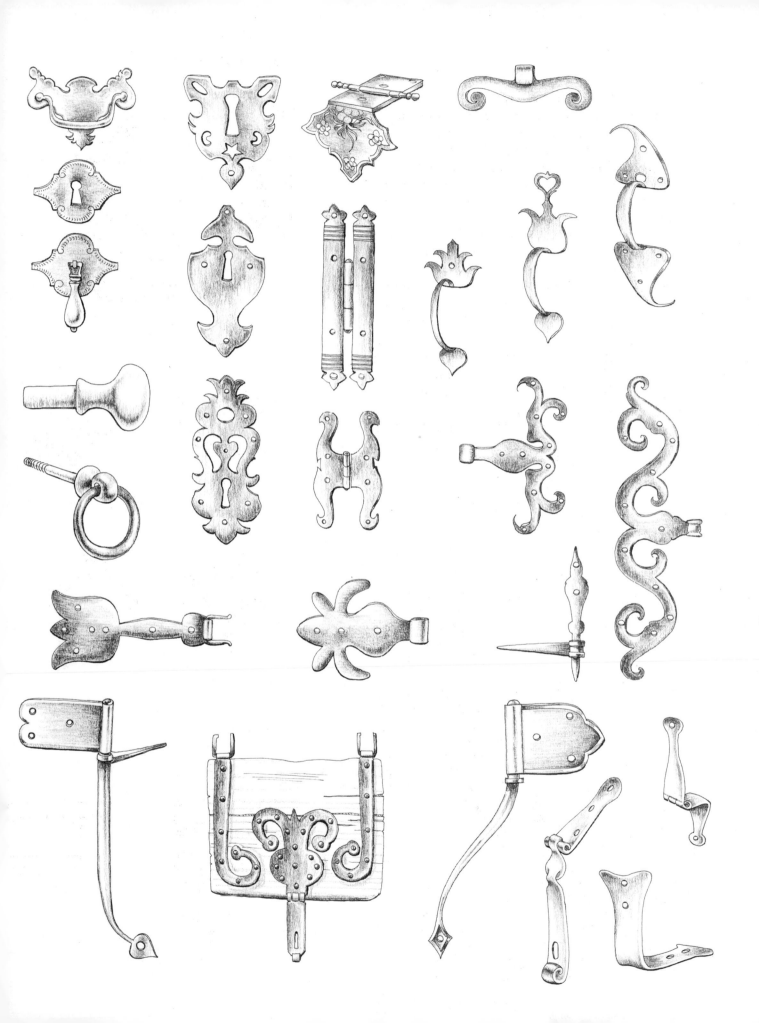

APPLIED MOLDINGS

There appears to be no limit to the shapes devised by our forefathers to fashion their many decorative moldings. These were used to trim dower chests, cupboards, schranks, chests of drawers and dressers. As is illustrated on these pages, no two were shaped exactly alike.

The hand processes required for making these moldings involved the use of molding planes with specially ground cutters, as illustrated above. The craftsman's first procedure was to grind the cutter of the molding plane to the precise shape he wanted to reproduce on wood.

Some of the more massive *crown* molding designs, illustrated in the bottom row at right, required the assembly of several different-shaped strips and parts to make a composite molded design. These were used to form the heavy top molding of the massive schranks and cupboards.

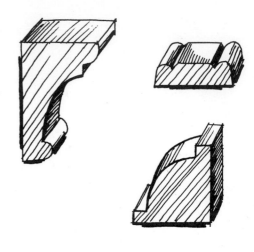

Molding plane, cutting edge molding. Note especially shaped cutter, which must be ground to exact shape of molding.

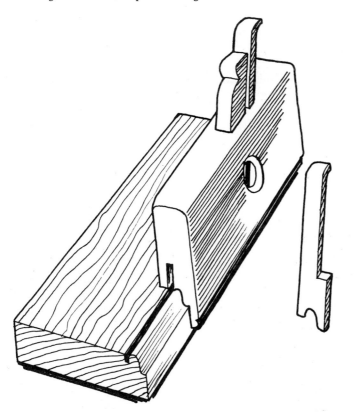

Crown Moldings

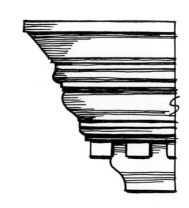

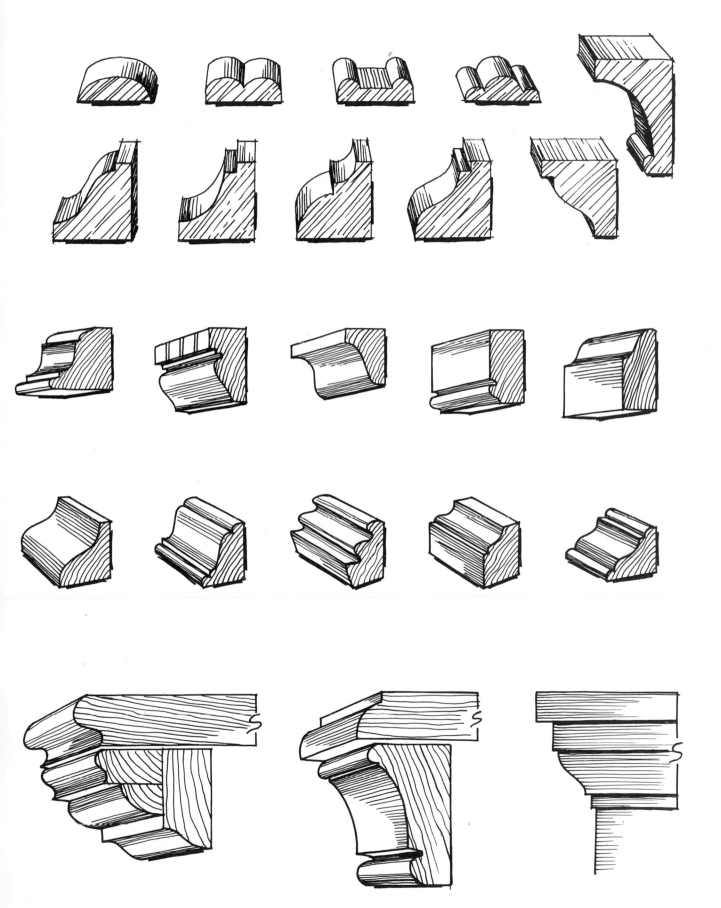

DADO JOINTS

Dadoes are grooves cut across the grain of a board. They are usually used for shelf construction. They may either be *open* (with the groove exposed at the intersection of shelf and attached member) or *closed* (with the groove inset from the front edge of the connecting piece). Another method is to cut a *tenon* on the connecting piece, which fits into the inset dado groove. Both of the concealed dado techniques are called *blind dadoes*.

Construction of the various designs of Pennsylvania Dutch furniture shown in this book frequently employ dadoes, particularly for cupboard shelves and other parts that require secure placement. Dado joints are often reinforced with glue and nails.

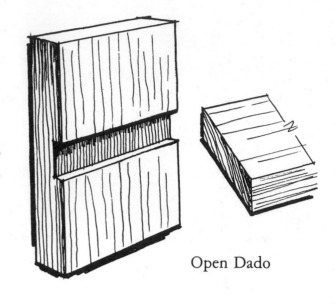

Open Dado

EDGE SHAPES

Tops of tables, chests and benches were usually shaped along the edges with distinctive edge molding. Sometimes this was extremely plain, consisting only of dulled edges; but for other types of work, more ornate shapes were employed.

Of the typical assortment of edge shapes shown at the right, several were produced with straight-cutting planes and abrasive tools. The more elaborate shapes, however, had to be made with molding planes with specially ground cutters.

The process of shaping edges is much the same as cutting the moldings shown on previous pages. Frequently, however, the "shoulder" cuts were made with a saw while the edge was planed to shape with an especially ground cutter. Edge shapes followed the style and function of the articles on which they appeared: the plainer the piece, the simpler the edge shape. The more sophisticated *thumb-nose* edge shapes seem to have been reserved for the more ornate pieces.

Edge Shapes

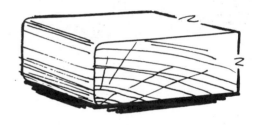

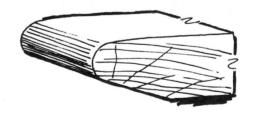

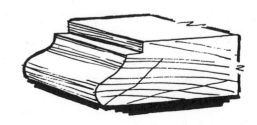

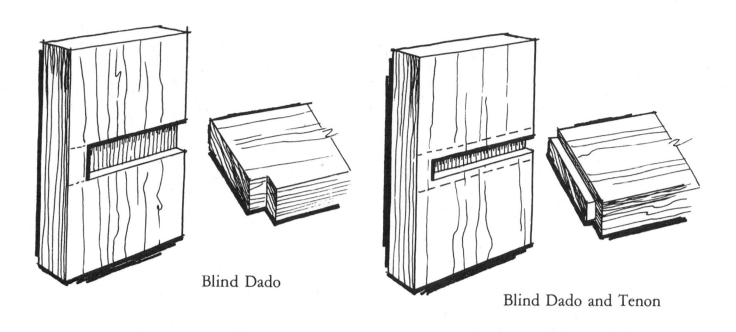

Blind Dado

Blind Dado and Tenon

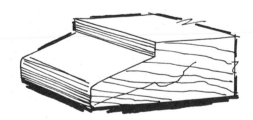

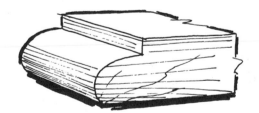

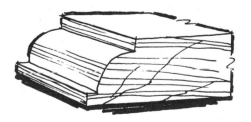

END CLEATS

To prevent the warping of broad wooden surfaces, separate strips of wood (or cleats) were fastened to the ends of tabletops, cabinets and chests. These were attached with hardwood pegs, or more frequently with *tongue-and-groove* or *mortise-and-tenon joints,* as shown at right. Before glue became commonly available, pegs were used to secure all joints. Nowadays, end cleats are generally *tongue-and-grooved* and permanently glued in place.

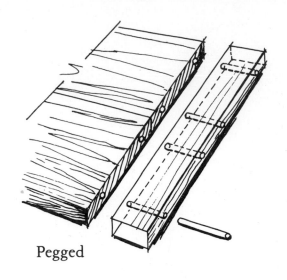
Pegged

EDGE JOINTS

The job of joining boards together to produce broad surfaces must have been formidable before modern woodworking machinery made its appearance. Some of the methods used for edge-joining tabletops of antique furniture are shown at right. These include simple *butt fastenings,* as well as the more complicated processes of *doweling, tongue-and-grooving, rabbeting, splining* and *inlaying* with *hardwood butterfly fasteners.* The last method was used before reliable glues became available.

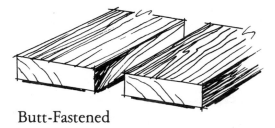
Butt-Fastened

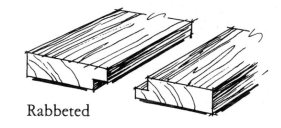
Rabbeted

SIMPLE CARVING

Many pieces of Pennsylvania Dutch furniture were decorated with simple carving. This might amount to nothing more than "chipped" cut-outs of fruit or floral patterns. Sometimes, however, the carved designs were more elaborate, requiring the artistic skill of a master carver.

For carving the simple design shown at right, it is first necessary to have the proper carving tools (as illustrated), which should be kept very sharp. First, proceed to transfer the design from a paper pattern to the wood. This is best accomplished with carbon paper. After the design is transferred, the outline is carefully cut with a "V," or *veining,* tool. Following this, the central areas are scooped out with a carving gouge.

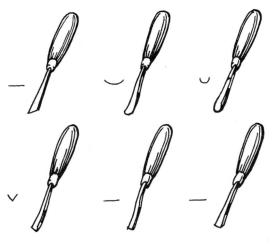
Carving Tools

110

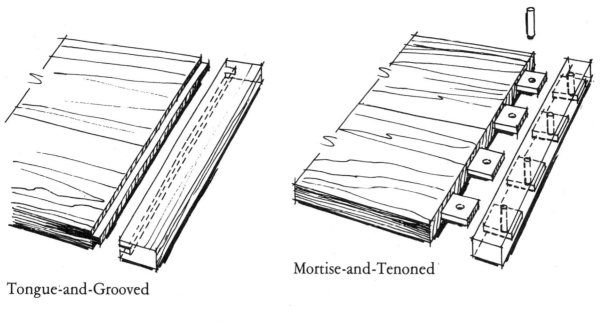

Tongue-and-Grooved

Mortise-and-Tenoned

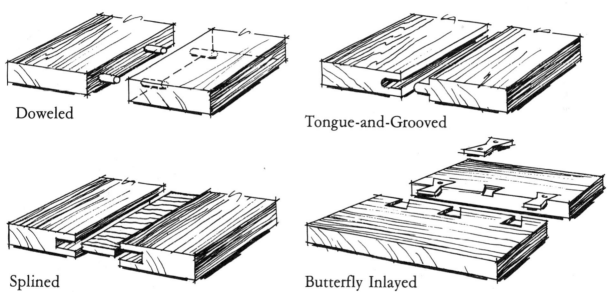

Doweled

Tongue-and-Grooved

Splined

Butterfly Inlayed

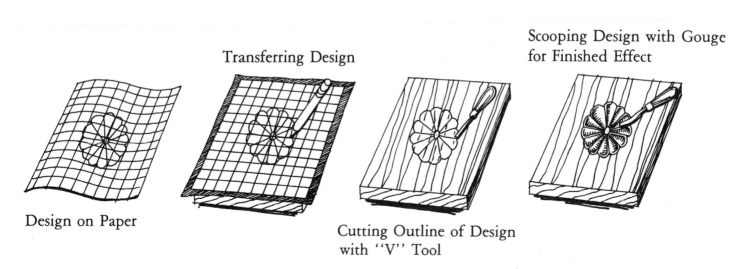

Transferring Design

Scooping Design with Gouge for Finished Effect

Design on Paper

Cutting Outline of Design with "V" Tool

LAPPED JOINTS

To make heavy bases for candlestands and stemmed tables, as well as for the construction of frames, the early craftsman frequently employed *lapped* joints. As shown at right, these included reciprocating *cross-laps, end-laps* and *middle-laps.* They were made by cutting away half of the wood of two connecting pieces and then fitting the cut-out portions together to form a flush connection. Usually, this connection was reinforced with glue, screws or nails.

Lapped joints, accurately cut, contributed additional strength to furniture construction. As illustrated at right, they were particularly useful for making the bases of early candlestands. In this construction, after the cross-laps were cut and fitted, the craftsman then proceeded to saw the scrolled shape of the foot design. When the foot shapes were smoothed to pattern, the cross-lap base was permanently joined together and then bored at the center to receive the stem tenon.

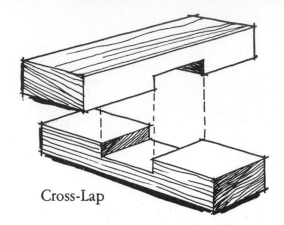

Cross-Lap

Cross-Lap Base Construction

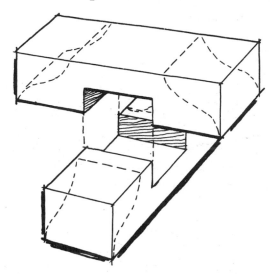

PEGLEG CONSTRUCTION

Many of the old stools, chairs and benches were constructed with peglegs which were mortised through or into the top. Usually this was performed with a *boring block,* prebored to the desired leg slant. The boring block was then clamped on the corners of the top, and holes were bored through the top to receive the leg tenons. The tenons were usually split with slots to receive hardwood wedges. These were driven in across the top again to spread the tenon and secure the assembly of legs and top. When the tenon was not intended to penetrate entirely through the top, the mortise holes were bored only part of the way through. For this assembly, the tenons were slotted to receive wedges which expanded the tenon when the leg was driven into the mortise hole.

Pegleg Construction

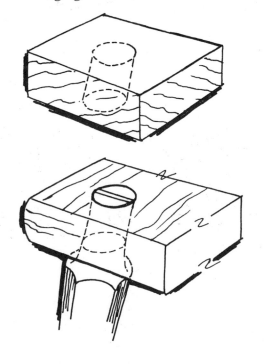

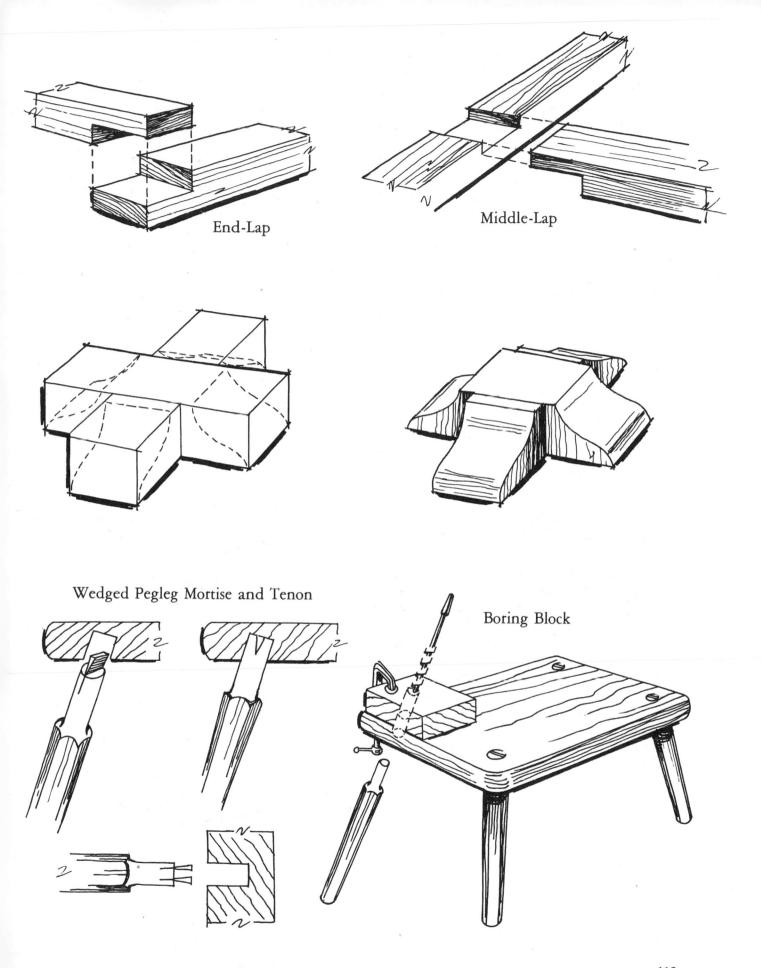

End-Lap

Middle-Lap

Wedged Pegleg Mortise and Tenon

Boring Block

DOVETAIL JOINTS

Dovetail joints were favored as a constructional technique by colonial craftsmen, and they were widely used in making the early furniture of Pennsylvania. In addition to their neatness of appearance, their exceptional strength and durability caused them to be used for many types of construction.

Basically, there are two types of dovetail joints—*open* and *concealed*. In drawer construction, both types are usually employed. As shown at right, *open dovetails* are made in such a way that each connecting member fully overlaps the other at the connection. For the *concealed dovetails*, the side members must be inset to occupy a marginal portion of the connecting edge. Thus, when the drawer is closed, the dovetail joints remain invisible.

As illustrated here, open dovetails are used at the back of the drawer, while concealed dovetails are used at the front where they can be seen from the side only when the drawer is opened.

Old dower chests, boxes, desks, cupboards and cabinets frequently employed open dovetails for corner construction. The types of dovetails varied in shape: some work called for the use of *single* dovetails, whereas other pieces required *multiple* dovetails. For neatness of appearance, many pieces were made with *feathered* dovetails, in which the size of the overlapping sections exceeded that of the slim, feathered slivers into which they were fitted.

Honesty of construction, as shown at right on the open-dovetailed corners of the chest, enhances this work in the eyes of antique admirers. For the superb handcraftsmanship this display adds a nostalgic note to its treasured antiquity.

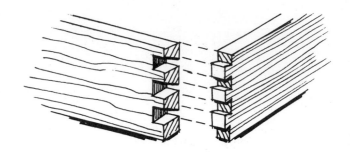

Open Dovetails

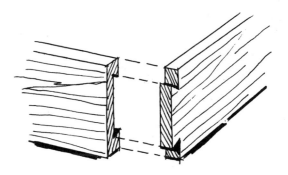

Concealed Single Dovetail

Concealed Multiple Dovetails

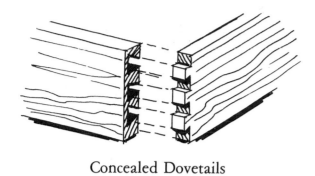

Concealed Dovetails

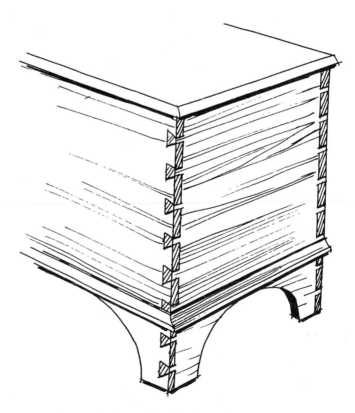

Dovetailed Drawer Construction

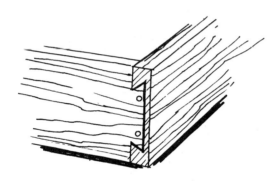

Concealed Single Dovetail

Concealed "Feathered" Dovetails

Open Dovetailed Chest Construction

115

DOVETAILED CONSTRUCTION

The dovetail form was also used for several other types of early construction. As shown at right, it offered the advantage of joining wooden parts together in such a way as to prevent their being pulled apart. Thus, dovetailed tenons were particularly effective for joining legs to the stems of pedestal tables, where the pressure of gravity would otherwise separate the connecting parts. For shelf construction, both *open* and *concealed sliding dovetailed dadoes* were used to hold the joining parts firmly together. Such construction was essential for early joinery before adequate glues were available to secure the connecting parts.

For bench *bracing,* early craftsmen used a distinctive type of *half-dovetail,* which was fitted into the cut-out of a connecting member. Reinforced with nails, such bracing provided a firm fix and prevented any possibility of connecting members working loose. Another type of *half-dovetail joint* was used to secure heavier construction. This was cut like a middle-lap joint, but the dovetailed shape of the lapped portion prevented the connecting pieces from pulling apart.

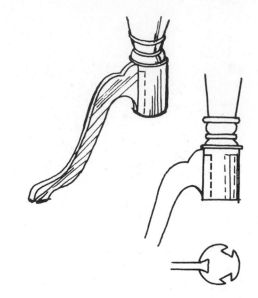

Dovetailed Stem-Lep Assembly

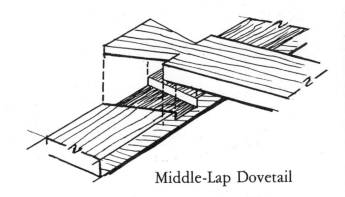

Middle-Lap Dovetail

HINGED JOINTS

Three types of hinged joints were used to secure the leaves of early drop-leaf tables. Of these, the plain *butt-hinged joint* was most common. The *tongue-and-groove-hinged joint* was also widely used—as well as the *rule joint,* which was the neatest. With all three types, the butt hinges were mortised in flush to the undersurfaces of the leaves and top.

As illustrated on previous pages, other types of hinges, which were attached to lids and outer surfaces of chests and doors, included wrought-iron "H" and "H-L" shapes, *rat-tail hinges, pintle hinges, strap hinges, butterfly hinges* and *staghorn hinges.* All of these were ornately shaped, and were made in various sizes.

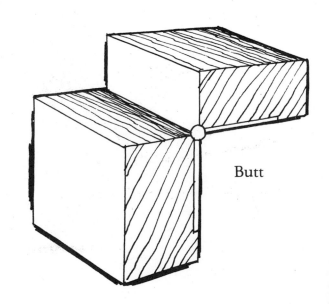

Butt

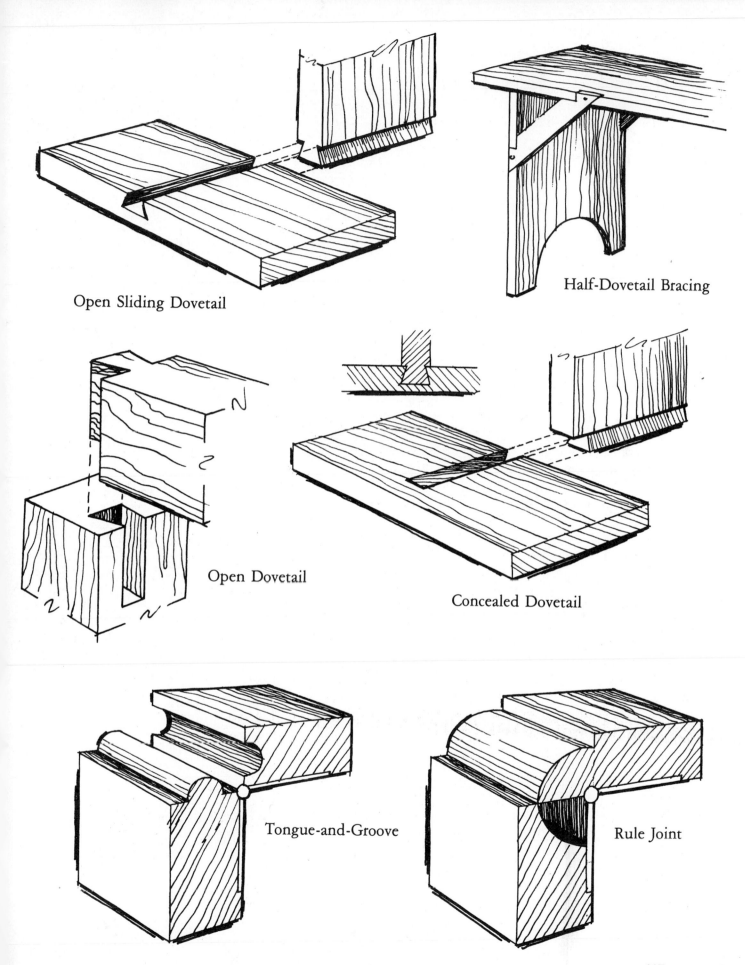

Open Sliding Dovetail

Half-Dovetail Bracing

Open Dovetail

Concealed Dovetail

Tongue-and-Groove

Rule Joint

117

MORTISE & TENON JOINTS

Ever since furniture was first built, *mortise-and-tenon joints* have been widely used to join furniture parts together. These joints have been made in various ways, depending on the practices of regional craftsmen. Before strong glues became available, the mortise-and-tenon joint was most frequently reinforced with hardwood pegs. This was done in accordance with the *drawbore-pin* method, which involved boring a hole slightly nearer the tenon shoulder than a corresponding hole that was bored through the mortised member. Thus, when the hardwood peg was pounded in place, the tenon was drawn snugly within the mortise.

Haunched mortise-and-tenon joints were used for paneled construction, where an inside groove was first cut to receive the panel. In most early work, the tenon was cut long enough to penetrate entirely through the connecting mortise. The *through-tenons* were further strengthened with hardwood wedges driven into slots at their ends. The wedges spread the tenons to produce an enduring joint.

Old trestle tables were usually made with cross-rail tenons that pierced the end posts and protruded beyond the mortise. The rails were secured with tapered keys driven either horizontally or vertically through the protruding end of the tenon. As the tapered key was driven into place, the post was drawn snugly against the shoulders of the protruding tenon. This was sometimes varied by using a straight rail, without tenons, which was secured on *both* sides of the post mortise with keyed wedges.

All types of mortise-and-tenon joints were designed to contribute to the long life of the furniture on which they were used. Examination of sturdy old chairs and tables in museums throughout the country offers ample testimony to the strength and endurance of this construction.

Hardwood Pegs

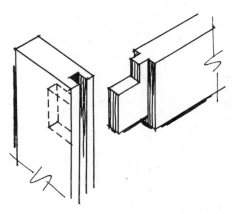

Haunched Mortise-and-Tenon

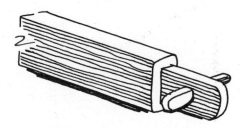

Horizontally Keyed Tenon

118

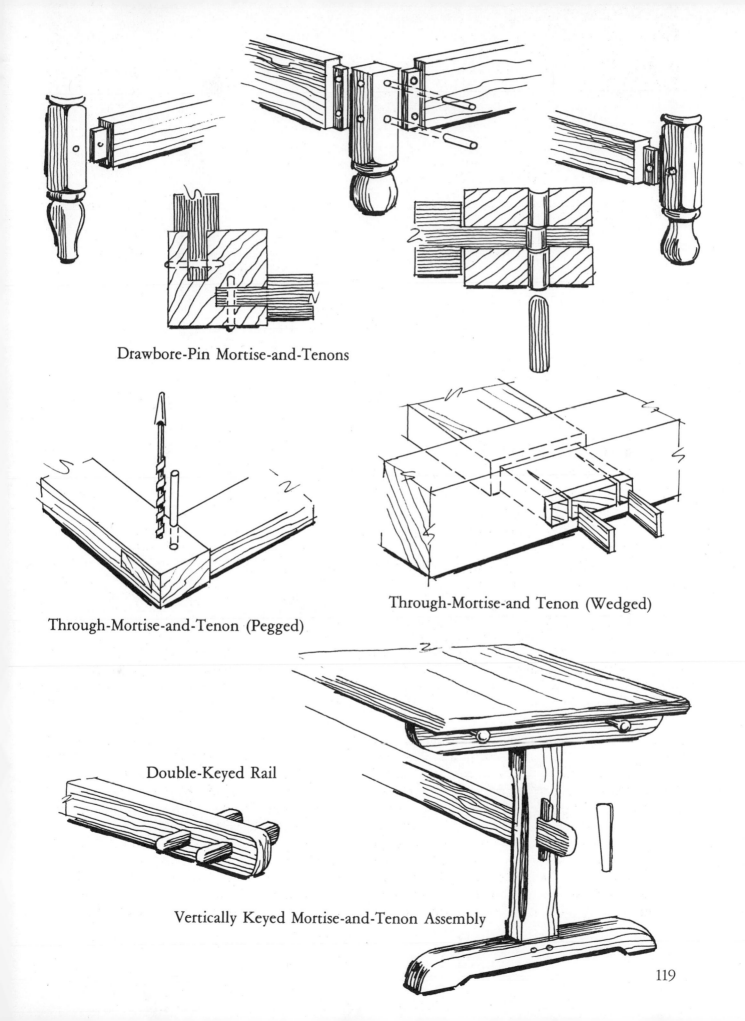

Drawbore-Pin Mortise-and-Tenons

Through-Mortise-and-Tenon (Pegged)

Through-Mortise-and Tenon (Wedged)

Double-Keyed Rail

Vertically Keyed Mortise-and-Tenon Assembly

119

HOW TO REPRODUCE A PENNSYLVANIA DUTCH DOWER CHEST

The dower chest shown above was originally built and decorated in 1784 by Christian Selzer of Berks County, Pa. However, in the building of this reproduction, some liberties were taken in the materials of its construction and decoration.

Actually, this dower chest was reproduced of the best quality (S2S) plywood. This choice was made primarily to obtain parts of required widths without joining boards together. Then, too, a good quality of plywood remains in stable condition, and is not vulnerable to warps and cracks.

As well as constructing the chest body of materials unknown to the original Mr. Selzer, we went one better by painting the panel decorations on one-eighth-inch *tempered hardboard,* and then cementing them to the chest after construction was completed. (It had to be done this way, because the artist who did the painting lived some 2,000 miles from where the chest was built!) Otherwise, this dower chest was carefully hand-made with dovetailed joints, antique molding and all details of mitering and fitting, faithfully following the original construction.

For those who desire to duplicate this dower chest, step-by-step construction photographs are shown on the following pages. After the parts have been cut to required sizes, the entire chest (like the original) can be built with hand tools. Following the same steps of construction, you may even make the chest of solid lumber. This, of course, will involve joining boards together to obtain required widths.

Decoration of the dower chest is performed in accordance with instructions given in Chapter 5. The same instructions apply whether the decorations are painted on separate panels or on the chest itself.

For finishing, give the chest body and lid three coats of semigloss paint. A "federal blue" color (a light shade of blue) was used with this work. However, you may choose any other bright basic colors, including greens, reds, browns or darker shades of blue.

If you build this dower chest, remember that you are building it for the centuries. So be sure to inscribe the name of the loved one (for whom you are building it) directly on target in the center of the valentine heart.

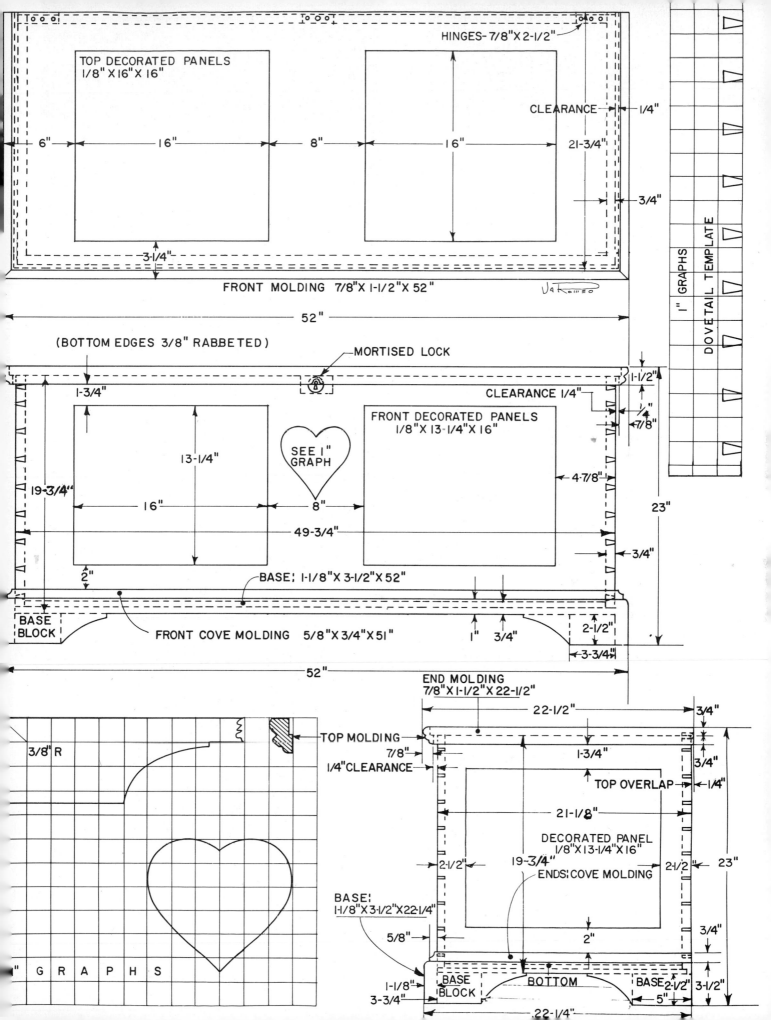

TOP DECORATED PANELS
1/8"×16"×16"

6"   16"   8"   16"

HINGES—7/8"×2-1/2"

CLEARANCE   1/4"

21-3/4"

3/4"

3-1/4"

FRONT MOLDING 7/8"×1-1/2"×52"

52"

(BOTTOM EDGES 3/8" RABBETED)   MORTISED LOCK

1-3/4"   1-1/2"

CLEARANCE 1/4"

1/4"

7/8"

FRONT DECORATED PANELS
1/8"×13-1/4"×16"

SEE 1"
GRAPH

13-1/4"   4-7/8"

19-3/4"   23"

16"   8"   3/4"

49-3/4"

2"

BASE: 1-1/8"×3-1/2"×52"

BASE
BLOCK

FRONT COVE MOLDING   5/8"×3/4"×51"   1"   3/4"

2-1/2"

3-3/4"

52"

END MOLDING
7/8"×1-1/2"×22-1/2"

22-1/2"   3/4"

TOP MOLDING

7/8"   1-3/4"   3/4"

1/4"CLEARANCE   TOP OVERLAP   1/4"

3/8" R   21-1/8"

DECORATED PANEL
1/8"×13-1/4"×16"

2-1/2"   19-3/4"   2-1/2"   23"

BASE:
1-1/8"×3-1/2"×22-1/4"

5/8"   2"   3/4"

" G R A P H S

BASE
BLOCK   BOTTOM   BASE 2-1/2"   3-1/2"

1-1/8"

3-3/4"   22-1/4"   5"

1" GRAPHS

DOVETAIL TEMPLATE

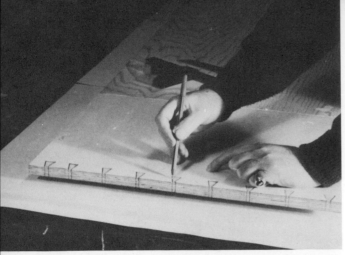

1 Cardstock template is used to mark dovetails on side pieces.

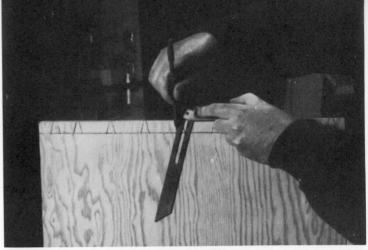

2 Bevel gauge is then used to strengthen marking of side dovetails.

3 Backsaw is used to saw side dovetails to *depth*. Note metal strip clamped on depth line to safeguard depth of saw cuts.

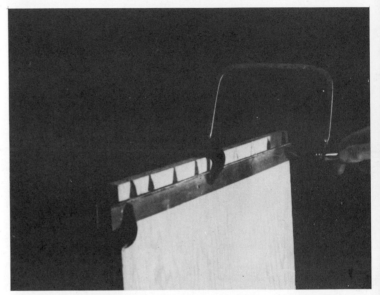

4 Coping saw and/or sharp chisel are used to clean out dovetails above depth line. File and sandpaper are also used.

5 Finished side dovetails are held over end edges to act as pattern for marking dovetail shapes. Lines are then squared to depth.

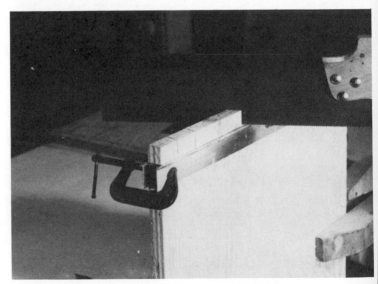

6 Backsaw is used to saw end dovetails to depth.

7 Coping saw is used to cut along depth line. "Spurs" of end dovetails are then filed to shape.

8 Dovetailed end pieces are fitted into dovetailed sides. Glue is then applied to connecting parts.

9 Dovetailed sides and ends, their joining parts glued, are clamped together for final assembly.

10 Rabbeted chest bottom is fitted to pre-rabbeted sides and ends. Bottom is then nailed and glued in place.

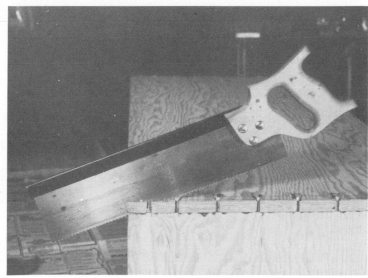

11 After glue has dried, protruding dovetail ends are carefully sawed off. Dovetailed corners are then planed and sanded flush.

12 Corner blocks are glued and clamped to bottom of chest. When glue has dried, they are planed flush to corners.

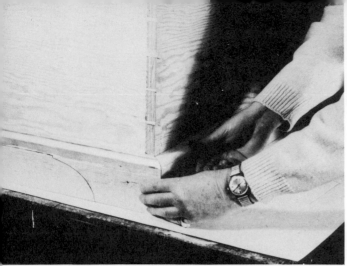

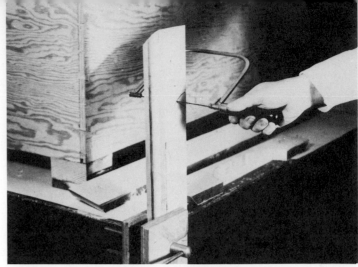

13 Baseboards have 3/8″ rounded shape on outside edges. They are fitted and mitered at corners.

14 Corner, foot shapes are cut on baseboards with coping saw.

15 Glue is spread on corner blocks and within 7/8″ margin of bottom edge.

16 Base is nailed in place. Nail heads are set and indentations filled with plastic wood. Cove molding is then attached.

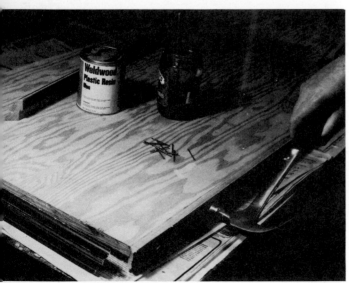

17 Rabbeted top edge molding is nailed and glued along front and end edges of top.

18 Edge molding is planed flush and then thoroughly sanded to obtain smooth top surface.

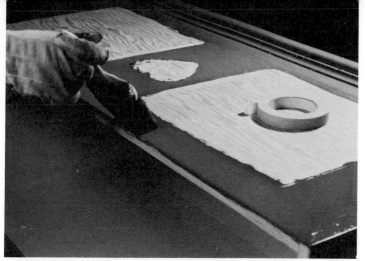

19 Areas where decorative panels are later attached are bordered with masking tape. Body of chest is then painted.

20 Lid of chest, with decorative panel areas left bare, are protectively masked and given three coats of paint.

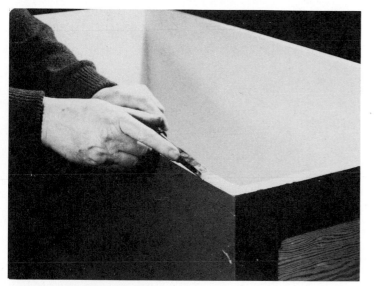

21 After making saw cuts 1/8″ deep, sharp chisel is used to cut insets for hinges.

22 Pilot holes are first drilled to receive screws which are driven to attach hinges.

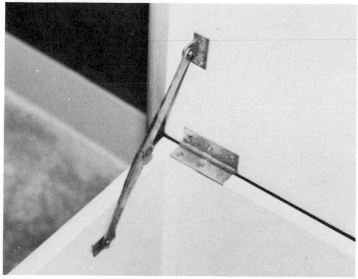

23 Lid brace is attached to hold lid open.

24 Chest lock is mortised into place on center front edge.

25 Masking tape is attached over paint to protect against spatter of contact cement.

26 Contact cement is spread over bare areas where decorative panels are attached.

27 Backs of decorative panels are thoroughly brushed with contact cement.

28 After contact cement has become "tacky," decorative panel is permanently attached to chest.

29 Finished dower chest, with lid open, shows inside painted white and all panels and parts in place.

30 This dower chest, carefully made, will last just as long as the antique Selzer original, from which it was copied.

126

Chapter 5

Furniture Painting
& Decorating

FURNITURE PAINTING & DECORATING

The painting and decoration of Pennsylvania Dutch furniture played an important part in its development. Indeed, as is shown in this book, many of the early pieces were most noteworthy because of their painted decorations.

However, as well as being attractively decorated with paintings, much of this furniture was also finished *naturally* with oil, stains and luster-producing agents, such as varnish, shellac and lacquer. Furniture made of walnut or cherry was frequently finished with linseed oil. This tended to darken and enrich the wood, as well as to bring out its grain.

Stain, compounded in oil, water or spirits, was applied to the wood, allowed to penetrate, and then wiped off with a rag. This process brought out the wood grain, which was darkened to the tone of the stain. After the stain dried, two or three coats of varnish (or other luster-producing top coating) were applied. As each coat dried, it was thoroughly rubbed with pumice stone and oil to obtain a highly polished finish.

On the following pages, specific information is offered to guide the application of painted decorations. This is intended to help in the projection of authentic decorative designs and to show how these designs may be painted and transferred to wood surfaces.

Unfortunately, because of space limitations, it is possible to offer only a few typical, detailed designs. However, with practice, the prospective artist may be able to interpret other painted decorations shown on other furniture pictures in this book.

Typical colors include blues, reds, yellows, oranges, greens and browns. These colors, as they appear on pieces displayed in museums, are somewhat faded. This may or may not contribute to their antique appeal. It would seem that fresh paint, of the desired colors would serve better when reproducing this work.

Hex sign designs, shown at the end of this chapter, were popularly used for decorating furniture as well as for adorning barns. These designs appear frequently on the lids and ends of dower chests. Their design variations appear to be limitless.

Corner cupboard, right, made in Pennsylvania between 1830 and 1840, has sponged decorations painted in swirled designs. Considerable artistry was invested in sponging process, as indicated by matching of decorative designs on each side of cupboard. (*Courtesy, The Henry Ford Museum, Dearborn, Mich.*)

Dower chest, below, self-dated "1797," is painted basically in mottled-stippled patterns. Variations of such painted decorations were commonly used for adornment of chests. (*Photo by author. Courtesy, Rock Ford Plantation, Lancaster, Pa.*)

DECORATIVE PAINTING

Many Pennsylvania Dutch cupboards, chests, beds, tables and chairs were *spatter-painted* for decorative embellishment. The *spatter* that distinguishes such work is applied by hand, with an assortment of tools, to obtain *stippled* or *mottled* designs on the painted surfaces. Sometimes such designs, applied with moist paint over a dried coat, would simulate wood graining. Otherwise, as shown on the corner cupboard at left, a rhythmic arrangement of sponge strokes produced the swirled designs.

Various processes were employed to produce the many different painted effects. These included graining, marbling, mottling-stippling-sponging, scumbling, feather-painting, fingerpainting, simulated tortoise shell painting and japanning. All these techniques were based on overcoats of contrasting colors, which were manipulated—while they were still wet—with fingers, sponge, graining tools, feathers or other means to produce decorative designs on painted surfaces.

HOW TO APPLY PAINTED DECORATIONS

For the decoration of dower chests, the Pennsylvania Dutch craftsmen let their imaginations run wild. All manner of decorative devices and motifs were employed, including displays of flowers and fruits (tulips were the favorite), vines, leaves, unicorns, horsemen, birds, soldiers, hex signs, hearts and adaptations of sgraffito designs. These colorful adornments were usually applied over stippled or mottled painted surfaces. Frequently, the name of the maiden for whom the chest was built was boldly inscribed on the front, along with the date when it was made.

As indicated on the dower chest shown above, colors were bright and contrasting. It should be noted that on the two front panels, although the designs are *almost* identical, they vary enough to require separate patterns.

Incidentally, a different design is applied to each end of the chest.

The following pages try to show how the typical Christian Selzer decorations of 1789 are applied to reproduce this Selzer chest. If you decide to paint the decorations directly on the chest, start by taping off, with masking tape, the areas of the chest which are to be decorated. The rest of the chest is then given three coats of basic color. After the paint has dried, the masked areas are *remasked* over the paint, leaving the squares to be painted white. This provides background for the painted decorations.

By following the steps shown on the facing page, a full-scale pattern is made to outline the painted designs. This is then traced on the panel. After this, the painting procedures shown on the next two pages should be carefully followed.

HOW TO TRANSFER DECORATIVE DESIGNS

1 Using graphed design in book as guide, spot off on full-scale 1″ graphed pattern paper, the positions of all points which outline the design.

2 Following design in book, connect dots with "french curve" to outline design on paper pattern.

3 With complete outline of design drawn on paper pattern, transfer design to chest panel with carbon paper and ballpoint pen.

4 Do not *overdraw* when tracing design on chest panel. Light carbon copy outline of design will suffice for painting steps which follow.

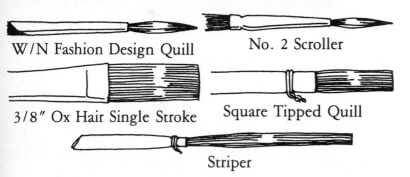

W/N Fashion Design Quill

No. 2 Scroller

3/8" Ox Hair Single Stroke

Square Tipped Quill

Striper

TOOLS & MATERIALS

Stylus or ballpoint pen (for tracing); brushes (as shown above); pencil; palette knife; medicine dropper; tracing paper; graphite paper; Staedtler Mars eraser; gum spirits of turpentine; jars (for mixed colors); paper disposable palettes; newspaper; waxed paper; varnish (Pratt & Lambert #61, or similar.); paper towels; rags; and oil paints—cadmium yellow, cadmium red, light Prussian blue, titanium white, yellow ochre, burnt umber, raw umber, and lamp black.

PAINTING PROCEDURES

Following the steps shown on the preceding page, trace the outlines of decorative designs on panels. Trace designs on *all* panels *first*, and then paint them *one color at a time*.

Mix each color and thin with turpentine. Keep the colors in small jars ready to be used as needed. When you are ready to apply paint, spread a small amount on your palette. Thin with varnish to make a smooth-flowing mixture.

Paint the yellow petals of the upper and lower flowers *first*. After the paint has dried (allow 24 hours), brush the central flower and pot in red. Following another drying period, paint the stems and leaves in green.

Next, paint the outlines of border scrolls and let it dry for 24 hours. Then, with blue paint, fill in the petals on the upper and lower flowers. After drying, add stamens, leaf veins and central flower details in black-green. Then paint dots in red and also paint the petals of the lower flowers.

Complete the panel by filling in the colors on the border scrolls. Then give the entire painted composition a thin coat of varnish. After the varnish dries, make a narrow marginal stripe around the design with a *striper* brush. Let it dry and then apply a second coat of varnish.

Observe the photo sequence, starting below, for step-by-step instructions on painting procedure. Note particularly the positions of the hands for holding brushes properly to produce the various painted designs.

1 With *square-tipped quill brush*, paint yellow petals on top and bottom flowers. Observe how hand is supported with little finger.

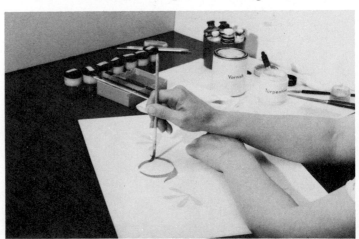

2 Again, using *square-tipped quill brush*, paint center flower red. Note method of supporting hand with other arm to steady full sweep of stroke.

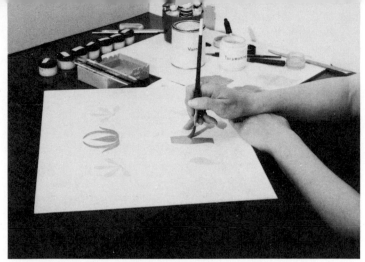

3 Using *ox-hair stroke brush*, apply red paint to fill outline of pot. Strokes slightly overlap from top to bottom. Handles are painted last using *fashion design quill* or *scroller brushes*. Note position of hands.

4 With *scroller brush*, paint green stems. Stroke from top to bottom. Support arm with other hand to avoid smudging.

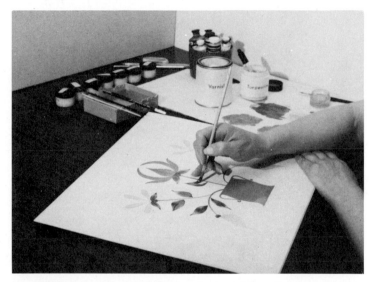

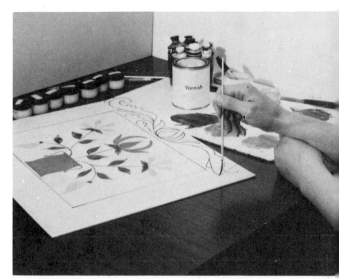

5 With *square tipped quill brush*, paint green leaves. Support arm as shown.

6 Mixing black-green paint with varnish, and using *fashion design quill brush* or *scroller*, paint outline of border design. To make free strokes, rest arm on fist, as shown.

7 With *fashion design quill brush*, paint veins of leaves. Same brush, held perpendicularly, is used to drip dots of flowers.

8 After varnishing finished painting, apply border stripes using ruler as a guide. Note ruler is raised slightly to allow freedom for brush stroke. *Scroller brush* is used. After drying period, finished painting is given a second thin coat of varnish.

black

red

136

Key Cupboard. *(Courtesy, The Metropolitan Museum of Art, New York, N.Y.)* See measured drawing, page 192.

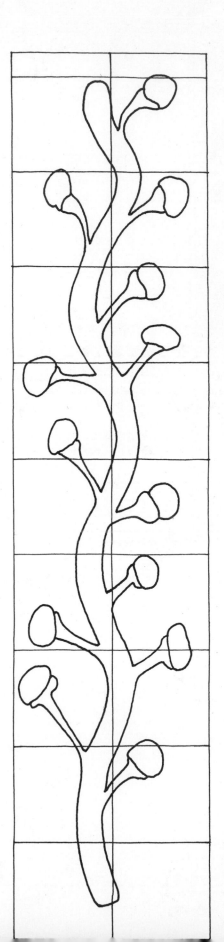

Candle Box. (*Courtesy, The National Gallery of Art, Index of American Design, Washington, D.C.*) See measured drawing, page 186.

Distelfink decorated chest of drawers, made in Snyder
County, Pa., around 1834. See measured drawing, page 208.
(*Courtesy, Philadelphia Museum of Art, Philadelphia, Pa.*)

½ Front

½ End

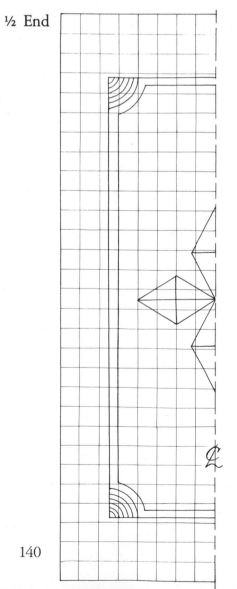

140

Unicorn decorated dower chest, made in Berks County, Pa. in 1803. See measured drawing, page 170. *(Courtesy, Philadelphia Museum of Art, Philadelphia, Pa.)*

Front (Center) Panel

Front Panels (Sides)

STENCILS

Stenciling is an ancient art that is used frequently for the decoration of Pennsylvania Dutch homes and furniture. It involves the accurate cutting of stencils, or *patterns*, to guide the painting of assorted designs. Stencils are generally cut of stiff card stock to prevent saturation and distortion of painted colors along their edges. They are usually taped to the surfaces when they are being used.

Pennsylvania stencil motifs include baskets, urns, fruits, stars, flowers and birds—all having brilliance of color and boldness of design associated with this peasant art. *Striping,* or bordering with repetitious symmetrical designs, was also common practice. Sometimes the use of stencils was combined with free-hand painting.

Stencils provide a *guarded* way to uniformly produce painted shapes. Although the free-hand method of painting described before offered attractive results, not everyone could paint free-hand designs in an accurate and artistic manner. Hence, the stencil was used to guide an applicator or brush within the cut-out portions of the design; and it masked the areas to remain unpainted. With reasonable care, this provided a safe and uniform means of producing ornamental paintings.

The stencil designs on these pages are intended to be reproduced in the same sizes as are shown. To transfer them to your work, start by tracing a cardboard stencil of the desired design. This is best accomplished by placing a sheet of carbon paper behind the book page and tracing directly from the printed page onto the sheet of cardboard. Use a *french curve* to accurately trace the design.

After the design has been traced on the cardboard, use a *stencil knife* and sharp scissors to cut out the inside portions of the design. Before using the stencil, make sure that all inside edges are thoroughly smooth.

In most cases, it is easier to reproduce the design with a *sponge-pad applicator,* moistened with paint. The color is simply *daubed* and *patted* into open areas of the stencil. If caution is employed, brushes may also be used. Care must be exercised to avoid dripping or smearing paint along the cut-out edges.

144

STENCILS

Hex signs on barn at Monterey, near Kutztown, Pa. These designs were laid out geometrically and painted in vivid colors. They were also used for the decoration of furniture. (*Courtesy, Henry J. Kauffman, Lancaster, Pa.*)

HEX SIGNS

The belief that hex signs (decorative stars and other geometrical designs shown on the following pages) were painted on barns and furniture to ward off witches and defy the devil, is largely discounted by families of the Pennsylvania Dutch. According to a survey recently made of farmers on whose barns hex signs were painted, all denied any belief in witches or in any other superstitious influence that would cause them to paint hexes on their buildings. In fact, most replied by inquiring, "Aren't they pretty?" This indicated a desire on their part merely to decorate their barns with these colorful designs and thus relieve the barns' plainness of appearance.

Actually, hex signs were not painted on Pennsylvania barns until well into the 19th century. (Barns built earlier were mostly unpainted.) However, hex signs were used during the 18th century for decorating dower chests, chests of drawers, utility boxes and other items of furniture.

Hex signs originated in Europe and have been used since the Middle Ages, when they did have definite religious significance. Several of the designs shown on following pages were painted on barns in the Rhine Valley, sometimes with religious initials *I.H.S.* and a cross inscribed on them. Obviously, such religious applications would contradict the use of holy symbols as an antidote for their demonic, "witch-warding" powers. As with any other religious symbols, hex signs were probably painted on barns both to decorate and to bring blessings of good fortune.

148

VARIATIONS OF HEX DESIGNS

yellow, black

red, yellow, black

red, black

green, black

blue, yellow, black

yellow, black

HOW TO LAY OUT
HEX DESIGNS

As illustrated on these pages, the variations of hex designs are almost limitless. The 24 designs shown here simply highlight the more interesting varieties that are geometrically produced with pencil, compass, protractor, french curve, ruler—and *patience!* The diagrams at right show the intricate steps of layout. It would be well to practice these on scrap paper before transferring design outlines to your work.

It will be noted that all of these designs require accurate measuring and marking, and that any slight miscalculations caused by a blunt pencil or inaccurate measurements can damage the entire composition. So be careful to develop the designs to required sizes. Then, when the outline has been established, proceed to paint the inner portions for desired coloration.

Caution should also be observed in painting. Since all hex signs are painted a variety of colors, be sure to allow one color to become thoroughly dry before brushing on another color. If you have the good fortune to possess a steady hand with a paint brush, you should be able to separate the colors into distinct divisions of lines and curves. However, to safeguard against paint runs and smears, you may wish to protect the painted divisions with masking tape. This should help secure sharp separations of contrasting painted areas.

In addition to being used to decorate barns and furniture, hex signs are becoming increasingly popular for decorating homes—both inside and out—because of their variety of intricate shapes and configurations. In fact, some of these signs can now be bought at country stores in the Pennsylvania Dutch region. They are painted on *tempered hardboard,* and can be bought in sizes ranging from 6 inches in diameter up to 3 feet.

Perhaps you would like to try your hand at making an enlargement of one of the hex designs shown here. If so, simply study the design, follow the layout steps shown on these pages, and choose good, bright colors to illuminate your handiwork.

150

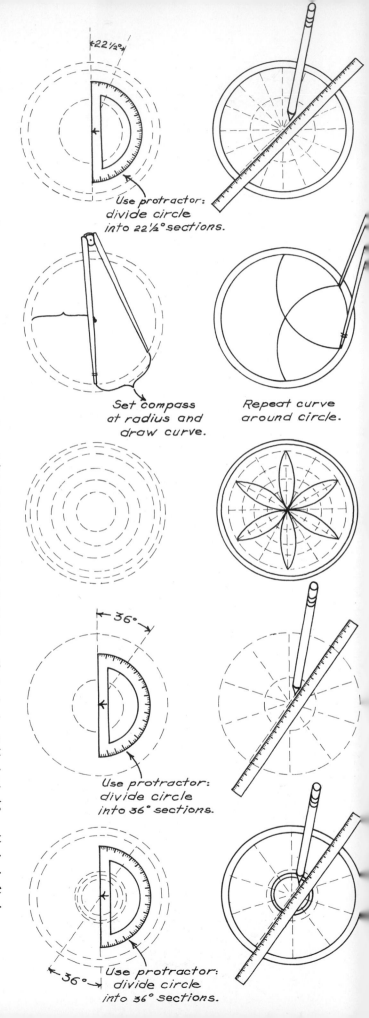

Use protractor: divide circle into 22½° sections.

Set compass at radius and draw curve.

Repeat curve around circle.

Use protractor: divide circle into 36° sections.

Use protractor: divide circle into 36° sections.

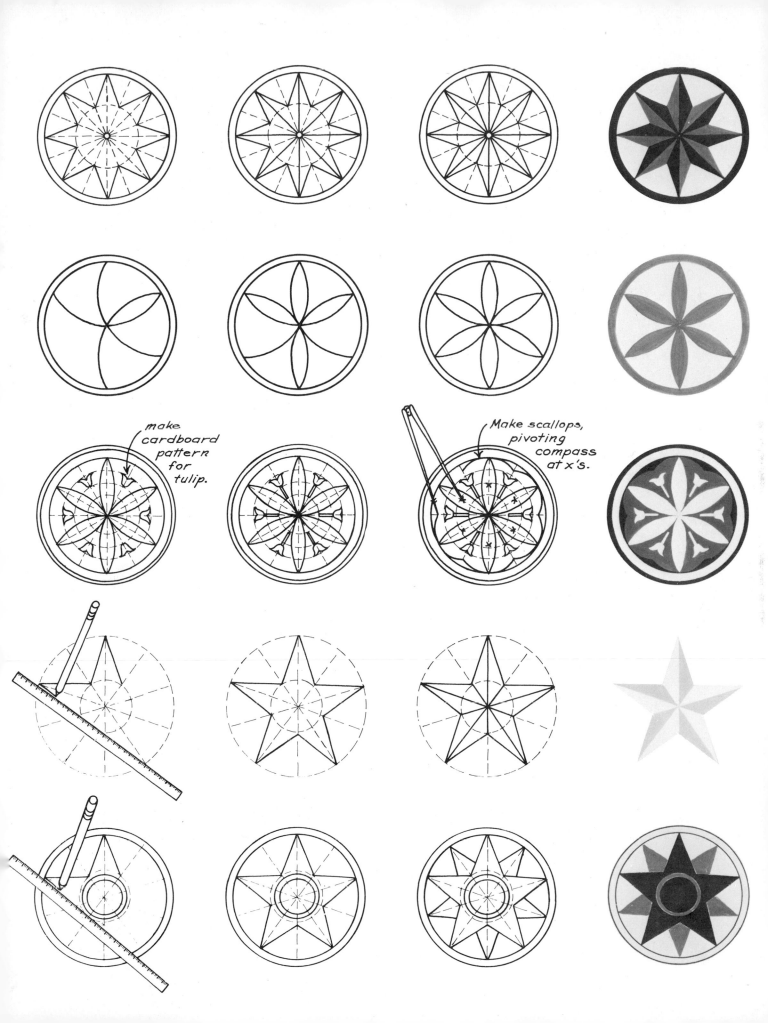

make
cardboard
pattern
for
tulip.

Make scallops,
pivoting
compass
at x's.

VARIATIONS OF HEX DESIGNS

green, black

red, yellow, black

red, gray, black

red, yellow, blue, gray

red and black

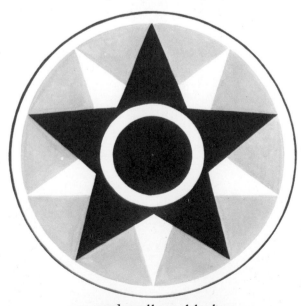

red, yellow, black

VARIATIONS OF HEX DESIGNS

red, yellow, black

red, yellow

green, yellow, black

red, yellow, black

red, yellow, gray

blue, yellow

VARIATIONS OF HEX DESIGNS

blue, yellow, black

red, black

red, yellow

red, gray, black

red, yellow, black

green, yellow

Chapter 6

Furniture Measurements

PAINTED KITCHEN CHAIR

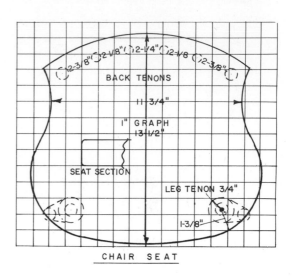

Painted kitchen chair of early 19th century, Pennsylvania-German origin. Note typical floral decorations. (*Courtesy, Hershey Museum of American Life, Hershey, Pa.*)

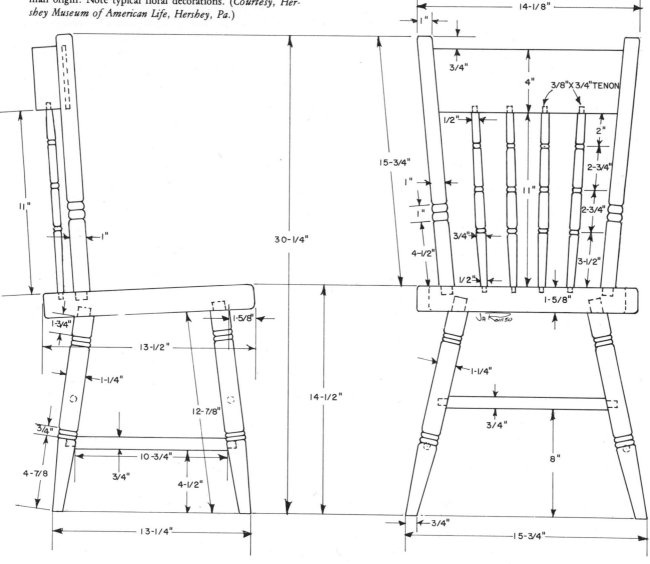

"JUDGE'S CHAIR"

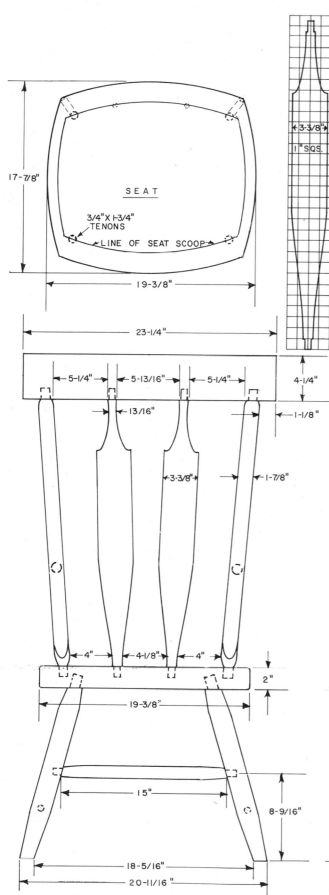

SEAT

3/4"X 1-3/4" TENONS

17-7/8"

19-3/8"

LINE OF SEAT SCOOP

3-3/8"

1"SQS.

"Judge's chair" of tiger maple, built in Pennsylvania between 1835 and 1840, apparently used by an unknown rural judge. *(Courtesy, Hershey Museum of American Life, Hershey, Pa.)*

23-1/4"

5-1/4" 5-13/16" 5-1/4"

4-1/4"

13/16"

1-1/8"

3-3/8"

1-7/8"

4" 4-1/8" 4"

2"

19-3/8"

15"

8-9/16"

18-5/16"

20-11/16"

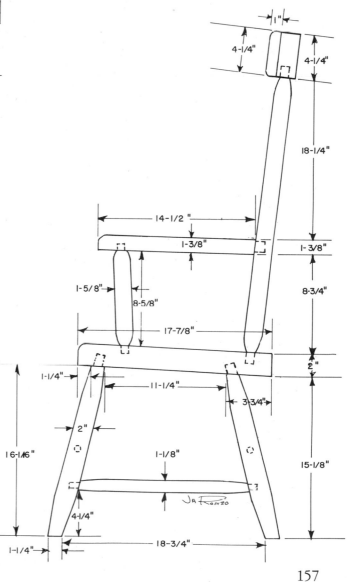

1"

4-1/4"

4-1/4"

18-1/4"

14-1/2 "

1-3/8"

1-3/8"

1-5/8"

8-5/8"

8-3/4"

17-7/8"

2"

1-1/4"

11-1/4"

3-3/4"

2"

1-1/8"

16-1/16"

15-1/8"

4-1/4"

1-1/4"

18-3/4"

157

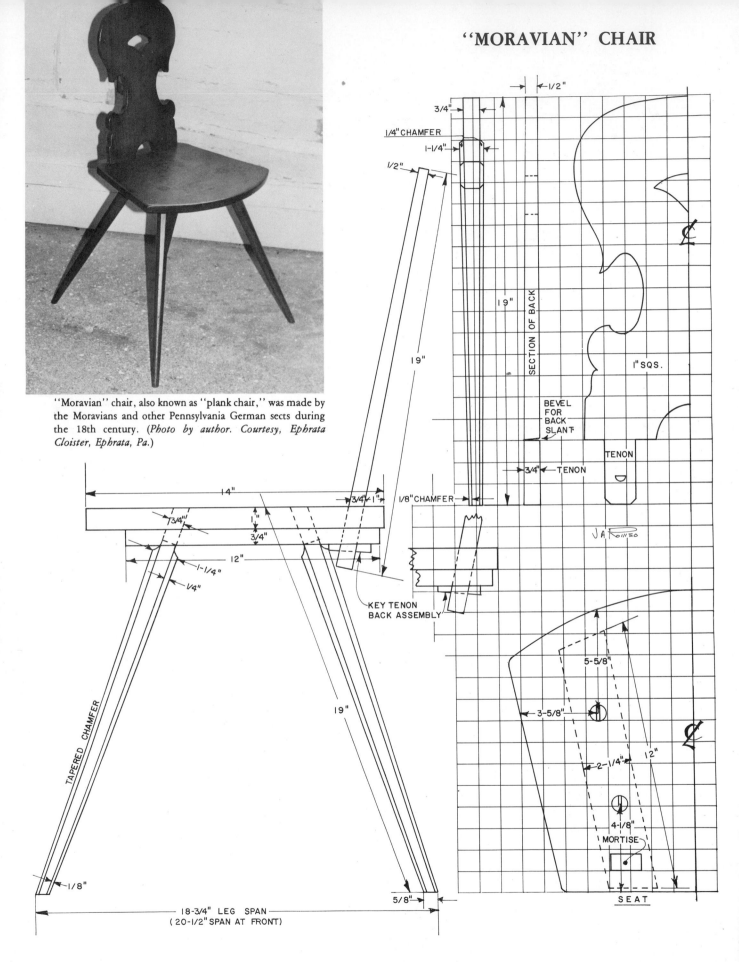

"MORAVIAN" CHAIR

"Moravian" chair, also known as "plank chair," was made by the Moravians and other Pennsylvania German sects during the 18th century. (*Photo by author. Courtesy, Ephrata Cloister, Ephrata, Pa.*)

KITCHEN STOOL

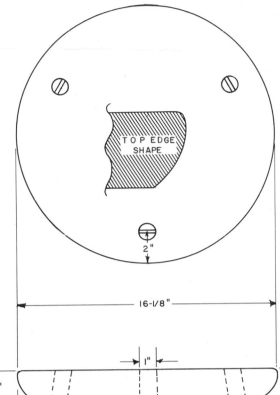

TOP EDGE SHAPE

2"

16-1/8"

Kitchen stool, circa 1800. Top of poplar, legs and rungs of maple. (*Photo by author. Courtesy, Hershey Museum of American Life, Hershey, Pa.*)

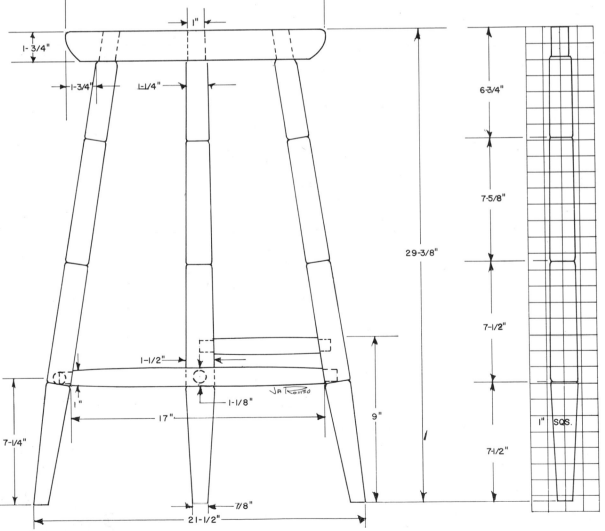

1"

1-3/4"

1-3/4"   1-1/4"

29-3/8"

6-3/4"

7-5/8"

7-1/2"

1-1/2"

JA Romeo

1"

1-1/8"

17"

9"

7-1/4"

7-1/2"

1" SQS.

7/8"

21-1/2"

Pine side bench, made in Pennsylvania during mid-18th century. (*Courtesy, William Penn Memorial Museum, Harrisburg, Pa.*)

PINE SIDE BENCH

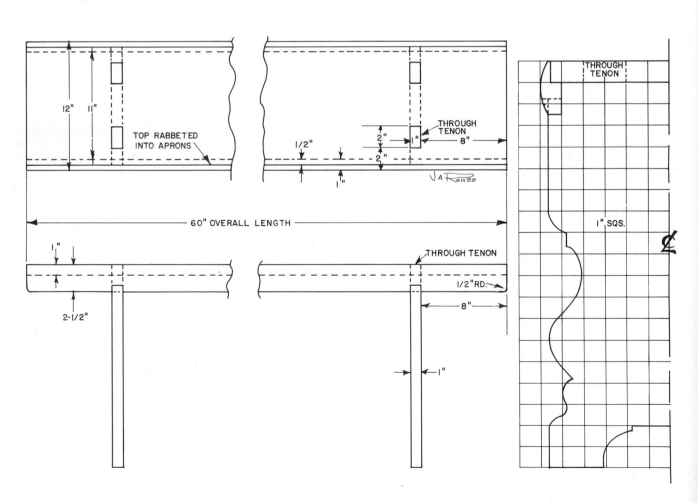

Cricket-on-the-hearth. One of a variety of little foot stools made during the 18th and 19th centuries. (*Photo by author. Courtesy, Rock Ford Plantation, Lancaster, Pa.*)

CRICKET-ON-THE-HEARTH

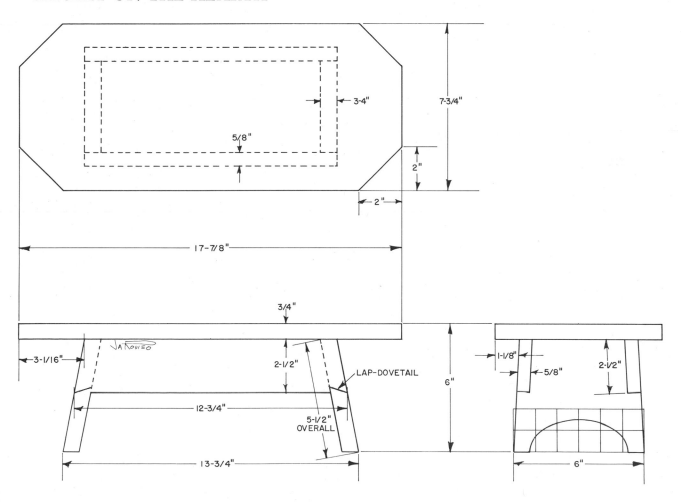

Joint table of yellow pine, made in Pennsylvania around 1750, was constructed of pegged mortise and tenon joints. Top was made of one width of pine, 14½″ wide. It is attached with square pegs to tops of legs. (*Courtesy, The Metropolitan Museum of Art, New York, N.Y.*)

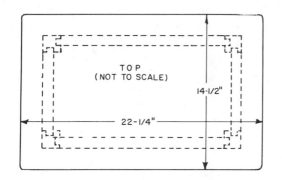

TOP
(NOT TO SCALE)

14-1/2"

22-1/4"

JOINT TABLE OF YELLOW PINE

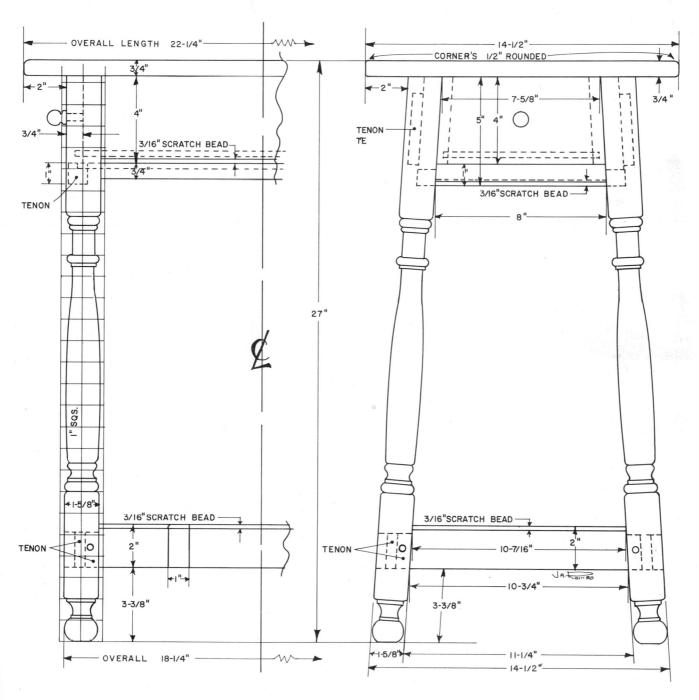

OVERALL LENGTH 22-1/4"

3/4"

2"

4"

3/4"

3/16" SCRATCH BEAD

3/4"

TENON

1" SQS.

1-5/8"

3/16" SCRATCH BEAD

2"

1"

TENON

3-3/8"

OVERALL 18-1/4"

27"

14-1/2"

CORNER'S 1/2" ROUNDED

2"

7-5/8"

3/4"

5" 4"

TENON
TE

3/16"SCRATCH BEAD

8"

3/16"SCRATCH BEAD

TENON

10-7/16"

2"

10-3/4"

3-3/8"

1-5/8"

11-1/4"

14-1/2"

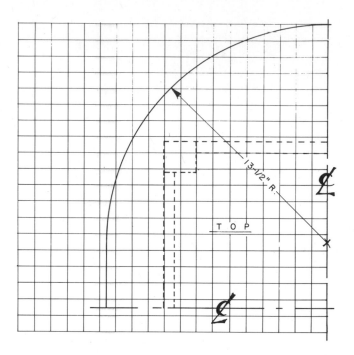

SCROLLED-APRON BEDSIDE TABLE

Scrolled-apron bedside table. Typical Pennsylvania German 18th century table design has unusually wide slant of legs. Scrolled apron designs differ on front and sides. (*Courtesy, Philadelphia Museum of Art, Philadelphia, Pa.*)

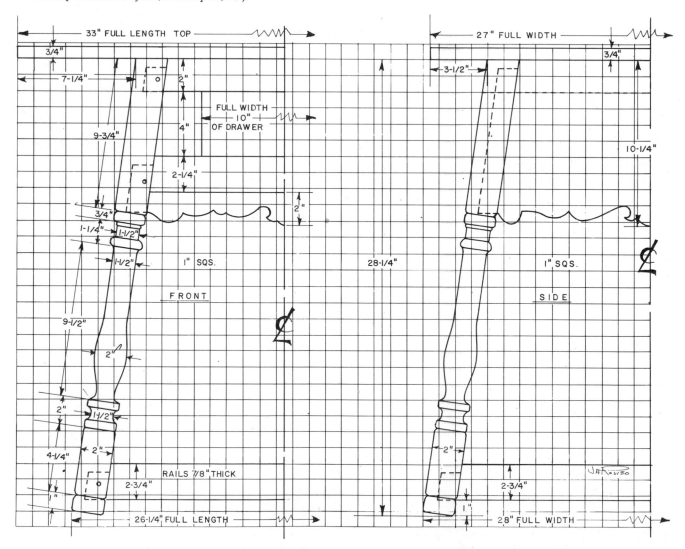

PENNSYLVANIA DESK-TABLE

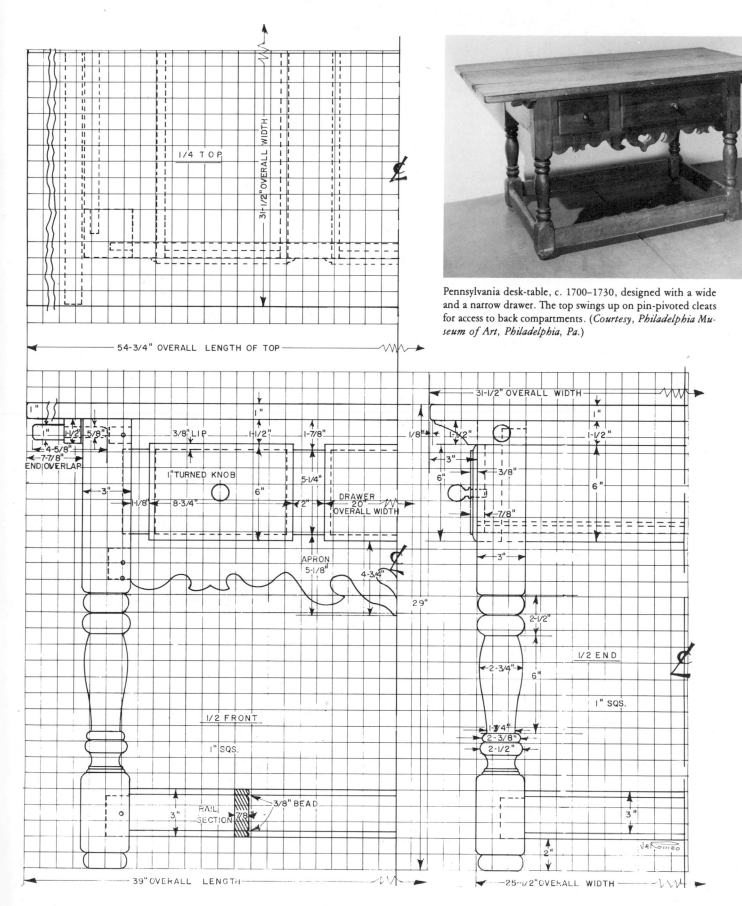

1/4 TOP

31-1/2" OVERALL WIDTH

54-3/4" OVERALL LENGTH OF TOP

Pennsylvania desk-table, c. 1700–1730, designed with a wide and a narrow drawer. The top swings up on pin-pivoted cleats for access to back compartments. (*Courtesy, Philadelphia Museum of Art, Philadelphia, Pa.*)

1"
1" 1-1/2" 5-8"
4-5/8"
7-7/8"
END OVERLAP

3/8" LIP 1-1/2" 1-7/8"

1" 1"

1" TURNED KNOB

3" 5-1/4"
1-1/8" 8-3/4" 6" 2"

DRAWER
20"
OVERALL WIDTH

APRON
5-1/8" 4-3/4"

29"

1/2 FRONT

1" SQS.

RAIL
SECTION 7/8" 3/8" BEAD
3"

39" OVERALL LENGTH

31-1/2" OVERALL WIDTH

1/8" 1-1/2" 1"
1-1/2"
3"
6" 3/8"
6"

7/8"

3"

2-1/2"

2-3/4" 6"

1/2 END

1" SQS.

1-3/4"
2-3/8"
2-1/2"

3"

2"

JAR 01 1120

25-1/2" OVERALL WIDTH

OVAL-TOP SAWBUCK TABLE

Oval-top sawbuck table, made of tulip-wood and walnut, was built during the 18th century at Ephrata Cloister. (*Photo by author. Courtesy, Ephrata Cloister, Ephrata, Pa.*)

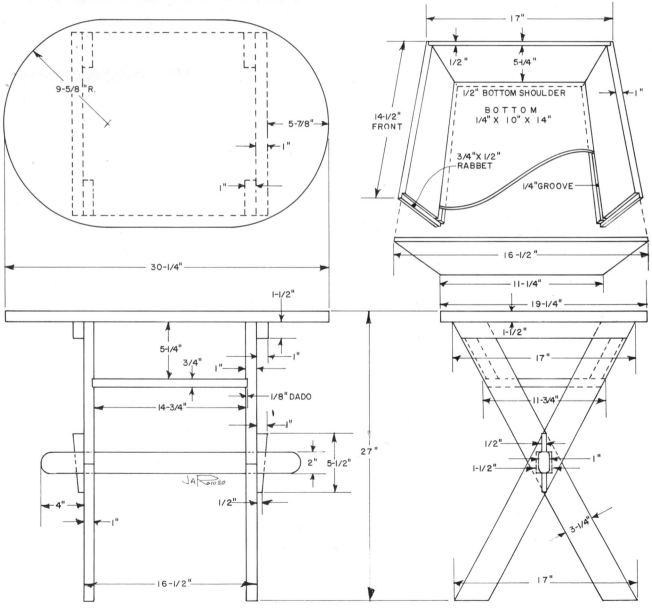

OCCASIONAL TABLE

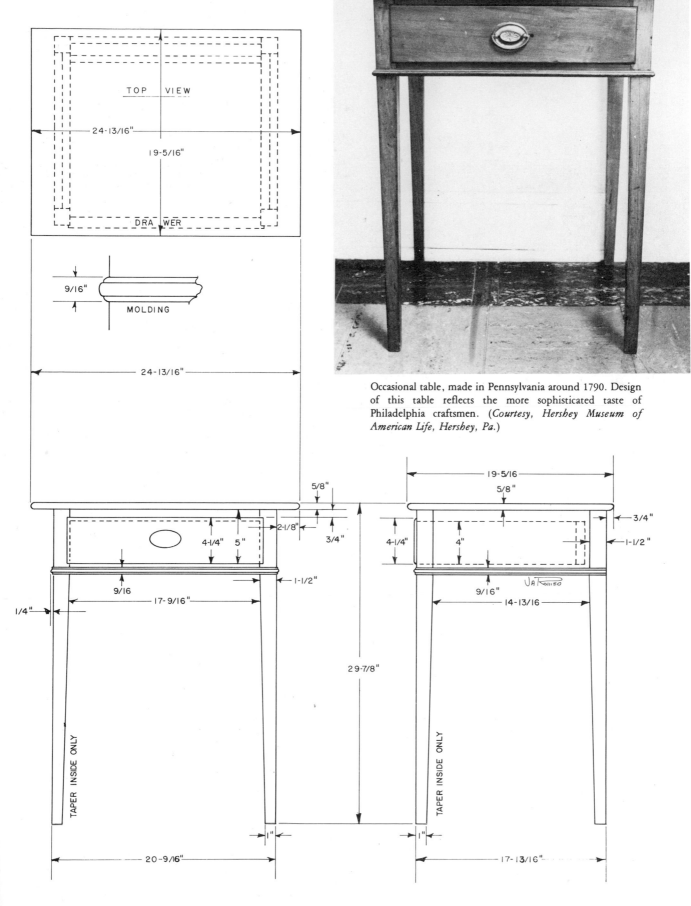

Occasional table, made in Pennsylvania around 1790. Design of this table reflects the more sophisticated taste of Philadelphia craftsmen. (*Courtesy, Hershey Museum of American Life, Hershey, Pa.*)

Dower chest, built and decorated by Christian Selzer of Berks County, Pa., in 1784, this chest shows variations of painted motifs. Designs are blended into space for harmonious effect. See graphs of painted designs, page 120. *(Courtesy, The Henry Ford Museum, Dearborn, Mich.)*

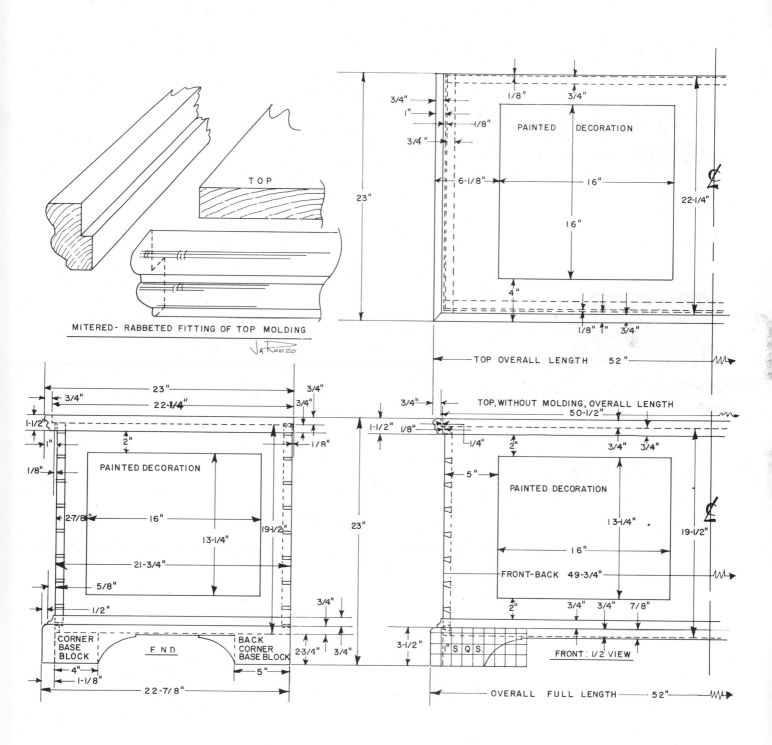

MITERED- RABBETED FITTING OF TOP MOLDING

J. A. Romeo

PAINTED DECORATION

23"

3/4"
1"
3/4"

1/8"
3/4"
1/8"

6-1/8"
16"
16"
22-1/4"

4"

1/8" 1" 3/4"

TOP OVERALL LENGTH   52"

TOP

TOP, WITHOUT MOLDING, OVERALL LENGTH
50-1/2"

23"
22-1/4"
3/4"
3/4"

3/4"

1-1/2" 1/8"
1/4"

1-1/2"
1"
2"
1/8"

3/4" 3/4"

1/8"

5"

PAINTED DECORATION

PAINTED DECORATION

2-7/8"
16"
13-1/4"
19-1/2"

13-1/4"

23"

16"

19-1/2"

21-3/4"

FRONT-BACK 49-3/4"

5/8"

1/2"

2"

CORNER
BASE
BLOCK

E N D

BACK
CORNER
BASE BLOCK

3/4"
3/4" 3/4" 7/8"

3-1/2"

1" S.Q.S.

FRONT: 1/2 VIEW

4"
5"

2-3/4" 3/4"

1-1/8"

22-7/8"

OVERALL FULL LENGTH — 52"

169

Dower chest with drawers, also made in Berks County, Pa., in 1803, is basically painted in stippled and swirled effects, but with panels painted in typical unicorn and tulip motifs. See graphs of painted designs on page 141. *(Courtesy, Philadelphia Museum of Art, Philadelphia, Pa., Gift of Arthur Sussel.)*

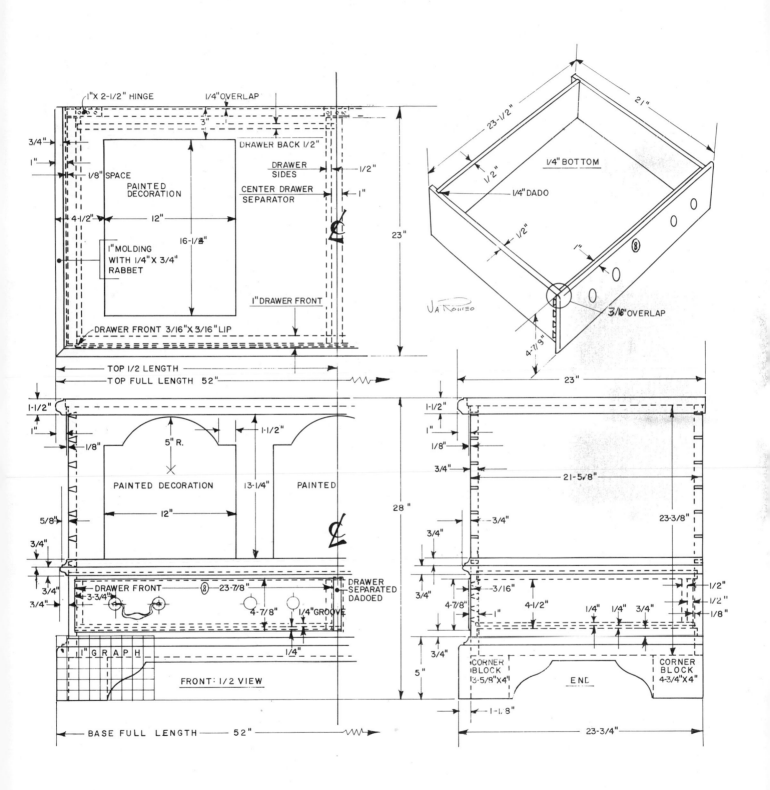

1"X 2-1/2" HINGE 1/4"OVERLAP

3"

DRAWER BACK 1/2"

3/4"

1"

1/8" SPACE

PAINTED
DECORATION

DRAWER
SIDES

1/2"

CENTER DRAWER
SEPARATOR

1"

4-1/2"   12"

23"

16-1/2"

1" MOLDING
WITH 1/4" X 3/4"
RABBET

1" DRAWER FRONT

DRAWER FRONT 3/16" X 3/16" LIP

23-1/2"   21"

1/4" BOTTOM

1/2"

1/4" DADO

1/2"

1"

JA ROMEO

3/16" OVERLAP

4-7/8"

23"

TOP 1/2 LENGTH

TOP FULL LENGTH 52"

1-1/2"   1-1/2"

1"

1/8"

5" R.

PAINTED DECORATION   PAINTED

13-1/4"

12"

28"

21-5/8"

23-3/8"

5/8"

3/4"

3/4"

3/4"

3/16"

DRAWER FRONT   23-7/8"

DRAWER
SEPARATED
DADOED

3/4"   3-3/4"

4-7/8"

1/4" GROOVE

4-7/8"   4-1/2"

1"

1/4"   1/4"   3/4"

1/2"

1/2"

1/8"

1/4"

1" GRAPH

FRONT: 1/2 VIEW

3/4"

5"

BASE FULL LENGTH   52"

CORNER
BLOCK
3-5/8"X4"

END

CORNER
BLOCK
4-3/4"X4"

1-1/8"

23-3/4"

Kitchen storage cabinet, made at Ephrata Cloister during the 18th century, has unusual fittings of hardwood hinges and latches. Cabinet is constructed of tulipwood and walnut. (*Photo by author. Courtesy, Ephrata Cloister, Ephrata, Pa.*)

KITCHEN STORAGE CABINET

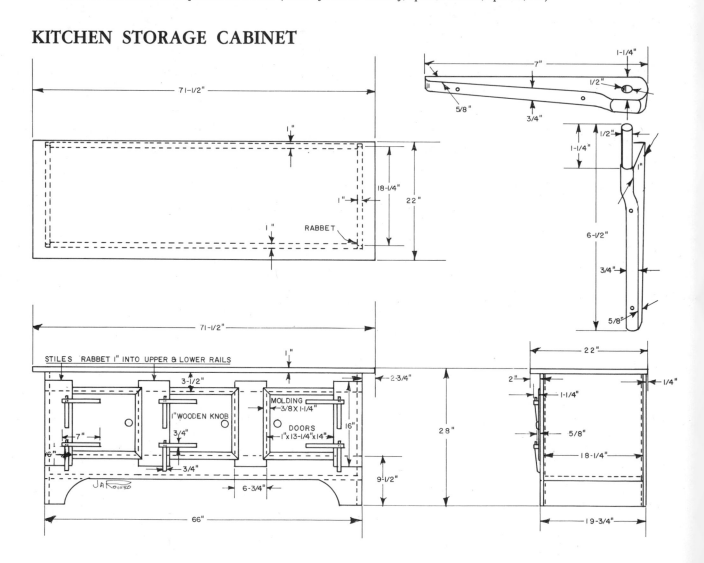

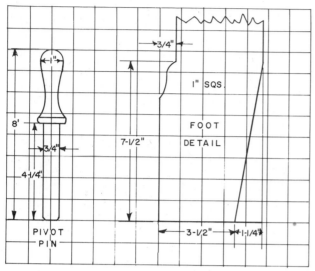

1" SQS.

FOOT

DETAIL

PIVOT PIN

Hutch table made of pine and maple was commonly used in Pennsylvania and other colonies during the 18th and 19th centuries. (*Photo by author. Courtesy, Rock Ford Plantation, Lancaster, Pa.*)

HUTCH TABLE

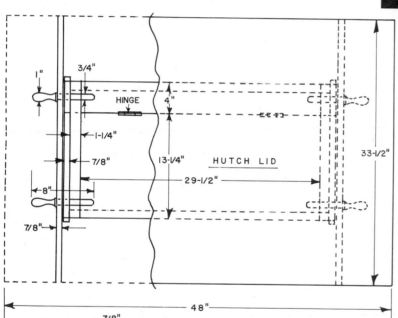

HINGE

HUTCH LID

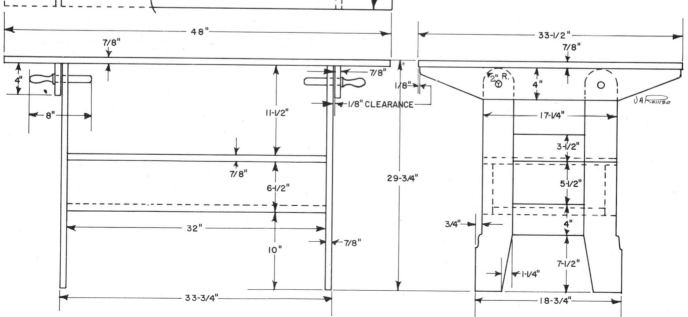

1/8" CLEARANCE

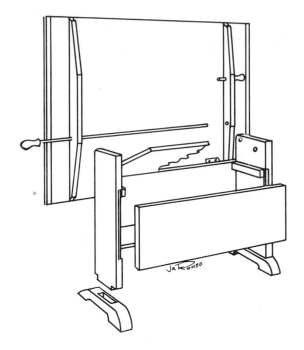

Bench table with hutch. These generic designs were built in Pennsylvania, as well as in the other colonies, during the 18th and early 19th centuries. (*Pen-sketched from museum original.*)

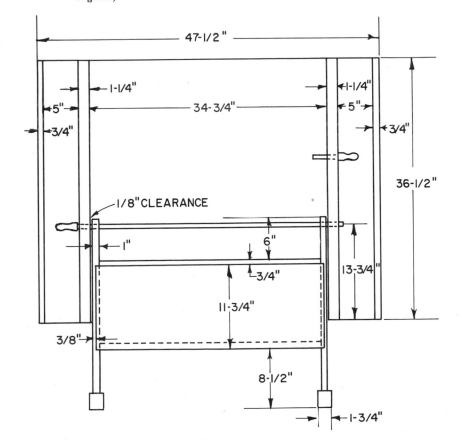

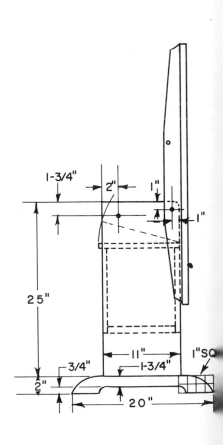

CHAIR TABLE WITH HUTCH

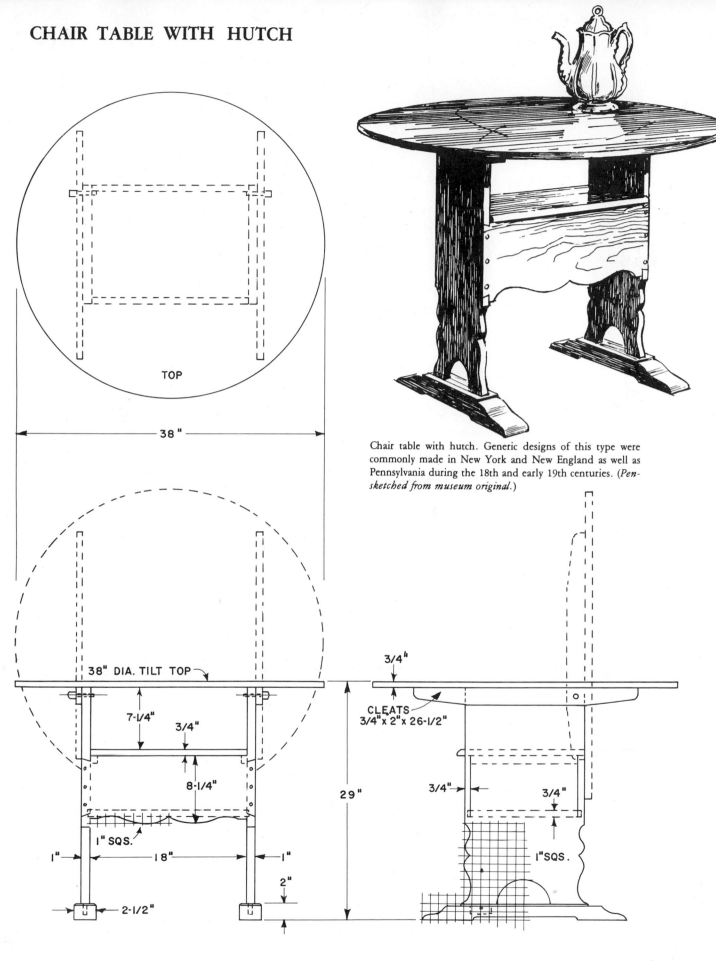

TOP

38 "

Chair table with hutch. Generic designs of this type were commonly made in New York and New England as well as Pennsylvania during the 18th and early 19th centuries. (*Pen-sketched from museum original.*)

38" DIA. TILT TOP

7-1/4"

3/4"

8-1/4"

1" SQS.

1"   18"   1"

2-1/2"

29"

2"

3/4"

CLEATS
3/4"x 2"x 26-1/2"

3/4"   3/4"

1"SQS.

CARPENTER'S TOOL BOX

Carpenter's tool box. Made in Pennsylvania during mid-19th century, this box is neatly arranged with a slotted rack for chisels and ample space for other tools. (*Courtesy, William Penn Memorial Museum, Harrisburg, Pa.*)

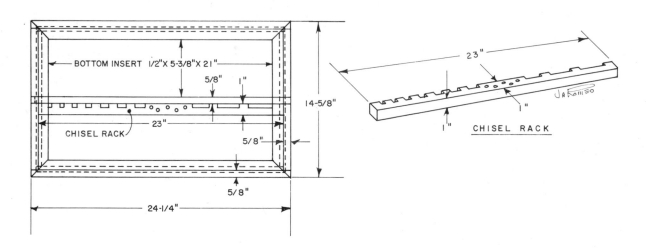

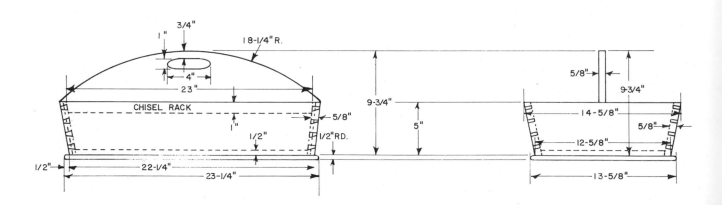

DOUGH BIN

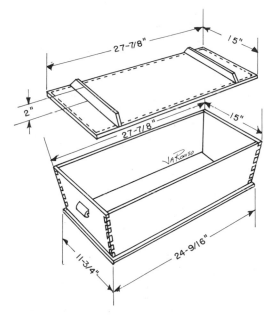

Dough bin. Built in Pennsylvania in the mid-19th century, this bin was made of pine and poplar, all neatly dovetailed at the corners. (*Courtesy, Hershey Museum of American Life, Hershey, Pa.*)

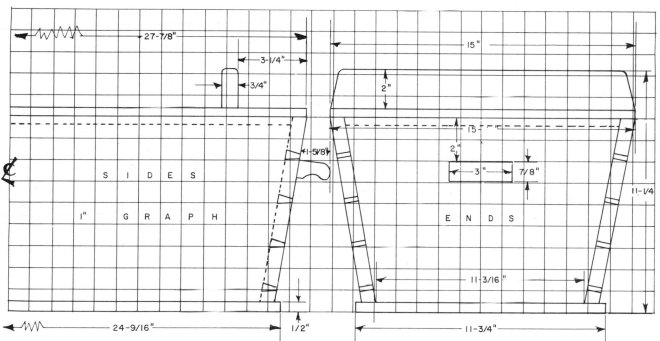

DOUGH TROUGH TABLE

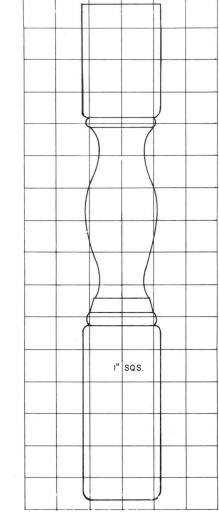

Dough trough table. Made in southeastern Pennsylvania during the early 19th century, this could be used as a regular kitchen eating table—as well as a large-sized trough for kneading dough. Table top, held in place with loose wooden pins, was easily removed. (*Courtesy, Mercer Museum, Doylestown, Pa.*)

1" SQS.

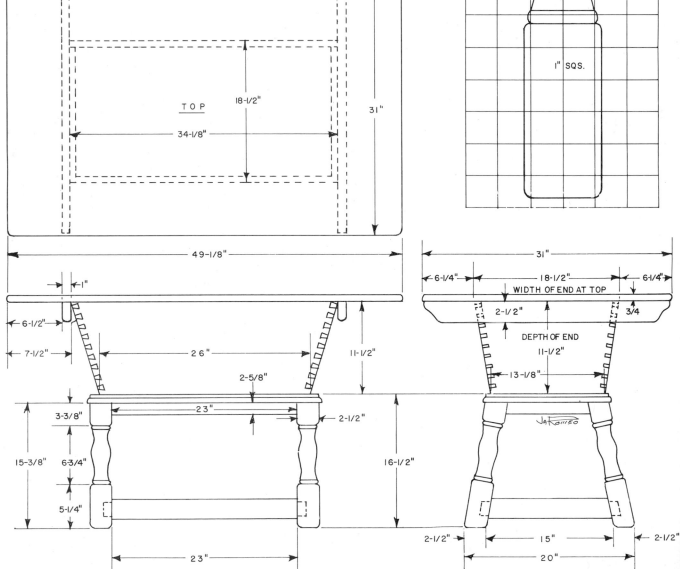

TOP

18-1/2"

34-1/8"

31"

49-1/8"

1"

6-1/2"

7-1/2"

26"

11-1/2"

2-5/8"

3-3/8"

23"

2-1/2"

15-3/8"

6-3/4"

5-1/4"

23"

31"

6-1/4"

18-1/2"

6-1/4"

WIDTH OF END AT TOP

2-1/2"

3/4

DEPTH OF END

11-1/2"

13-1/8"

16-1/2"

2-1/2"

15"

2-1/2"

20"

DOUGH TROUGH TABLE
(DESIGN VARIATION)

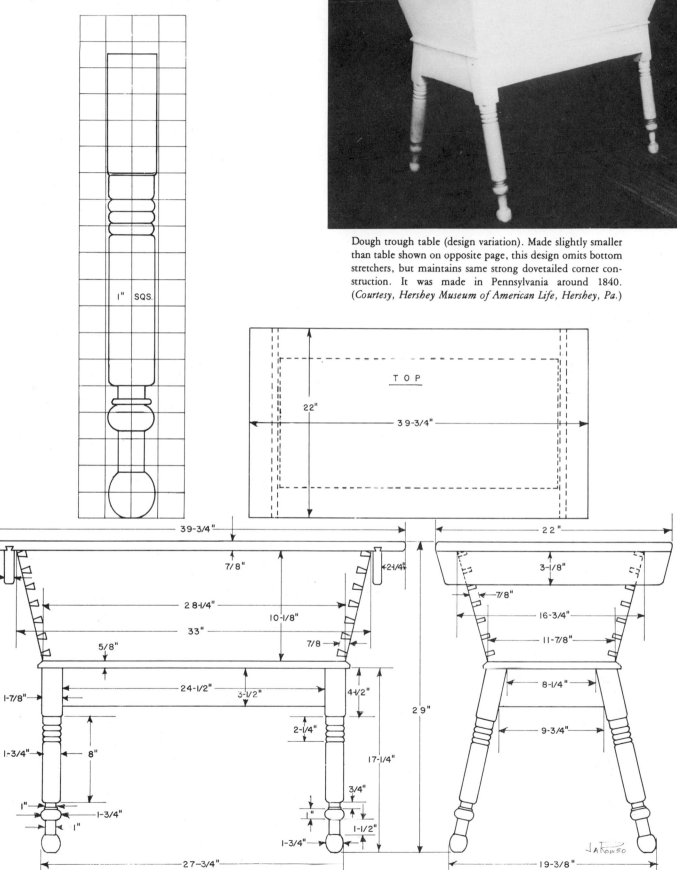

1" SQS.

Dough trough table (design variation). Made slightly smaller than table shown on opposite page, this design omits bottom stretchers, but maintains same strong dovetailed corner construction. It was made in Pennsylvania around 1840. (*Courtesy, Hershey Museum of American Life, Hershey, Pa.*)

TOP

22"

39-3/4"

39-3/4"

7/8"

2 8-1/4"

10-1/8"

33"

7/8

5/8"

24-1/2"

3-1/2"

4-1/2"

2-1/4"

17-1/4"

8"

1-7/8"

1-3/4"

1"

1-3/4"

1"

3/4"

1-1/2"

1-3/4"

27-3/4"

7/8"

2 2"

3-1/8"

7/8"

16-3/4"

11-7/8"

8-1/4"

9-3/4"

2 9"

19-3/8"

179

PLATE RACK

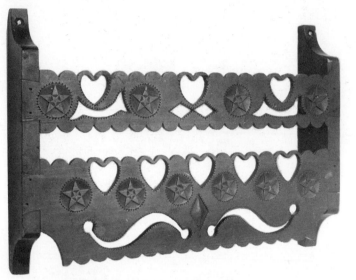

Plate rack. Of early 19th century origin, with typical Pennsylvania German detailing of fretwork, heart-shaped apertures and incised carving of circles enclosing five-pointed stars. *(Photo by Ron Sprules. Courtesy, The American Museum in Britain, Bath, England.)*

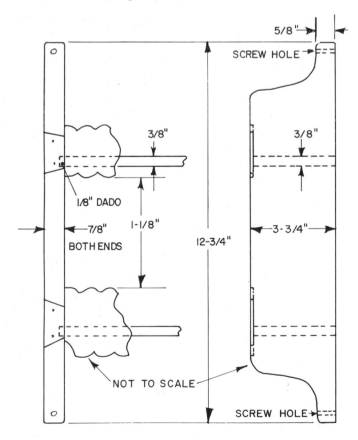

5/8"

SCREW HOLE

3/8"

3/8"

1/8" DADO

7/8"
BOTH ENDS

1-1/8"

12-3/4"

3-3/4"

NOT TO SCALE

SCREW HOLE

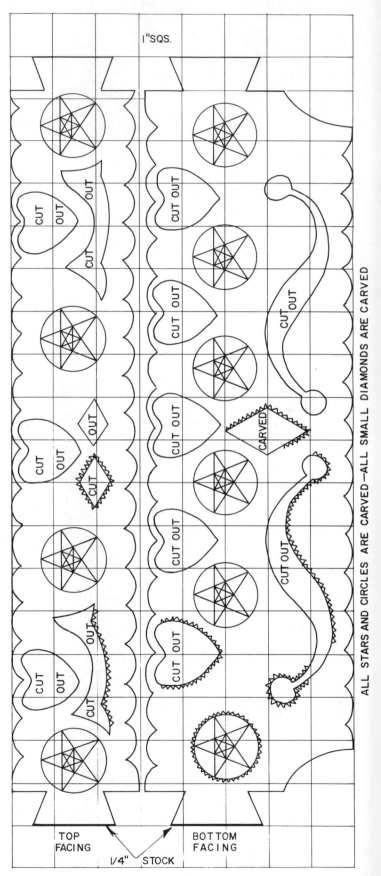

1"SQS.

CUT OUT

CUT OUT

CUT OUT

CUT OUT

CUT OUT

CARVED

CUT OUT

CUT OUT

CUT OUT

CUT OUT

CUT OUT

CUT OUT

CUT OUT

CUT OUT

ALL STARS AND CIRCLES ARE CARVED—ALL SMALL DIAMONDS ARE CARVED

TOP FACING

BOTTOM FACING

1/4" STOCK

180

"MARBLEIZED" SHELF

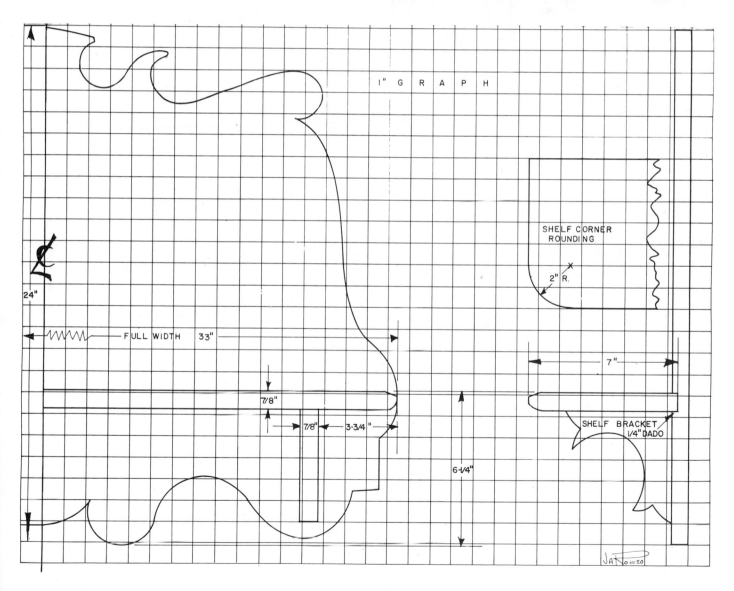

"Marbleized" shelf. This unusual scrolled shelf, which may be made of slate, is finished with pink and white paint to simulate marble effect. It was made near Slatington, Pa., in 1830. (*Courtesy, The American Museum in Britain, Bath, England.*)

1" GRAPH

SHELF CORNER ROUNDING

2" R.

24"

FULL WIDTH 33"

7/8"

7/8" 3-3/4"

7"

SHELF BRACKET 1/4" DADO

6-1/4"

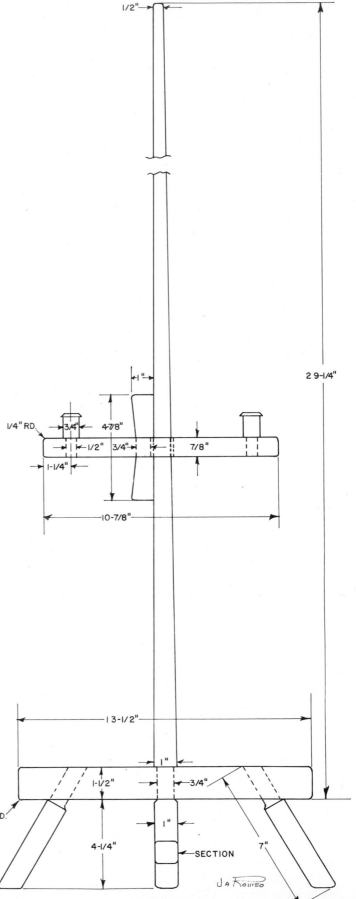

ADJUSTABLE CANDLE STAND

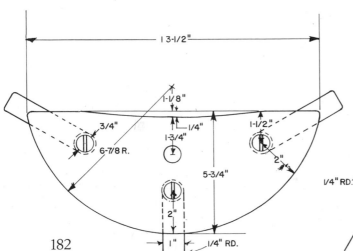

Adjustable candlestand. Of the many candlestands which were made and used throughout the colonies, this early Pennsylvania example is unique in its use of a two-way wedge to secure the candle arm at desired elevation. (*Courtesy, Rock Ford Plantation, Lancaster, Pa.*)

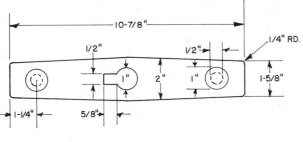

BETTY LAMPS WITH THREADED STANDARD

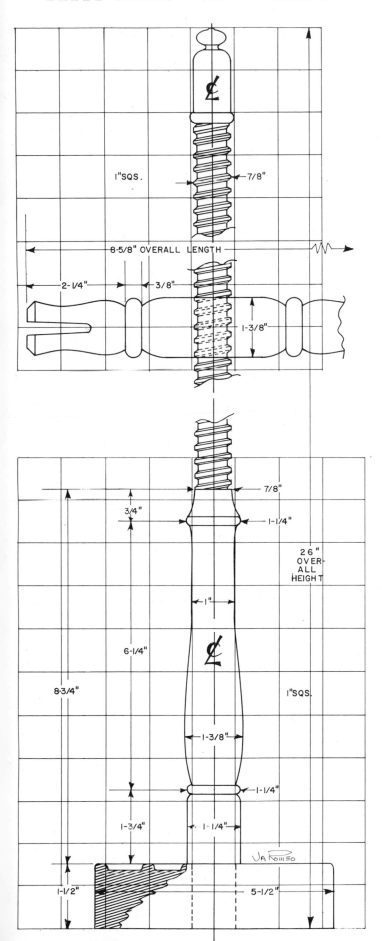

1"SQS.
7/8"
8-5/8" OVERALL LENGTH
2-1/4"
3/8"
1-3/8"

7/8"
3/4"
1-1/4"
26"
OVER-
ALL
HEIGHT
1"
6-1/4"
8-3/4"
1"SQS.
1-3/8"
1-1/4"
1-3/4"
1-1/4"
1-1/2"
5-1/2"

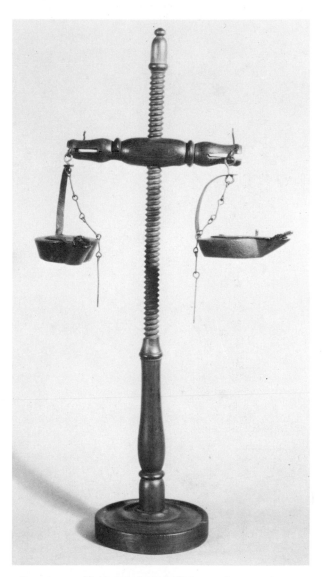

Betty lamps with threaded standard. Late 18th century betty lamps were mounted on cross-arms, with threaded stems for height adjustment. Lamps burned whale oil. They were used as a substitute for candles. (*Courtesy, Philadelphia Museum of Art, Philadelphia, Pa.*)

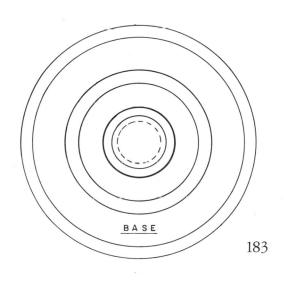

BASE

183

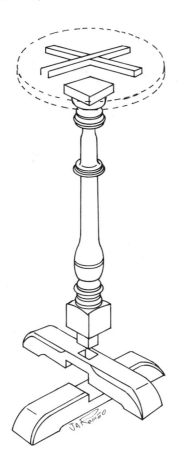

Turned candlestand. Of early 18th century Pennsylvania origin. This stand is strongly built with through mortises and tenons connecting cross-lapped base and top cleats. (*Courtesy, Philadelphia Museum of Art, Philadelphia, Pa., The Titus C. Geesey Collection.*)

TURNED CANDLE STAND

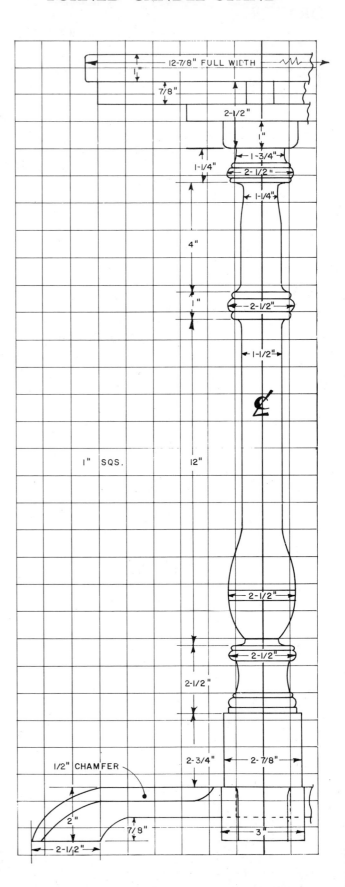

12-7/8" FULL WIDTH

1"

7/8"

2-1/2"

1"

1-3/4"

1-1/4"

2-1/2"

1-1/4"

4"

1"

2-1/2"

1-1/2"

1" SQS.

12"

2-1/2"

2-1/2"

2-1/2"

1/2" CHAMFER

2-3/4"   2-7/8"

2"

7/8"

3"

2-1/2"

MINIATURE CHEST OF DRAWERS

Miniature chest of drawers. While it serves admirably as a trinket or jewelry chest, this small 19th century chest of drawers probably originated as a manufacturer's model. Rather than burden themselves with full-size pieces of furniture, many salesmen from urban centers represented their merchandise with accurately built small-scale models. (*Photo by author. Courtesy, Rockford Plantation, Lancaster, Pa.*)

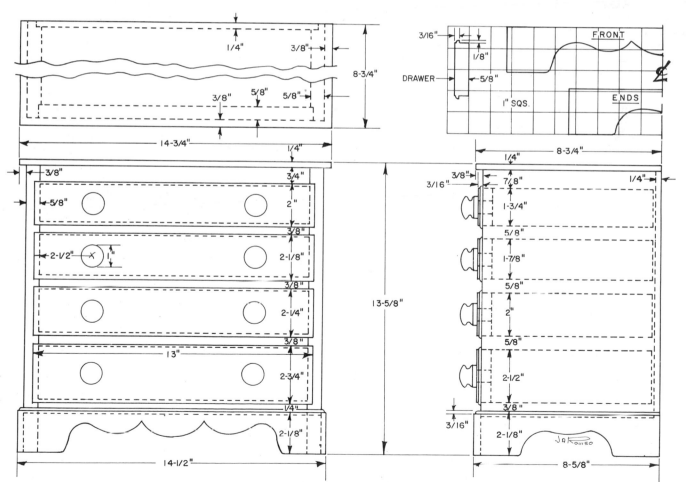

CANDLE BOX

Candle box. Elaborate painted decorations of this slide-lid Pennsylvania candle box identify it with the early German school of decorative art. It was made in 1783. See graphed decorative pattern, page 139. (*Courtesy, National Gallery of Art, Index of American Design, Washington, D.C.*)

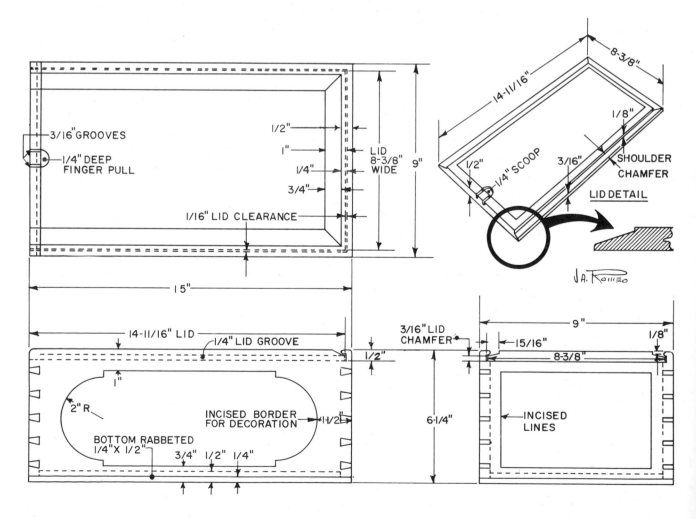

SALT BOX

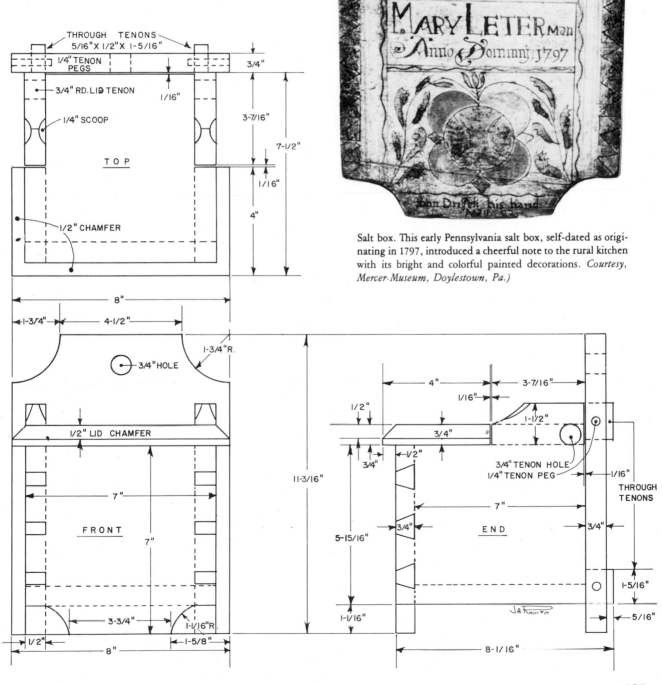

Top view labels:
THROUGH TENONS
5/16"X 1/2"X 1-5/16"
1/4" TENON PEGS
3/4"
3/4" RD. LID TENON
1/16"
3-7/16"
1/4" SCOOP
7-1/2"
T O P
1/16"
1/2" CHAMFER
4"
8"

Front view labels:
1-3/4"
4-1/2"
1-3/4"R.
3/4" HOLE
1/2" LID CHAMFER
7"
11-3/16"
FRONT
7"
3-3/4"
1-1/16"R.
1/2"
8"
1-5/8"

End view labels:
4"
3-7/16"
1/16"
1/2"
1-1/2"
3/4"
3/4"
3/4" TENON HOLE
1/4" TENON PEG
1/16"
7"
THROUGH TENONS
5-15/16"
3/4"
E N D
3/4"
1-5/16"
1-1/16"
5/16"
8-1/16"

Salt box. This early Pennsylvania salt box, self-dated as originating in 1797, introduced a cheerful note to the rural kitchen with its bright and colorful painted decorations. *Courtesy, Mercer-Museum, Doylestown, Pa.)*

Wall box.

WALL BOXES & SPOON RACK

Wall boxes and spoon rack. A variety of quaint wall boxes and racks were made in Pennsylvania and other colonies during the 18th century. These generic designs were used mostly for containing salt, sugar, herbs, candles—and as cutlery racks. They were sometimes carved with simple surface designs or painted in vivid colors. (*Photo by author. Courtesy, Sleepy Hollow Restorations, Tarrytown, N.Y.*)

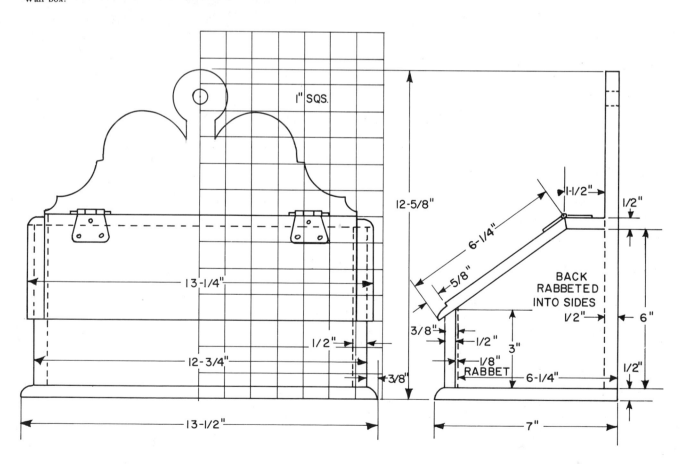

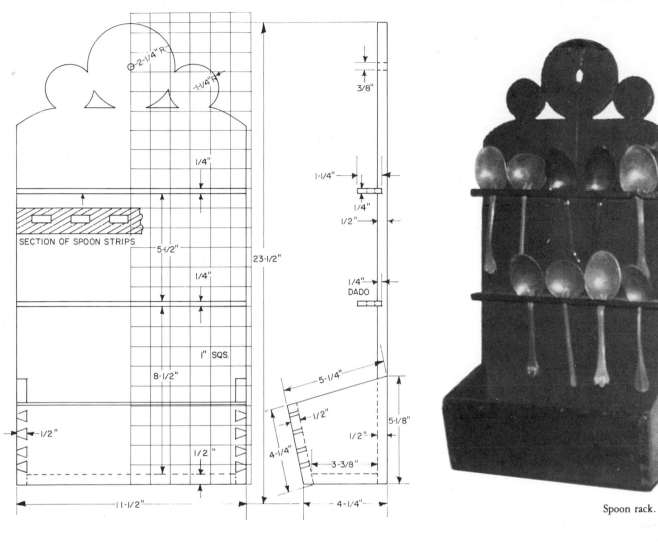

SECTION OF SPOON STRIPS

1/4"

5-1/2"

1/4"

1" SQS.

8-1/2"

1/2"

1/2"

11-1/2"

23-1/2"

3/8"

1-1/4"

1/4"

1/2"

1/4"
DADO

5-1/4"

1/2"

5-1/8"

4-1/4"

1/2"

3-3/8"

4-1/4"

Spoon rack.

Salt box.

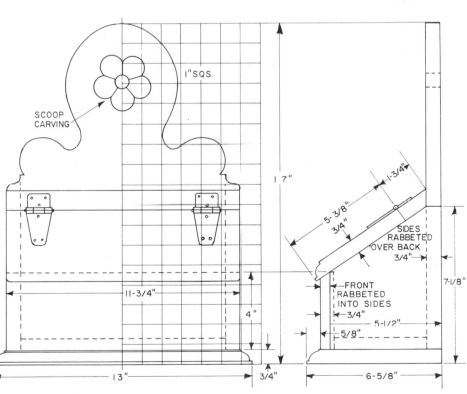

SCOOP
CARVING

1" SQS.

17"

11-3/4"

4"

13"

3/4"

1-3/4"

5-3/8"

3/4"

SIDES
RABBETED
OVER BACK

3/4"

FRONT
RABBETED
INTO SIDES

3/4"

5/8"

5-1/2"

7-1/8"

6-5/8"

189

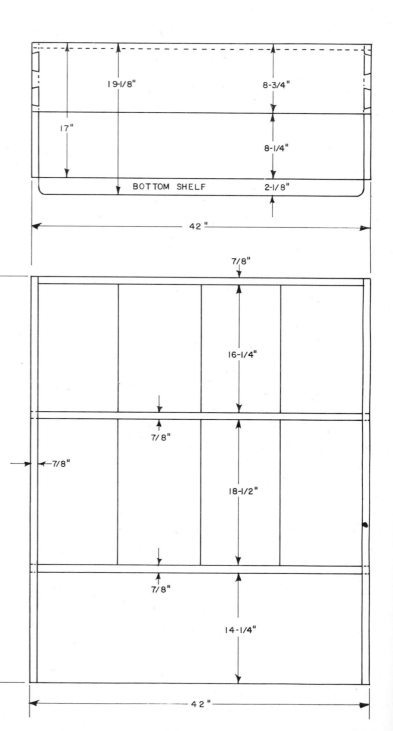

KITCHEN UTILITY SHELVES

Kitchen utility shelves. Strongly built, with dovetailed top and with shelves interlocking sides with piercing mortise and tenon joints, these shelves were built to last for centuries—which is precisely what they are doing! (*Photo by author. Courtesy, Rock Ford Plantation, Lancaster, Pa.*)

PIE SAFE WITH PIERCED TIN PANELS

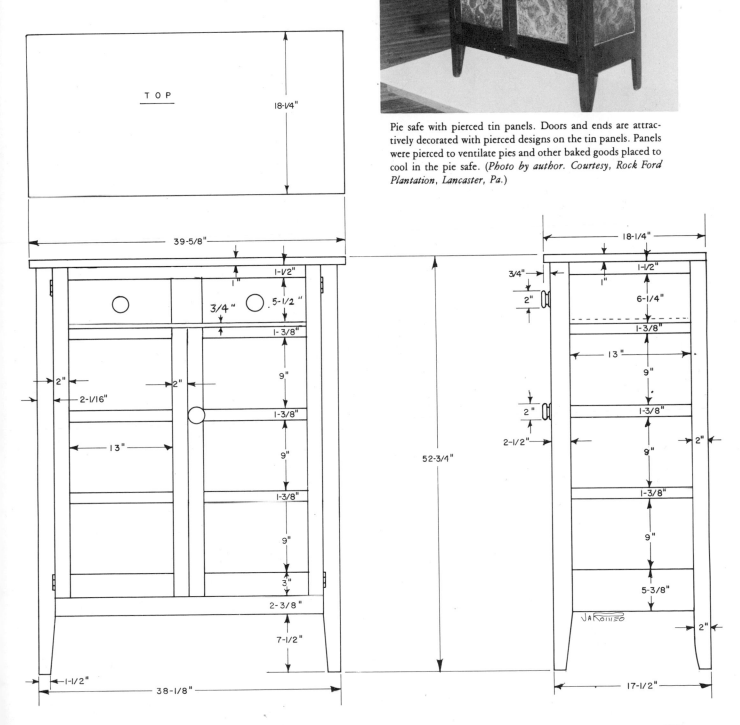

Pie safe with pierced tin panels. Doors and ends are attractively decorated with pierced designs on the tin panels. Panels were pierced to ventilate pies and other baked goods placed to cool in the pie safe. (*Photo by author. Courtesy, Rock Ford Plantation, Lancaster, Pa.*)

TOP

18-1/4"

39-5/8"

1-1/2"
1"
5-1/2"
3/4"
1-3/8"
9"
1-3/8"
9"
1-3/8"
9"
3"
2-3/8"
7-1/2"

2"
2-1/16"
2"
13"

1-1/2"
38-1/8"

18-1/4"

3/4"
2"
2"
2-1/2"

1-1/2"
1"
6-1/4"
1-3/8"
13"
9"
1-3/8"
9"
2"
1-3/8"
9"
5-3/8"
2"

52-3/4"

17-1/2"

JAROMEO

PINE KEY CUPBOARD

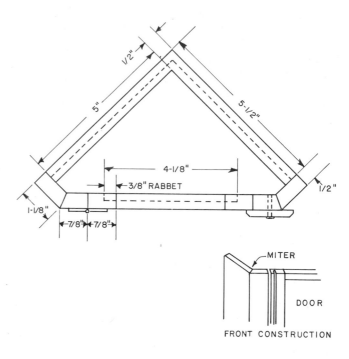

MITER

DOOR

FRONT CONSTRUCTION

Pine key cupboard. Ingeniously designed and decorated with painted motifs, this little cupboard—which originated in Pennsylvania around 1800—displays graceful blending of design and decorative elements. See graphed decorative patterns, page 138. *(Courtesy, The Metropolitan Museum of Art, New York, N.Y.)*

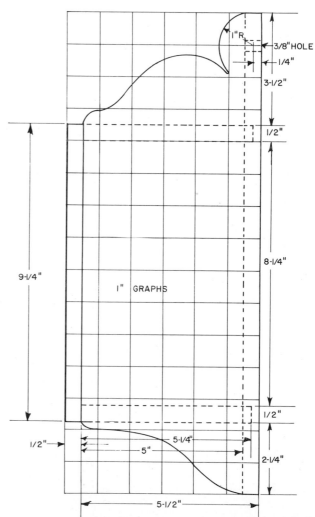

192

STAGHORN-HINGED HANGING CUPBOARD

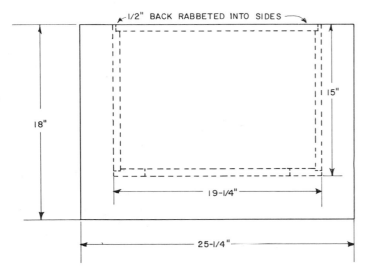

1/2" BACK RABBETED INTO SIDES

15"

18"

19-1/4"

25-1/4"

Staghorn-hinged hanging cupboard. This sturdy design originated in Pennsylvania around 1725—1750. Intricate molding of the top, bottom, and panel borders is particularly interesting. Staghorn hinges of the type shown were commonly forged in eastern Pennsylvania during the 18th century. (*Courtesy, Metropolitan Museum of Art, New York, N.Y.*)

A — TOP MOLDING

B — DOOR LIP

C — BASE MOLDING

D — DOOR PANEL

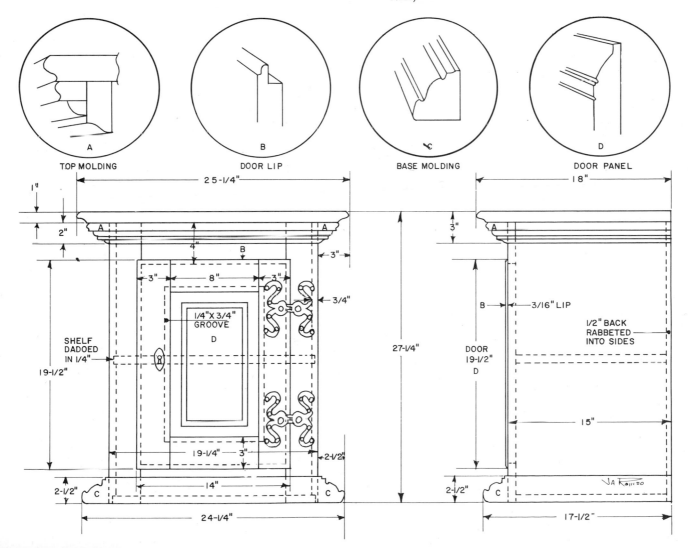

25-1/4"

1"

2"

A   A

4"

B

3"

3"   8"   3"

3/4"

1/4" X 3/4" GROOVE

D

SHELF DADOED IN 1/4"

19-1/2"

19-1/4"   3"

2-1/2"

14"

2-1/2"

C   C

24-1/4"

18"

3"

A

B   3/16" LIP

1/2" BACK RABBETED INTO SIDES

27-1/4"

DOOR 19-1/2" D

15"

2-1/2"

C

17-1/2"

JA Romeo

SCROLLED WALL CUPBOARD

Scrolled wall cupboard. Hanging wall cupboard of 18th century origin is decorated with elaborately scrolled apron, typical of early Pennsylvania German cabinet work. (*Courtesy, The American Museum in Britain, Bath, England.*)

1" SQS.

1/2 PATTERN OF APRON SCROLL

METAL LOCK PLATE

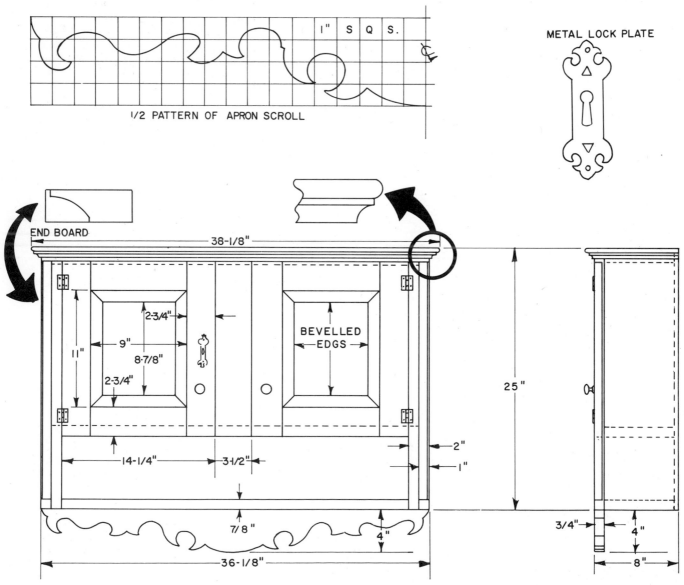

END BOARD

38-1/8"

2-3/4"

9"

8-7/8"

11"

2-3/4"

BEVELLED EDGS

25"

14-1/4"   3-1/2"

2"

1"

7/8"

4"

3/4"

4"

36-1/8"

8"

HANGING CUPBOARD

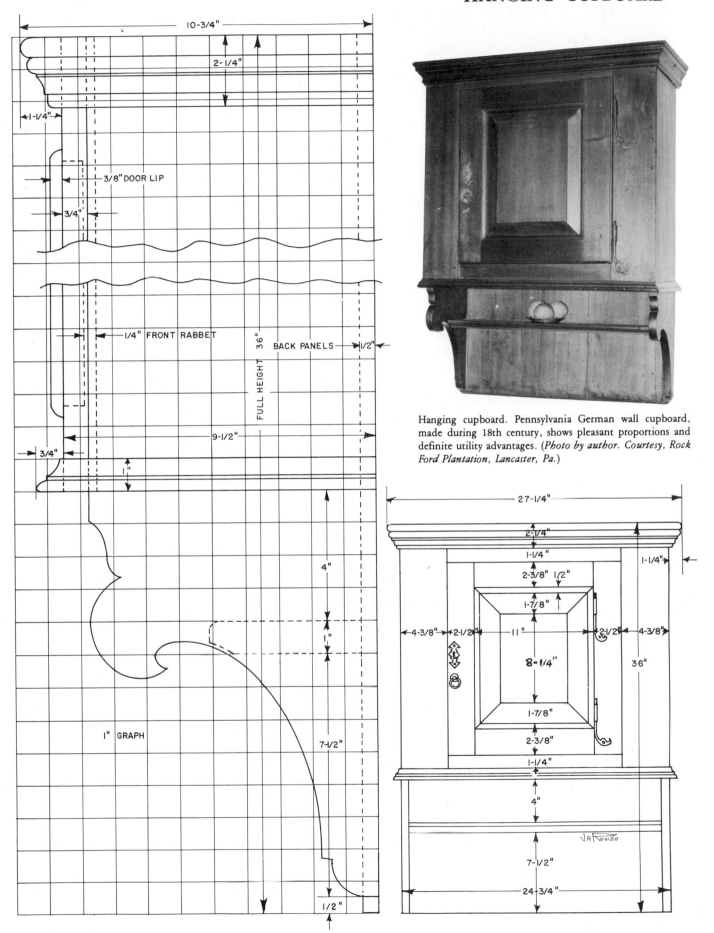

10-3/4"

2-1/4"

1-1/4"

3/8" DOOR LIP

3/4"

1/4" FRONT RABBET

FULL HEIGHT 36"

BACK PANELS

1/2"

9-1/2"

3/4"

1"

4"

1"

1" GRAPH

7-1/2"

1/2"

Hanging cupboard. Pennsylvania German wall cupboard, made during 18th century, shows pleasant proportions and definite utility advantages. (*Photo by author. Courtesy, Rock Ford Plantation, Lancaster, Pa.*)

27-1/4"

2-1/4"

1-1/4"

2-3/8" 1/2"

1-1/4"

1-7/8"

4-3/8" 2-1/2" 11" 2-1/2" 4-3/8"

8-1/4"

36"

1-7/8"

2-3/8"

1-1/4"

4"

7-1/2"

24-3/4"

JA Romeo

SMALL DOVETAILED CHEST

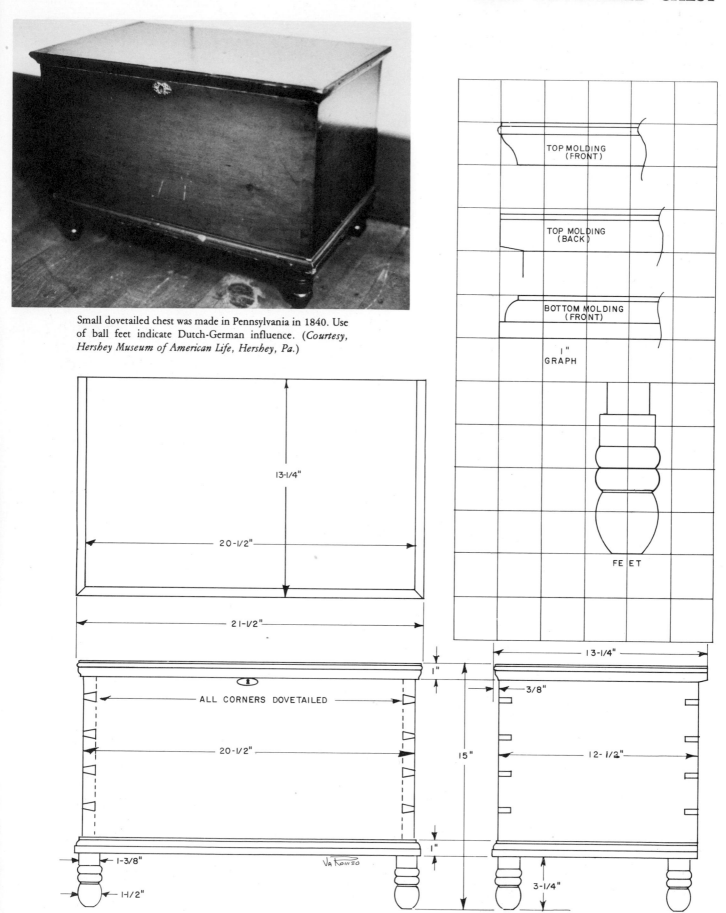

Small dovetailed chest was made in Pennsylvania in 1840. Use of ball feet indicate Dutch-German influence. (*Courtesy, Hershey Museum of American Life, Hershey, Pa.*)

TOP MOLDING (FRONT)

TOP MOLDING (BACK)

BOTTOM MOLDING (FRONT)

1" GRAPH

FEET

13-1/4"

20-1/2"

21-1/2"

ALL CORNERS DOVETAILED

20-1/2"

1"

15"

1"

1-3/8"

1-1/2"

13-1/4"

3/8"

12-1/2"

3-1/4"

WATER BENCH

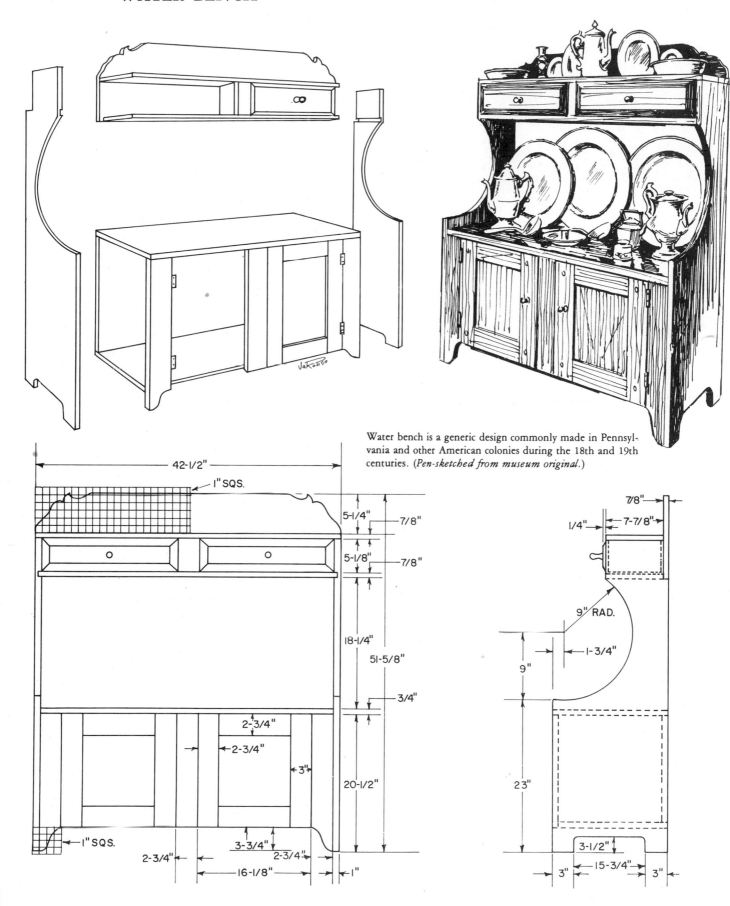

Water bench is a generic design commonly made in Pennsylvania and other American colonies during the 18th and 19th centuries. (*Pen-sketched from museum original.*)

197

Nazareth Hall school desk. This desk was used during the late 18th and early 19th centuries in the Moravian Boy's School at Nazareth, Pa. (*Photo by author. Courtesy, Moravian Museum of Bethlehem, Bethlehem, Pa.*)

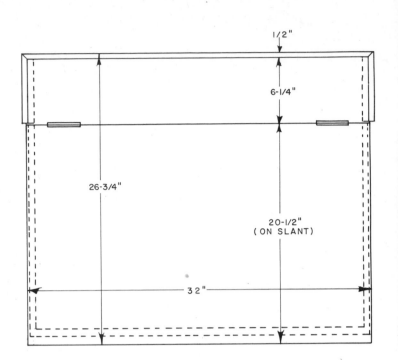

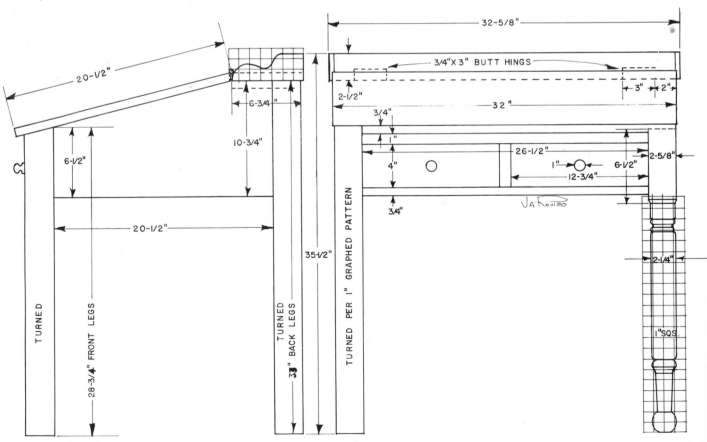

SCHOOLMASTER'S DESK

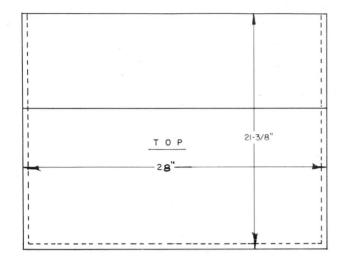

TOP

21-3/8"

28"

Schoolmaster's desk. Made around 1800 in central Pennsylvania, this standing desk was built of hard, yellow pine and finished with gray paint. (*Courtesy, Hershey Museum of American Life, Hershey, Pa.*)

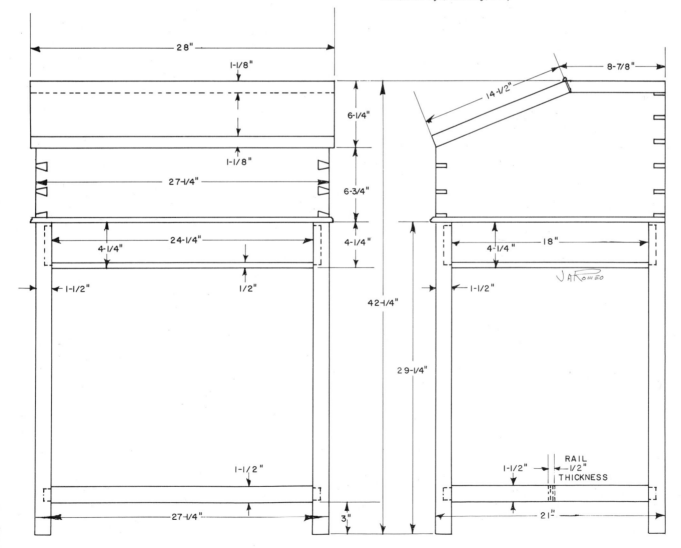

28"

1-1/8"

6-1/4"

1-1/8"

27-1/4"

6-3/4"

24-1/4"

4-1/4"

4-1/4"

1-1/2"

1/2"

42-1/4"

29-1/4"

1-1/2"

27-1/4"

3"

8-7/8"

14-1/2"

4-1/4"

18"

1-1/2"

JA Romeo

1-1/2"

RAIL
1/2"
THICKNESS

21"

Drop-lid desk. This desk, which is believed to have been made in Philadelphia in 1740, exemplifies the more sophisticated cabinet work which spread into rural areas of Pennsylvania from the urban centers. It is made of walnut, white cedar and spruce. (*Courtesy, Hershey Museum of American Life, Hershey, Pa.*)

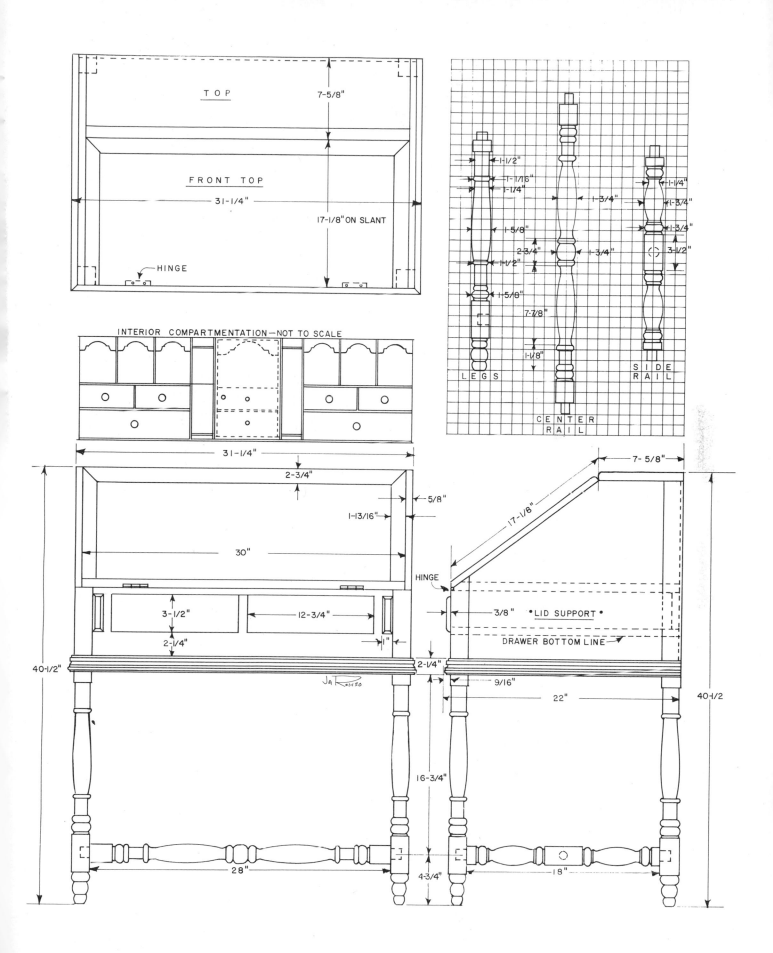

TOP

7-5/8"

FRONT TOP

31-1/4"

17-1/8" ON SLANT

HINGE

1-1/2"
1-1/16"
1-1/4"
1-3/4"
1-1/4"
1-5/8"
1-3/4"
1-3/4"
2-3/4"
1-3/4"
3-1/2"
1-1/2"
1-5/8"
7-7/8"
1-1/8"

LEGS

SIDE RAIL

CENTER RAIL

INTERIOR COMPARTMENTATION—NOT TO SCALE

31-1/4"

2-3/4"

5/8"

1-13/16"

30"

3-1/2"

12-3/4"

2-1/4"

1"

40-1/2"

7-5/8"

17-1/8"

HINGE

3/8"   • LID SUPPORT •

DRAWER BOTTOM LINE

2-1/4"

9/16"

22"

40-1/2

16-3/4"

28"

18"

4-3/4"

WALNUT CRADLE

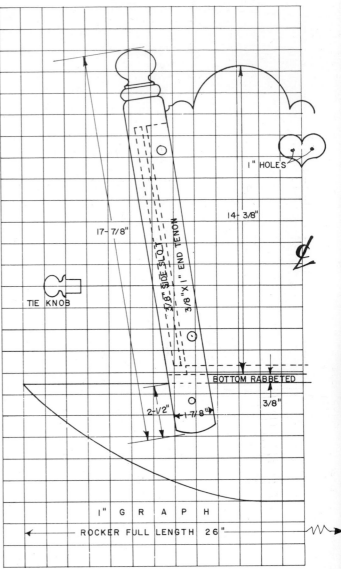

17-7/8"

TIE KNOB

1" HOLES

14-3/8"

3/8" SIDE SLOT

3/8" X 1" END TENON

2-1/2"

1-7/8"

BOTTOM RABBETED

3/8"

1" G R A P H

ROCKER FULL LENGTH 26"

Walnut cradle. Made in Bucks County, Pa., around 1815. Cradle is believed to have been built by Abraham Overholt in about 1765–1834. (*Courtesy, Mercer Museum, Doylestown, Pa.*)

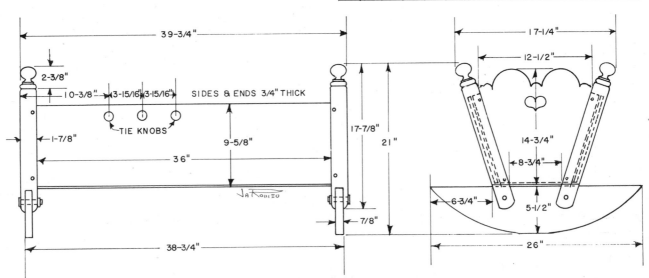

39-3/4"

2-3/8"

10-3/8"   3-15/16" 3-15/16"   SIDES & ENDS 3/4" THICK

TIE KNOBS

1-7/8"

9-5/8"

36"

17-7/8"

21"

7/8"

38-3/4"

17-1/4"

12-1/2"

14-3/4"

8-3/4"

6-3/4"

5-1/2"

26"

HOODED CRADLE

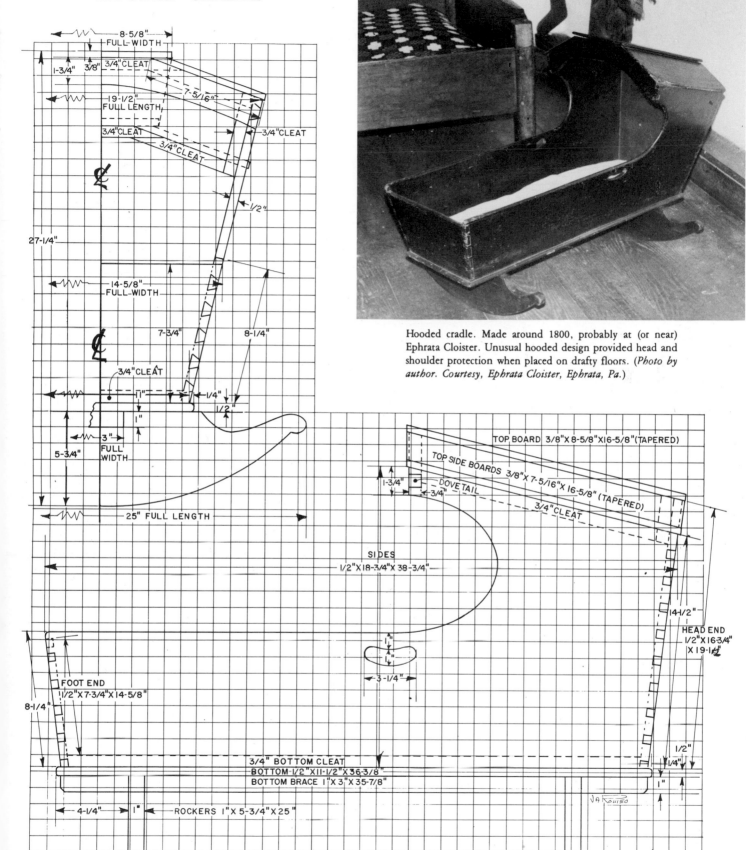

8-5/8"
FULL WIDTH

1-3/4"   3/8"   3/4" CLEAT

7-5/16"

19-1/2"
FULL LENGTH

3/4" CLEAT

3/4" CLEAT

3/4" CLEAT

3/4" CLEAT

1/2"

℄

27-1/4"

14-5/8"
FULL WIDTH

℄

7-3/4"   8-1/4"

3/4" CLEAT

1"   1/4"
1"   1/2"

3"
FULL WIDTH

5-3/4"

Hooded cradle. Made around 1800, probably at (or near) Ephrata Cloister. Unusual hooded design provided head and shoulder protection when placed on drafty floors. (*Photo by author. Courtesy, Ephrata Cloister, Ephrata, Pa.*)

TOP BOARD 3/8"X 8-5/8"X16-5/8"(TAPERED)

TOP SIDE BOARDS 3/8"X 7-5/16"X 16-5/8" (TAPERED)

1-3/4"
DOVETAIL
3/4"

3/4" CLEAT

25" FULL LENGTH

14-1/2"

SIDES
1/2"X18-3/4"X 38-3/4"

HEAD END
1/2"X163/4"
X 19-1/2"

3-1/4"

FOOT END
1/2"X7-3/4"X14-5/8"

8-1/4"

1/2"
1/4"

1"

3/4" BOTTOM CLEAT
BOTTOM 1/2"X11-1/2"X 36-3/8"
BOTTOM BRACE 1"X 3"X 35-7/8"

J A Romeo

4-1/4"   1"   ROCKERS 1"X 5-3/4"X 25"

203

"Cannonball" four-poster bed. This bed was built for the Miess family in 1840. It is massively constructed of poplar and white pine. (*Courtesy, Hershey Museum of American Life, Hershey, Pa.*)

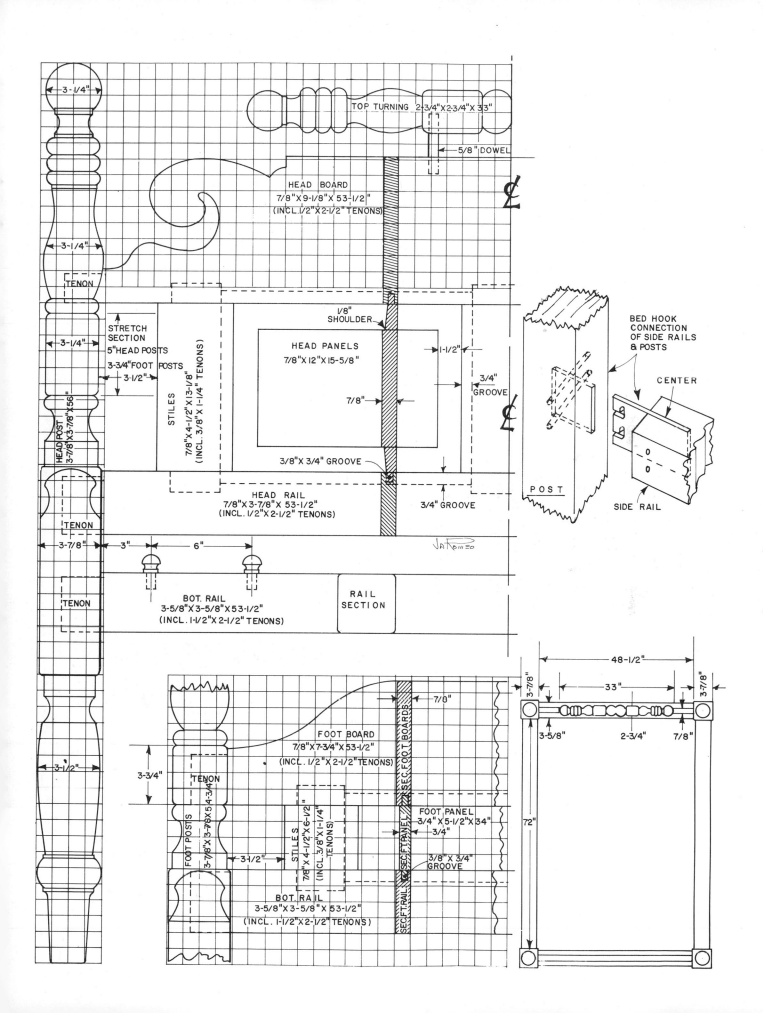

TOP TURNING 2-3/4"X2-3/4"X 33"

3-1/4"

3-1/4"

3-1/4"

5/8" DOWEL

HEAD BOARD
7/8"X9-1/8"X 53-1/2"
(INCL.1/2"X2-1/2" TENONS)

1/8"
SHOULDER

STRETCH
SECTION
5"HEAD POSTS
3-3/4"FOOT POSTS
3 1/2"

HEAD PANELS
7/8"X 12"X15-5/8"

1-1/2"

3/4"
GROOVE

7/8"

STILES
7/8"X4-1/2" X13-1/8"
(INCL. 3/8"X 1-1/4" TENONS)

HEAD POST
3-7/8"X3-7/8"X56"

3/8"X 3/4" GROOVE

HEAD RAIL
7/8"X 3-7/8"X 53-1/2"
(INCL. 1/2"X2-1/2" TENONS)

3/4" GROOVE

TENON

TENON

TENON

3-7/8"   3"   6"

BED HOOK
CONNECTION
OF SIDE RAILS
& POSTS

CENTER

POST

SIDE RAIL

RAIL
SECTION

BOT. RAIL
3-5/8"X 3-5/8"X 53-1/2"
(INCL. 1-1/2"X 2-1/2" TENONS)

3-1/2"

48-1/2"

3-7/8"

33"

3-7/8"

3-5/8"

2-3/4"

7/8"

72"

FOOT BOARD
7/8"X7-3/4"X 53-1/2"
(INCL. 1/2"X 2-1/2"TENONS)

7/8"

3-3/4"

TENON

FOOT POSTS
3-7/8"X 3-7/8"X 54-3/4"

STILES
7/8"X 4-1/2"X 6-1/2"
(INCL. 3/8"X 1-1/4"
TENONS)

3-1/2"

FOOT PANEL
3/4"X 5-1/2"X 34"

3/4"

3/8"X 3/4"
GROOVE

SEC.FOOT BOARD

SEC.F T.PANEL

SEC.F T.RAIL

BOT. RAIL
3-5/8"X 3-5/8"X 53-1/2"
(INCL. 1-1/2"X 2-1/2" TENONS)

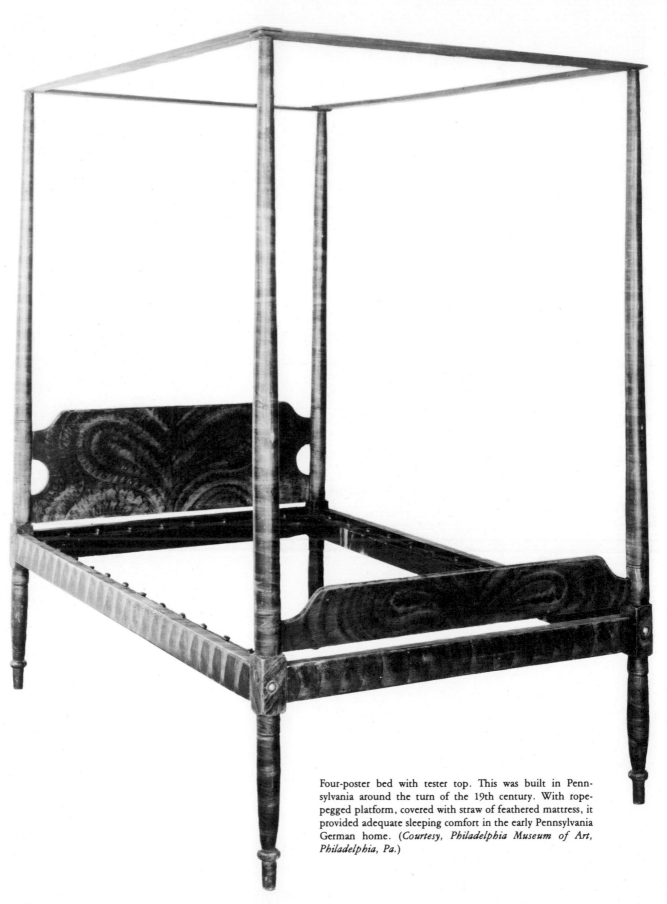

Four-poster bed with tester top. This was built in Pennsylvania around the turn of the 19th century. With rope-pegged platform, covered with straw of feathered mattress, it provided adequate sleeping comfort in the early Pennsylvania German home. (*Courtesy, Philadelphia Museum of Art, Philadelphia, Pa.*)

206

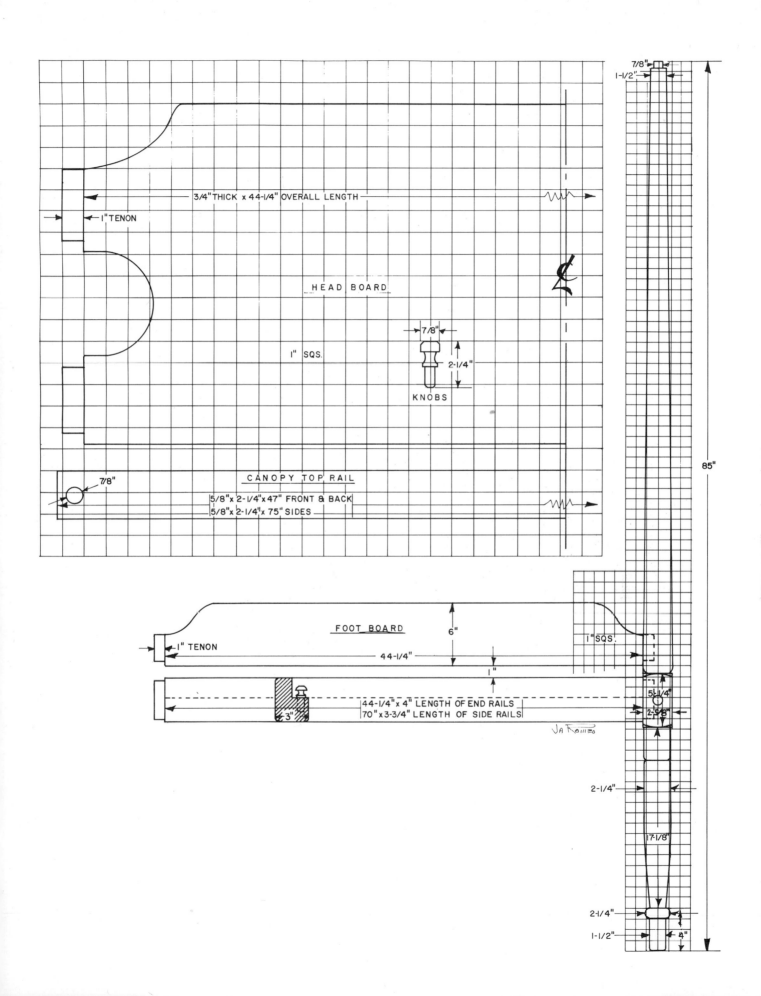

3/4" THICK x 44-1/4" OVERALL LENGTH

1" TENON

HEAD BOARD

1" SQS.

7/8"

2-1/4"

KNOBS

7/8"

CANOPY TOP RAIL

5/8"x 2-1/4"x 47" FRONT & BACK
5/8"x 2-1/4"x 75" SIDES

7/8"

1-1/2"

85"

FOOT BOARD

1" TENON

44-1/4"

6"

1"

1" SQS.

5-1/4"

2-5/8"

44-1/4"x 4" LENGTH OF END RAILS
70"x 3-3/4" LENGTH OF SIDE RAILS

3"

2-1/4"

17-1/8"

2-1/4"

1-1/2"

4"

CHEST OF DRAWERS

Chest of drawers. Elaborately decorated with floral and distel-fink designs, this chest of drawers was made in Snyder County, Pa., around 1834. See graphed decorative designs, page 140. *(Courtesy, Philadelphia Museum of Art, Philadelphia, Pa.)*

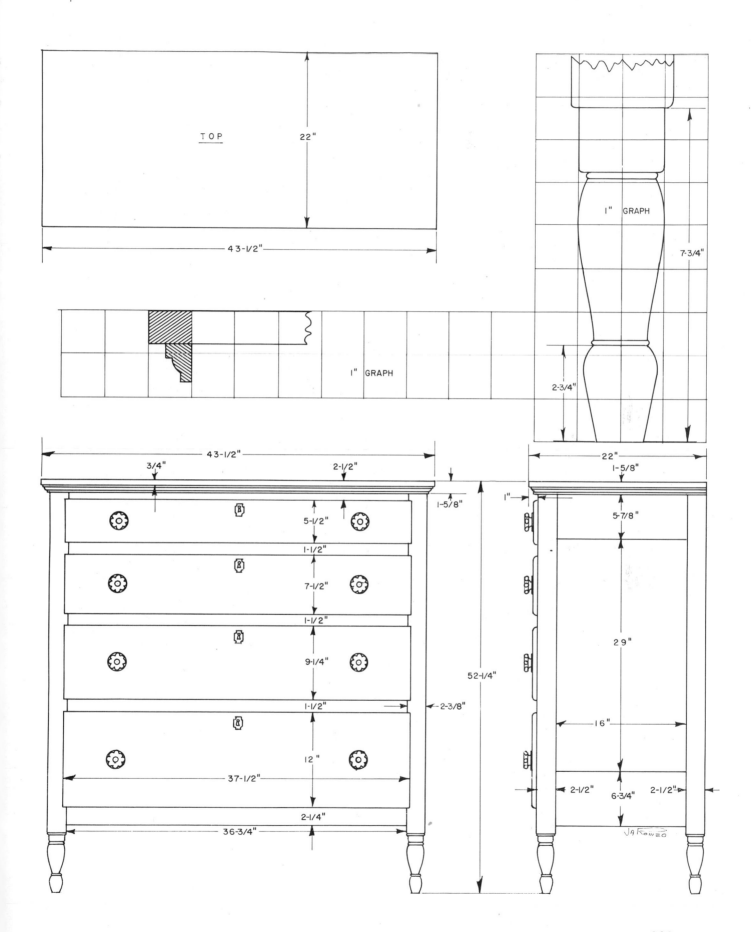

TOP

22"

43-1/2"

1" GRAPH

1" GRAPH

7-3/4"

2-3/4"

43-1/2"

3/4"

2-1/2"

1-5/8"

5-1/2"

1-1/2"

7-1/2"

1-1/2"

9-1/4"

1-1/2"

12"

37-1/2"

2-1/4"

36-3/4"

52-1/4"

2-3/8"

22"

1-5/8"

1"

5-7/8"

29"

16"

2-1/2"

6-3/4"

2-1/2"

JA Romeo

209

CHEST OF DRAWERS

Chest of drawers, less elaborately decorated than design shown on preceding pages, this chest originated in eastern Pennsylvania around 1780. (*Photo by Ron Sprules. Courtesy, The American Museum In Britain, Bath, England.*)

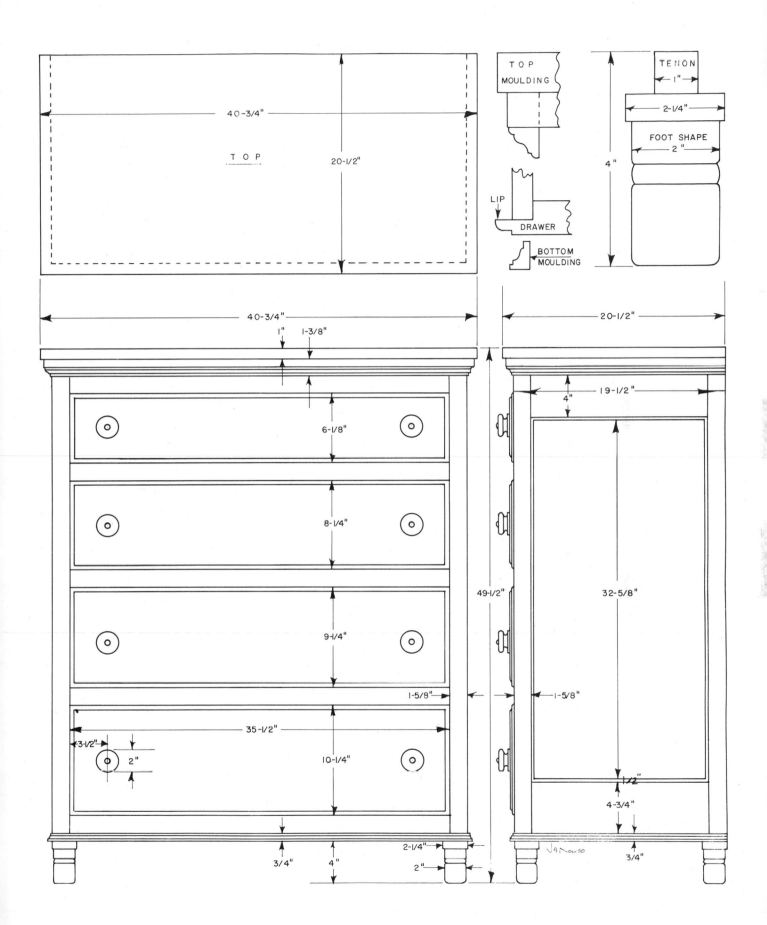

TOP
MOULDING

TENON
1"

2-1/4"

FOOT SHAPE
2"

4"

LIP

DRAWER

BOTTOM
MOULDING

40-3/4"

TOP

20-1/2"

40-3/4"

20-1/2"

1" 1-3/8"

19-1/2"

4"

6-1/8"

8-1/4"

49-1/2"

32-5/8"

9-1/4"

1-5/8"

1-5/8"

35-1/2"

3-1/2"

2"

10-1/4"

1/2"

4-3/4"

2-1/4"

3/4"

3/4"   4"

2"

CORNER CUPBOARD

Corner cupboard. Adapted from an original design of 1725 (now in the Philadelphia Museum of Art), this corner cupboard offers ample space for storage and display of prized pewter and crockery. (*Archive photo.*)

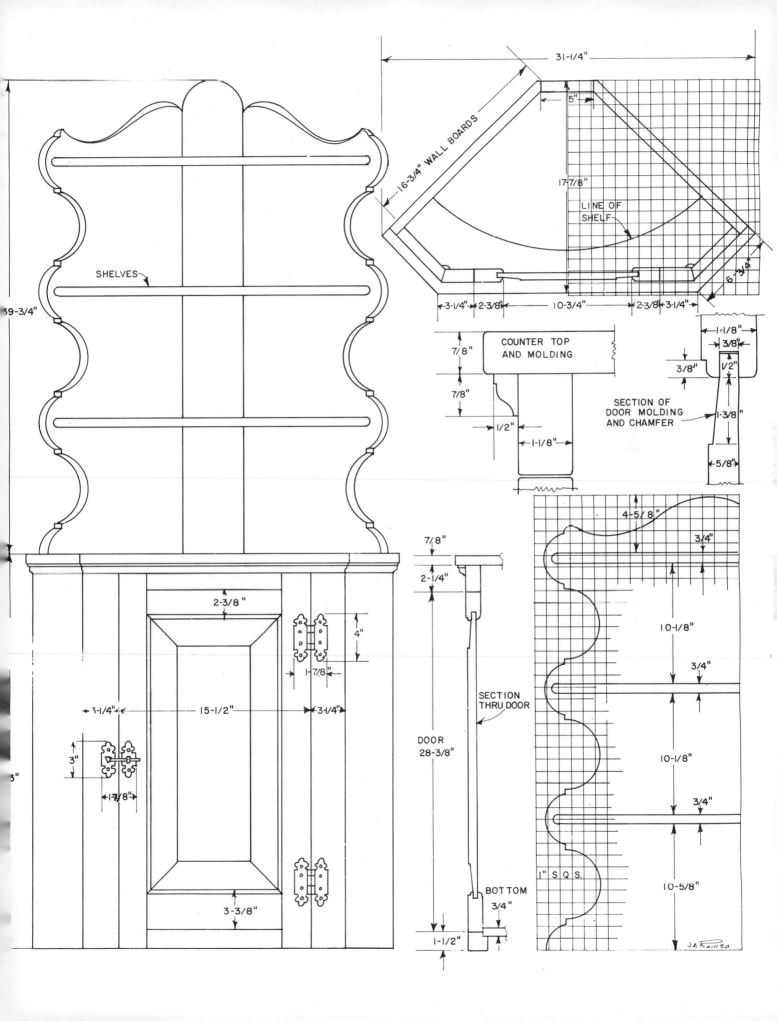

SHELVES

39-3/4"

3"

31-1/4"

5"

16-3/4" WALL BOARDS

17-7/8"

LINE OF SHELF

6-3/4"

3-1/4" · 2-3/8" · 10-3/4" · 2-3/8" · 3-1/4"

1-1/8"

3/8"

3/8"

1/2"

SECTION OF DOOR MOLDING AND CHAMFER

1-3/8"

5/8"

COUNTER TOP AND MOLDING

7/8"

7/8"

1/2"

1-1/8"

2-3/8"

4"

1-7/8"

3-1/4" · 15-1/2" · 3-1/4"

3"

1-7/8"

3-3/8"

7/8"

2-1/4"

SECTION THRU DOOR

DOOR 28-3/8"

BOTTOM

3/4"

1-1/2"

4-5/8"

3/4"

10-1/8"

3/4"

10-1/8"

3/4"

1" SQS.

10-5/8"

JARO1130

Open cupboard. This plain, open cupboard of early 19th century origin, came from Ephrata, Pa. It displays a prized collection of Pennsylvania Dutch decorated tinware. (*Courtesy, American Museum in Britain, Bath, England.*)

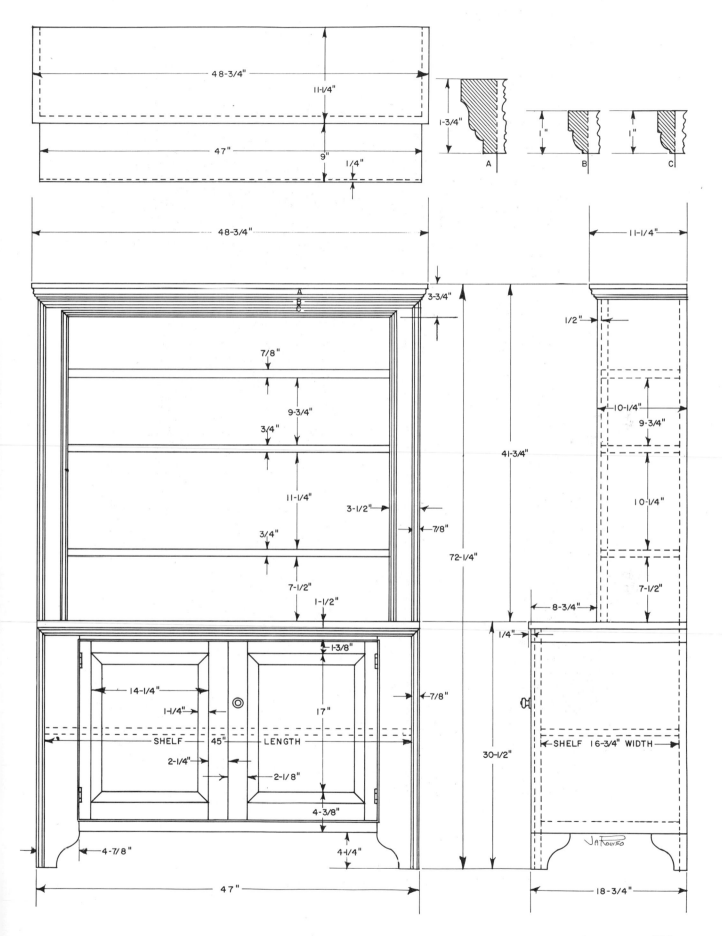

215

PENNSYLVANIA DUTCH DRESSER

Pennsylvania German Dresser. This masterpiece of Pennsylvania German craftsman's art originated in eastern Pennsylvania during the early 18th century. This is a highly decorative piece of somewhat complicated construction. Bail-handles, brasses, door hasps and rattail hinges are particularly noteworthy. (*Courtesy, Metropolitan Museum of Art, New York, N.Y.*)

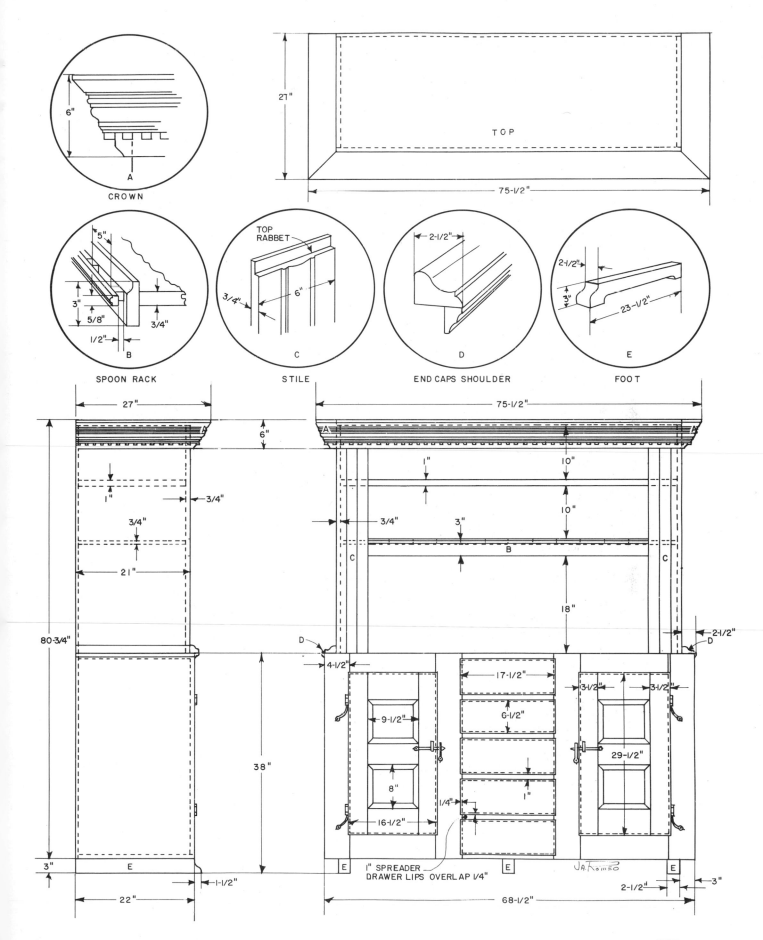

CROWN

SPOON RACK

STILE

END CAPS SHOULDER

FOOT

TOP

1" SPREADER
DRAWER LIPS OVERLAP 1/4"

J.A.Romeo

217

Selected Bibliography

BOOKS

Allen, Walser H. *Who Are the Moravians?* Bethlehem: Moravian Book Shop.

Applied Arts Publishers, Lancaster:
The Amish: An Illustrated Essay
Among the Amish
Antiques of Pennsylvania Dutchland
Bundling Among the Amish
Covered Bridges of Pennsylvania Dutchland
The Dunkard-Dutch Cook Book
The Folk Art of Pennsylvania Dutchland
Hex Signs and Other Barn Decorations
The Lancaster County Farm Cook Book
Meet the Mennonites
Pennsylvania Dutch Folklore
The Pennsylvania Dutch
The Plain People
Songs, Sayings and Stories of a Pennsylvania Dutchman

Barber, Edwin Attlee. *Tulipware of the Pennsylvania German Potters.* Harrisburg: The Pennsylvania Museum School of Industrial Art.

Bealer, Alex W. *Old Ways of Working Wood.* Barre, Massachusetts: Barre Publishing Co., 1972.

Bining, Arthur C. *Pennsylvania Iron Manufacture in the Eighteenth Century.* Harrisburg: Pennsylvania Historical and Museum Commission.

Bishop, Adele, and Lord, Gile. *The Art of Decorative Stenciling.* New York: The Viking Press, 1976.

Bishop, Robert. *The American Chair.*
———. *How to Know Antique Furniture.* New York: E. P. Dutton, 1973.

Borneman, Henry S. *Pennsylvania Illuminated Manuscripts.* Philadelphia: Pennsylvania German Society.

Brand, Millen. *Fields of Peace—A Pennsylvania German Album.* New York: Doubleday & Co. Inc.

Butler, Joseph F. *American Antiques.* New York: The Odyssey Press.
———. *American Furniture.* London: Triune Books.

Comstock, Helen. *American Furniture.* New York: The Viking Press.
———. *Concise Encyclopedia of American Antiques.* New York: The Viking Press.

Cornelius, C. O. *Early American Furniture.* New York: Appleton-Century-Crofts.

Daniel, Joseph. *Building Early American Furniture.* Harrisburg: Stackpole Books.

Day, Jo Anne C. *Pennsylvania Dutch Cut and Use Stencils.* New York: Dover Publications Inc., 1975.

De Jonge, Eric. *Country Things.* New York: Weathervane Books.

Downs, Joseph. *The House of the Miller at Millbach.* Philadelphia: Pennsylvania Museum of Art.

Dreppard, Carl W. *Handbook of American Chairs.* New York: Doubleday & Co. Inc.

Dunway, Wayland Fuller. *A History of Pennsylvania.* Englewood Cliffs, N.J.: Prentice-Hall, Inc.

Durant, Mary. *American Heritage Guide to Antiques.* New York: McGraw-Hill, 1970.

Fales, Dean A., Jr., and Bishop, Robert. *American Painted Furniture—1660–1880.* New York: E. P. Dutton, 1979.

Gamon, Albert T. *Pennsylvania Country Antiques.* Englewood Cliffs, N.J.: Prentice-Hall, Inc.

Gould, Mary Earle. *Antique Tin and Toleware*. Rutland, Vermont: Charles E. Tuttle Co., 1957.

Greenfield Village and the Henry Ford Museum (3 vols). New York: Crown Publishers Inc., 1972.

Halsey, R. T. H. *A Handbook of the American Wing Opening Exhibition*. New York: Metropolitan Museum of Art.

Harbeson, Georgiana. *American Needlework*. New York: Coward-McCann and Geohegan Inc.

Hayden, Arthur. *Chats on Old Furniture*. New York: Stokes, 1979.

Hillerbrand, Hans J. *The World of the Reformation*. New York: Charles Scribner's Sons.

Hinckley, Frederick L. *A Directory of Antique Furniture*. New York: Crown Publishers Inc.
———. *Directory of Historic Cabinet Woods*. New York: Crown Publishers Inc.

Hunter, Frederick William. *Stiegel Glass*. New York: Houghton Mifflin Co.

Iverson, Marion Day. *The American Chair—1630–1890*. New York: Hastings House Publishers Inc.

Jordan, Mildred. *The Distelfink Country of the Pennsylvania Dutch*. New York: Crown Publishers Inc., 1978.

Kauffman, Henry J. *Pennsylvania Dutch American Folk Art*. New York: Crown Publishers Inc.
———. *Early American Ironware*. New York: Weathervane Books.
———. *Early American Copper, Tin and Brass*. New York: Medill McBride.
———. *The Pennsylvania-Kentucky Rifle*. Harrisburg: The Stackpole Co.
———. *Early American Gunsmiths*. Harrisburg: The Stackpole Co.

Keith, Charles P. *Chronicles of Pennsylvania from the English Revolution to the Peace of Aix-La-Chapelle*. Philadelphia: Patterson & White Co., 1917.

Kettell, Russell Hawes. *The Pine Furniture of Early New England*. New York: Dover Publications Inc., 1929.

Kirk, John T. and Maynard, Henry P. *Early American Furniture: How to Recognize, Buy And Care for the Most Beautiful Pieces—Highstyle, Country, Primitive and Rustic*. New York: Alfred A. Knopf Inc., 1970.

Klees, Frederick. *The Pennsylvania Dutch*. New York: Macmillan, 1950.

Klein, H. M. J. *Lancaster County, Pennsylvania*. Lancaster: Lewis Historical Publishing Co.

Knittle, Rhea Mansfield. *Early American Glass*. New York: The Century Co.

Kovel, Ralph and Kovel, Terry. *American Country Furniture 1780–1875*. New York: Crown Publishers Inc., 1965.

Kuhns, Oscar. *The German and Swiss Settlements of Colonial Pennsylvania*. New York: Henry Holt & Co.

Laughlin, Leslie Irwin. *Pewter in America*. New York: Houghton Mifflin Co.

Lichten, Frances. *Folk Art of Rural Pennsylvania*. New York: Bonanza Books.
———. *Folk Art Motifs of Pennsylvania*. New York: Dover Publications Inc., 1976.

Lipman, Jean. *Techniques in American Folk Decoration*. New York: Dover Publications Inc.

Lockwood, Luke Vincent. *Colonial Furniture in America*. New York: Castle Books Inc.

Lorrimar, Betty and Hickson, Margaret. *Ideas for Decoupage and Decoration*. New York: Van Nostrand Reinhold Co., 1975.

McKearin, Helen and McKearin, George S. *American Glass*. New York: Crown Publishers Inc., 1941.

Mercer, Henry C. *Ancient Carpenter's Tools*. Doylestown, Pa.: Bucks County Historical Society.
———. *The Bible in Iron*. Doylestown, Pa.: Bucks County Historical Society.
———. *The Survival of the Medieval Art of Illuminative Writing among the Pennsylvania Germans*. Doylestown, Pa.: Bucks County Historical Society.
———. *The Origin of Log Houses in the United States*. Doylestown, Pa.: Bucks County Historical Society.

Metropolitan Museum of Art. *Pennsylvania German Arts and Crafts.* New York: Metropolitan Museum of Art.

Miller, Edgar G., Jr. *American Antique Furniture.* New York: Dover Publications Inc., 1966.

Mitchell, Edwin Valentine. *It's an Old Pennsylvania Custom.* New York: Bonanza Books.

Moore, N. H. *The Old Furniure Book.* New York: Stokes.

Nutting, Wallace. *Pennsylvania Beautiful.* New York: Bonanza Books.
———. *Furniture of the Pilgrim Century* (2 vols). New York: Dover Publications Inc., 1965.

Omwake, John. *Conestoga Six Horse Bell Team 1750–1850.* Cincinnati: Ebbert & Richardson Co.

Palmer, R. R. and Colton, Joel. *A History of the Modern World.* New York: Alfred A. Knopf Inc., 1977.

Powers, Beatrice Farnsworth and Floyd, Olive. *Early American Decorated Tinware.* New York: Dover Publications Inc.

Robacker, Earl F. *Pennsylvania Dutch Stuff.* New York: Bonanza Books.

Rosenberger, Jesse Leonard. *In Pennsylvania German Land.* Chicago: University of Chicago Press.
———. *The Pennsylvania Germans.* Chicago: University of Chicago Press.

Ritz, Gislind M. *The Art of Painted Furniture.* New York: Van Nostrand Reinhold Co., 1970.

Sabine, Ellen S. *American Folk Art.* New York: Van Nostrand Reinhold Co.
———. *Early American Decorative Patterns.* New York: Bonanza Books.

Sack, Albert. *Fine Points of Furniture: Early American.* New York: Crown Publishers Inc., 1950.

Schiffer, Margaret B. *Furniture and Its Makers of Chester County, Pennsylvania.* Margaret B. Schiffer, 1978.

Schwartz, Mervin D. *Country Style.* New York: Brooklyn Museum.

Shea, John G. *Antique Country Furniture of North America,* 1975;

———. *The American Shakers and Their Furniture,* 1971;
———. *Colonial Furniture Making for Everybody,* 1964.
(All titles published by Van Nostrand Reinhold Co., New York.)

Silcock, Arnold and Avrton, Maxwell. *Wrought Iron and Its Decorative Uses.* New York: Charles Scribner's Sons.

Singleton, Esther and Sturgis, Russell. *Furniture of Our Forefathers.* New York: Doubleday & Co., Inc., 1969.

Slayton, Mariette Paine. *Early American Decorating Techniques.* New York: Macmillan Publishing Co. Inc., 1979.

Slivka, Webb and Patch. *The Crafts of the Modern World.* New York: Bramhall House.

Sonn, Albert. *Early American Wrought Iron* (3 vols). New York: Charles Scribner's Sons.

Stevens, Sylvester K. *Pennsylvania—Birthplace of a Nation.* New York: Random House Inc.

Stoudt, John Joseph. *Early Pennsylvania Arts and Crafts.* New York: Bonanza Books.
———. *Consider the Lilies How They Grow.* Pennsylvania German Folklore Society.

Sweeney, John A. H. *Winterthur Illustrated.* Winterthur, Del.: Winterthur Museum.

Taylor, H. H. *Knowing, Collecting and Restoring Early American Furniture.* Philadelphia: J. B. Lippincott Co.

Waring, Janet, *Early American Stencils on Walls and Furniture.* New York: Dover Publications Inc., 1937.

Watson, Aldren A. *Country Furniture.* New York: Thomas Y. Crowell Co. Inc., 1974.

Williams, Henry L. *Country Furniture of Early America.* Cranbury, N.J.: Barnes.

Winchester, Alice. *The Antiques Treasury.* New York: E. P. Dutton.
———. *How to Know American Antiques.* New York: Signet Books.
———. *Living with Antiques.* New York: E. P. Dutton.

Wood, Ralph. *The Pennsylvania Germans.* Princeton: Princeton University Press.

Wood, Stacey B. C., Kramer, Stephen, and Snyder, John J., Jr. *Clockmakers of Lancaster County.* New York: Van Nostrand Reinhold Co., 1977.

PERIODICALS:

Allen, Philip Meredith. "Old Iron." *The Antiquarian,* Vol. VIII, No. 2.

America. "Amish Education," 126:554, May 27, 1972.

Christian Century. "Amish," 90:223–224, February 21, 1973.
———. "Amish Court Decision," 88:95, January 1971.
———. "Mennonites," 90:70–73, January 17, 1973.

Christianity Today. "Mennonites," 19:62–63, September 12, 1975.
———. "Amish Education and Religious Freedom," 16:15–18, June 9, 1972.
———. "Mennonite Mandates," 15:47, September 1971.
———. "Mennonites," 16:36, May 12, 1972.

Commonweal. "Catholics and Amish," 96:331–332, June 16, 1972.

Current History. "Amish Education," 63:82, August 1972.

Education Digest. "Amish Religious Liberty," 38:36–37, December 1972.
———. "Education of the Amish," 40:48–50, January 1975.

Harper's. "Amish," 246:36, March–May 1973.

Holiday. "The Amish Are Wexelin," 49:60–63. April 1971.

National Review. "Amish Case—Supreme Court Decision," 24:747, July 7, 1972.

Newsweek. "Mennonites Disaster Relief," 84–85, October 21, 1974.

Old South Leaflets. Vol. IV #85, Old South Meeting House, Boston.

Senior Scholastic. "Mennonites," 104:13–14, April 25, 1974.

Swan, Mabel M. "The Village Tinsmith," *Antiques Magazine,* Vol. XIII, No. 3.

Index

agriculture, 23–24
  Amish, 15
  farmstead, 14
  Mennonites, 13
  practices in, 9, 11
  railroads, 42
Alden, John, 39
Alsace, 3
American Red Cross, 13
American Revolution, 12
Amish, 8, 11, 13–15, 16, 17
Amman, Jacob, 13
Anabaptists, 19–20
apostolic clock, 96
applied moldings, 106
  see also moldings
apron table, 57
  see also table(s)
Arnold, Charles V., 98
artisans, 8, 11, 23
  blacksmiths, 23, 26–27
  coopers, 11, 39
  tinsmiths, 23, 28
ash, 39
assimilation, 17
auger bits (antique), 100

Bach Festival, 19
Baden, 3
bank barns, 9
Baptist-Brethren (Dunkards), 8, 15
barn raising, 10, 12
barns, 9
"Barony of Nazareth," 18
Beck, J. P., 31
Beckel, Charles F., 94
beds, 84, 85
  "cannon ball" four-poster, 204
  four-poster with tester top, 85, 206
bedside table, 164
Beissel, Johann Conrad, 19
benches, 52, 53
  side bench, 160
  water bench, 197
bench table, 174
Berks County (Pa.), 8, 120
Bethlehem (Pa.), 8, 18, 19
Betty lamps, 64, 183
Bishop, Henry D., 94
Black Bumper Mennonites, 13
blacksmiths, 23, 26–27

block houses, 9
Boone, Daniel, 30
boring block, 112
bow drills, 102
boxes, 69, 86
  candle boxes, 86, 138, 186
  salt boxes, 86, 187
  wall boxes, 188
braces (antique), 100
Brennemans, 13
"Brethren in Christ" (River Brethren), 17
butternut tree, 23
butt fastenings, 110
butt-hinged joint, 116

cabinetmaker's workbench, 98
cabinets, 172
  see also cupboards
Calvin, John, 4
Calvinism, 20
canals, 41–42
candle box, 86, 138, 186
candlestand, 64, 182, 184, 186
  lapped joints, 112
"cannon ball" four-poster bed, 204
Carolinas, 19
carpenters, 11
carpenter's tool box, 176
carving, 38–39, 110
cast-iron decoration, 27
cast-iron production, 26
cedar, 23
celibacy, 19
ceramics, 35–36
chair(s), 44, 45, 46, 47–51, 54
  "judge's," 48, 157
  kitchen, 45, 46, 156
  "Moravian," 48, 158
  rockers, 50, 51
  trombone, 93
  Windsor, 48, 49, 89
chair table, 175
chalkware, 36
Charles II (k. of England), 4
cherry wood, 128
Chester County (Pa.), 61
chestnut, 39
chests, 69, 196
chests of drawers, 70, 71, 140, 185, 208, 210
Chippendale style, 54

Christ, John, 61
Church Amish, 14
"Church of the United Brethren in Christ" (United Brethren), 20
Church People, 11, 12, 17
class (social), 8, 11, 18
cleats, 110
clergy, 12, 13
clocks, 94, 95–96
cloth manufacture, 23
coal, 42
Colebrookdale furnace (Pa.), 26
Coleman, Robert, 31
Collegium Musicum, 18
Cologne (Germany), 37
colonization, 3
color
  application of, 132
  dower chest, 130
  selection of, 120, 128
communion, 17–18
Concord (ship), 9, 11, 12
Conestoga Wagons, 40–41
Congress Hall, 27
cooperage, 39
coopers, 11, 39
copper, 29
corner cupboards, 74, 75, 129, 212
cradles, 82, 83, 202, 203
craftsmen, 11
cricket-on-the hearth, 161
crop rotation, 15, 23
crops, 23–24
  see also agriculture
Cumberland Valley Railroad, 42
cupboards, 72, 73, 77, 78, 79
  corner, 74, 75, 129, 212
  hanging, 195
  open, 214
  pine key, 192
  schranks, 45, 80–81
  scrolled wall, 194
  staghorn-hinged, 193
  wall, 38, 72
cutlery rack, 87
Czechoslovakia, 11

dado joints, 108, 116
  see also joints
Danes, 9

Dauphin County (Pa.), 8
decoration
    hardware, 104
    stencils, 144–146
    see also paint and painting
decorative designs, 131
Denmark, 3, 18
desks, 54, 61
    desk-table, 58, 165
    drop-lid, 200
    Nazareth Hall school desk, 198
    school master's desk, 61, 199
    desk-table, 58, 165
diet, 19
Diet of Spires (1520), 20
dough tables and bins, 62, 63, 177, 178, 179
dovetailed chest, 196
dovetail joints, 114–116, 122–123
    see also joints
doweling, 110
dower chest, 44, 45, 54, 65–68, 141, 168, 170
    construction of, 120–126
    decoration of, 129, 130
drawbore-pin method, 118
dressers, 76, 77, 216
drills (antique), 102
drop-lid desk, 200
Dunkards (Baptist-Brethren), 11,15

Eby, Christian, 94
edge joints, 110
    see also joints
edge shapes, 108
education, 15, 18
Eisenhauer, Martin, 81
Eisenhower, Dwight D., 17
end cleats, 110
Ephrata Cloister, 6, 7, 34, 48
Ephrata Pietists, 11
Ephrata Society (Seventh Day Baptists), 6, 7, 19
Erie Canal, 42
Evangelical Association, 20
Evangelicals, 13

"Falckner's Swamp," 8
farmhouses, 9, 14, 25
fertilization, 15, 23
Fiester, John, 96
finishes (natural), 128
    see also paint and painting
firearms, 30–31
flax, 23, 32
food preparation, 23
foot stool, 87
forest clearing, 8–9, 22, 23, 98, 99
foundrymen, 23
four-poster beds, 204, 206
fractur, 19, 34, 35, 54
frame saws, 99, 100

France, 3, 9
Franklin, Benjamin, 3
french curve, 144
froe (tool), 100
Frueauff, John F., 61
funerals, 12
Funkites, 13
furniture construction, 97–120
furniture design, 43–96
    see also entries under types of furniture

Gaudy Dutch crockery, 36
Georgia, 18, 19
Germantown (Pa.), 6–7, 8, 15, 32
glass production, 11, 27, 37
Gothic style, 57
gouges (antique), 100
great wheel lathe, 102
Gregor, Christian, 93
gunsmiths, 11, 23, 30–31
Guthart, Jacob, 95

hanging cupboards, 73, 195
    see also cupboards
hanging shelves, 72
    see also shelves
Hapsburg empire, 4
hardboard
    dower chest construction, 120
    hex signs, 150
hardware, 27, 104–105
harpsichord, 93
hasps, 104
haunched mortise-and-tenon joints, 118
    see also joints
"Hausgemeine" Moravians, 19
hemp, 23
Herbein, Peter, 25
Heritage Center, 104
Herrites, 13
hewing, 99
hex signs, 128
    barns, 9
    lay out of, 148, 150
    purpose of, 148
    variations in, 149, 152–154
Heyne, Johann Christoph, 29
hickory, 23, 39, 99
hinged joint, 116
    see also joints
hinges, 104
Hoff, George, 95
Holy Roman Empire, 4
hooded cradles, 82, 203
horses, 40–41
Hotenstein, David, 54
House Amish, 14, 17
houses, 9, 14, 25
Huber, George, 80
Huguenots, 9
Hus, John, 18
hutch table, 174

immigrants and immigration
    causes of, 3–4
    class and, 8, 11, 18
    homes for, 8–9
    passage of, 5–7
    sources of, 3
    waves in, 7–8
indentured servitude, 8
Indians (native Americans), 11, 19
inlaying, 110
iron manufacture, 11, 26–27, 104

Jacquard loom, 3
jigsaws (antique), 102
John of Husinec, 18
joints, 108–120
    butt-hinged, 116
    dado, 108
    dovetail, 114–115, 122–123
    dovetailed dadoes, 116
    edge joints, 110
    end cleats, 110
    hinged, 116
    lapped joints, 112
    mortise-and-tenon, 110, 118
    rule joint, 116
    tongue-and-groove, 110
    tongue-and-groove hinged joint, 116
joint table (yellow pine), 162
"judge's chair," 48, 157

Kelpius, Johannes, 20
Kentucky rifle, 30
key plates, 104
Kiche shonk, 77
kitchen chair, 45, 46, 156
kitchen stool, 159
kitchen storage cabinet, 172
    see also cupboards
kitchen utility furniture, 88–89, 190
Krause, Samuel, 94
Krefeld (Pa.), 7
Krisheim (Pa.), 7

Lancaster County (Pa.), 8, 10, 15, 29, 31, 96, 104
lapped joints, 112
latches, 104
lathes (antique), 102
Lebanon County (Pa.), 8, 63, 65
Lehigh County (Pa.), 8
Lehigh Valley Railroad, 42
linen, 32–33
linseed oil finishes, 128
Linsey-Woolsey, 32
Lititz (Pa.), 18, 19
livestock, 23, 24, 32
log cabins, 9, 25
long saw, 99, 100
looms, 90, 91
Louis XIV (k. of France), 4
Luckenbach, Reuben, 51

lumber, 23
Luther, Martin, 3, 4, 17
Lutherans, 8, 9, 11, 17–18, 20

Manatawny (Pa.), 8
maple, 23, 99
"marbleized" shelf, 181
marriage, 12
Martinites, 13
Maryland, 19
materials, 132
Melthaner, John C., 92
Mennonites, 5, 8, 10, 11, 12–13, 15, 17
metalwork, 26–31
Methodist Revival, 20
"Millerites," 20
millers, 23
mining, 42
mirrors, 86, 87
missionaries, 11, 19
molding planes, 100
moldings, 106, 107, 108
"Moravian chair," 48, 158
Moravian Trombone Chair, 18
Moravians, 3, 8, 11, 18–19
mortise joints, 102
    see also joints
mortise-and tenon joints, 110, 118
    see also joints
music, 18–19
musical instruments, 92, 93

native Americans, 11, 19
natural finishes, 128
natural resources, 23, 26
Nazareth (Pa.), 18, 19
Nazareth County (Pa.), 8
Nazareth Hall school desk, 198
Neshaminy (Pa.), 8
Netherlands, 4, 9
New England, 19
"New-Geboren" sect, 20
New German Tract, The, 8
"New Mooners" sect, 20
newspapers, 11
New York, 19
Northampton County (Pa.), 8
Norway, 18

oak, 23, 39, 99
oaths, 13
occasional table, 167
Old Order Amish, 13–14
open cupboard, 214
oral culture, 17
orchards, 23
Otto, Frederick, 19
oval-top sawbuck table, 166

pacifism, 12, 15, 17
paint and painting, 127–154
    application of, 130

decorative, 129
dower chest construction, 120
procedures in, 132
stencils, 144–146
Palatinates, 9
paper mill, 11
passage, 5–7
Pastorious, Francis Daniel, 5, 6, 7, 8, 12
patterns (stencils), 144–146
Peace of Augsburg, 4
peasantry, 8
pegleg construction, 112
Penn, William, 4–5, 6, 8, 11, 15, 18
Pennsylvania Railroad, 42
Pennsylvania rifles, 31
Perkins, William, 27
pewter, 29
Philadelphia (Pa.), 6, 7, 8, 15, 41
Philadelphia & Reading Railroad, 42
pianos, 92, 93
pie safe, 89, 191
pietist movement, 17
Pietists, 8
pig iron production, 26
Pikers, 13
"Pilgergemeine" Moravians, 19
pine, 23, 63, 99
pitsawing, 99
Pittsburgh (Pa.), 41
Plain People, 9, 11–12, 14, 17
planes (antique), 100
planing jack, 102
plate rack, 73, 180
Plymouth colony, 39
plywood, 120
poplar, 63
Portsmouth, Mount Joy & Lancaster
    Railroad, 42
potters, 23
potters' clay, 35
pottery manufacture, 11
printing, 11
Protestant Reformation, 3–4, 17, 18
pumice stone, 128
pump drills, 102
punched tin, 28
Puritans, 17

Quakers, 4–5, 8, 12, 15, 37

rabbeting, 110
racks, 86, 87, 188
railroads, 42
Reading Railroad, 42
Red Cross, 13
Redemptioners, 8
reels, 91
refectory table, 57
Reformation, 3–4, 17, 18
Reformed Church, 8, 9, 11, 17, 18
religion
    ceremonies in, 14, 17–18

hex design, 9
immigration, 3–4
variety in, 11
see also entries under names of religions
Rhineland, 4, 9
Rhine Valley, 3
Rhode Island, 20
River Brethren (Brethren in Christ), 17
rockers, 50, 51
Roman Catholic Church, 3–4
Ruettynhuysen, Willem, 11
rule joint, 116

Saal kitchen, 6, 7
salt box, 86, 187
Salvation Army, 13
sawbuck tables, 44, 54, 55, 60, 89, 166
sawmills, 99
saws (antique), 99, 100
Saxony, 3
school masters' desk, 199
schranks, 44, 80, 81
see also cupboards
Schwenkfelders, 8, 15, 17
scrolled-apron bedside table, 164
scrolled wall cupboard, 194
seasoning, 99
seats, 52
Sectarians, 9, 11
Selzer, Christian, 65, 67, 120, 130
settees, 52
Seventh Day Baptists (Ephrata Society),
    6, 7, 19
sgraffito, 36
sheep raising, 32
shelves, 72, 73, 181
    kitchen utility shelves, 190
shoemakers, 23
shooks, 9
Shriner, Martin, 95
side bench, 160
Silesia, 3
silversmiths, 29
Simons, Menno, 12
slavery, 12
slip decoration, 36
small boxes, 69
    see also boxes
social class, 8, 11, 18
"Society of Women in the Wilderness,"
    20
Sommerhausen (Pa.), 7
Spangenberg, Bishop, 18
spatter-painting, 129
spatterware, 36
spinning wheels, 90, 91
splining, 110
spoon rack, 87, 188
spring-pole lathe, 102
Staffordshire (England), 36
staghorn-hinged hanging cupboard, 193
stains, 128

stands, 64
steel production, 26
stencils, 144–146
Stevenson, George, 26
Stiegel, Wilhelm, 26, 27, 37
stools, 52, 64, 86, 87, 159
stoves, 26, 89
striping, 144
Sweden, 3, 9, 18
Switzerland, 3, 9, 12, 13

table(s), 55, 56, 58–60
  apron, 57
  bedside, 164
  bench with hutch, 174
  chair, 175
  dough trough, 62, 178, 179
  hutch, 174
  occasional, 167
  oval-top sawbuck, 166
  refectory, 57
  sawbuck, 44, 54, 55, 69, 89, 166
  three-legged, 56
  yellow pine, 162
tanners, 11, 23
Tatery, Joshua, 37
taufscheine, 34
tempered hardboard
  dower chest, 120
  hex design, 150
textile production, 11, 32–33
Thirty-Fivers, 13
Thirty Years' War (1618–1648), 4
Thomas, George, 24
Thomme, Margretha, 19
three-legged table, 56
thumb-nose edge shapes, 108
Till, Jacob C., 92
tinkers, 23
tinsmiths, 23, 28
tinware, 28
toleware, 28
tongue-and-groove cutters, 102
tongue-and-groove hinged joint, 116
tongue-and-groove joints, 110
  see also joints
tool box, 176
tools, 132
  antique, 99–103
  edge shapes, 108
trades, see artisans
transportation, 40–42
treadle lathe, 102
trees, 23
Trinity Church, 27
trombone chair, 93
trucking, 42

turnpikes, 41
twible (tool), 100

Union Canal, 42
"United Brethren," 20
utility dressers, 76
utility furniture, 88–89

Valley Forge (Pa.), 41
varnish, 128, 132
vegetarianism, 19
veining tool, 110
Virginia, 19
von Ossig, Kasper Schwenkfeld, 15, 17
vorsschrift, 34

wagonmakers, 23
wall boxes, 188
  see also boxes
wall cupboards, 38, 72, 73, 194
  see also cupboards
walnut, 23, 55, 63, 69, 128, 202
Washington, George, 41
washstands, 61
water bench, 197
waterways, 23
weavers, 11, 23, 32, 33
  see also looms
Weavers (sect), 13
weddings, 12
Weis, Noah, 38
Weiss, Jedediah, 94
Wengerites, 13
wheat, 23
Wheeler, S., 27
wheelwrights, 11
Whitefield, 18
white oak, 39
Windsor chairs, 48, 49, 89
Windsor turned stool, 64
Wislerites, 13
Wolle, J. Fred, 92
women
  clothing of, 15
  role of, 12, 23
woodenware, 38–39
woodworking, 26
wool, 23, 32
workbench, 98
World War II, 13
Wurtemberg, 3

York County (Pa.), 8

Zinzendorf, Count, 18
Zwingli, Ulrich, 4, 18